The Image of God in the Theology of Gregory of Nazianzus

Gregory of Nazianzus, known best for his Christology and Trinitarian doctrine, presents an incomparable vision of the image of God. In this book, Gabrielle Thomas offers a close analysis of his writings and demonstrates how Nazianzen depicts both the nature and experience of the image of God throughout his corpus. She argues that Nazianzen's vision of the human person as an image of God is understood best in light of biblical and extra-biblical themes. To establish the breadth of his approach, Thomas analyses the image of God against the backdrop of Nazianzen's beliefs about Christology, Pneumatology, creation, sin, spiritual warfare, ethics and theosis. Interpreted accordingly, Nazianzen offers a dynamic and multifaceted account of the image of God, which has serious implications both for Cappadocian studies and contemporary theological anthropology.

Gabrielle Thomas is a postdoctoral research associate at Durham University and a priest in the Church of England, serving as a Minor Canon in Durham Cathedral. Her articles have appeared in *Scottish Journal of Theology*, *Studia Patristica*, *Exchange*, and *A Forum for Theology in the World*.

The Image of God in the Theology of Gregory of Nazianzus

GABRIELLE THOMAS

Durham University

CAMBRIDGE
UNIVERSITY PRESS

Shaftesbury Road, Cambridge CB2 8EA, United Kingdom

One Liberty Plaza, 20th Floor, New York, NY 10006, USA

477 Williamstown Road, Port Melbourne, VIC 3207, Australia

314–321, 3rd Floor, Plot 3, Splendor Forum, Jasola District Centre, New Delhi – 110025, India

103 Penang Road, #05–06/07, Visioncrest Commercial, Singapore 238467

Cambridge University Press is part of Cambridge University Press & Assessment, a department of the University of Cambridge.

We share the University's mission to contribute to society through the pursuit of education, learning and research at the highest international levels of excellence.

www.cambridge.org
Information on this title: www.cambridge.org/9781108742528

DOI: 10.1017/9781108593410

First published 2019
First paperback edition 2023

A catalogue record for this publication is available from the British Library

Library of Congress Cataloging-in-Publication data
NAMES: Thomas, Gabrielle, 1974- author.
TITLE: The image of God in the theology of Gregory of Nazianzus / Gabrielle Thomas, University of Durham.
DESCRIPTION: 1 [edition]. | New York : Cambridge University Press, 2019. | Includes bibliographical references and index.
IDENTIFIERS: LCCN 2018058432| ISBN 9781108482196 (hardback : alk. paper) | ISBN 9781108742528 (pbk. : alk. paper)
SUBJECTS: LCSH: Gregory, of Nazianzus, Saint. | Image of God–History of doctrines–Early church, ca. 30-600.
CLASSIFICATION: LCC BR65.G66 T46 2019 | DDC 233/.5092–dc23
LC record available at https://lccn.loc.gov/2018058432

ISBN   978-1-108-48219-6   Hardback
ISBN   978-1-108-74252-8   Paperback

I too am also an *eikon* of God ... you should worship me

Εἰκών εἰμι καὶ αὐτὸς Θεοῦ ... σύ με προσκύνησον

Gregory of Nazianzus, *On Baptism*, Oration 40.10

Contents

Preface

'Why choose Gregory of Nazianzus?' I have lost count of the times I have been asked this question, often accompanied by a mystified expression on the face of the enquirer. On more than one occasion I have asked myself, 'Why have I chosen to spend so many years exploring, translating, and grappling with the work of this particular theologian?' Like many before me, who have delved into these texts, I resonate with Gregory's writing. He theologises on Scripture, doctrine, pastoral care, prayer, and faith within the context of his own experience. Gregory's love of God, Father, Son, and Holy Spirit, radiates through the pages of his work and is contagious. The more time I spend in his company, the more I find myself aspiring to be a good theologian.

This book represents the culmination of nearly a decade of research; no reader would thank me for acknowledging the generosity of every person who has contributed to its formation and completion. I am thankful for the friends and near-strangers who have given invaluable feedback on my ideas, commented on translations, read through drafts, provided encouragement, and more.

The seeds of this book began during my training for ordained ministry in the Church of England. Desiring to continue to explore Gregory's theological anthropology, I pursued doctoral work at the University of Nottingham. During this time, I was funded fully by the Church of England Research Degrees Panel, the Sylvanus Lysons Trust, and St Luke's Trust. I am grateful for their support, which allowed me the luxury of being a full-time researcher.

My supervisor, Mary Cunningham, went far beyond the call of duty at every stage of my research and writing. The fellowship and friendship we shared through reading ancient texts together contributed significantly both to my academic and spiritual formation. My other supervisors, Simon Oliver and Alison Milbank, provided essential, critical feedback whilst demonstrating what it means to be a scholar-priest.

Crispin Fletcher-Louis, Ben Fulford, Nick Wilshere, Suzanne Abrams Rebillard, Ian Paul and Mark Cartledge gave particularly helpful advice at various stages of the research. Fr. Andrew Louth, Scot Ray Douglass, Dragoş Giulea, Sophie Cartwright and Alistair McFadyen kindly shared unpublished work with me, which made the research run more smoothly. Thanks also to Terry J. Wright, Alex Williams, Carole Schultz, Lavinia Cerioni, and Judy Nesbit. Long conversations with Tarah Van de Wiele prevented me from becoming a curator of the texts. I am grateful to her and her husband Brady for the open door to their home in Nottingham during the two years I was based near London, making trips back and forth.

Fr. John Behr made the journey from Crestwood, New York to examine the thesis. I have long been influenced by his work and value his support. Along with Simeon Zahl, my other discerning examiner, he encouraged me to pursue publication; both shared valuable insights that contributed to the revision.

I moved from Nottingham to an equally rich and rewarding time at Durham University, working as a Postdoctoral Research Associate within the Centre for Catholic Studies. I am grateful for the funding from the National Board of Catholic Women and The Caulfield Foundation, which made this possible. During this period, I have continued to develop the book, receiving excellent advice from Karen Kilby and Lewis Ayres. Encouragement from them ensured that I saw the manuscript through to completion (although, is a book ever really finished!?). My thanks also to Beatrice Rehl and the editorial team at CUP.

Finally, my family. I am so very thankful for a mother and father who raised me to believe that almost anything is possible through prayer and perseverance. This belief has served me well through hitting the troughs of research, writing, and editing. My sister, whose belief in my abilities far exceeds reality, has refused to collaborate with me when I have doubted my ability to complete this book.

My husband, Matthew, has been a longsuffering companion from the day I first enthused about Gregory's theology. He has consistently cheered me on every step of the way; he has listened to ideas, read countless drafts, and allowed generously Gregory into almost every aspect of our life together. As an image of God, Matthew is indeed 'divine'. I dedicate this book to him.

Abbreviations

	Comm. Jn.	*Commentarii in evangelium Joannis*
	Dial.	*Dialogus cum Heraclide*
	Hom. Gen.	*Homiliae in Genesim*
	Princ.	*De Principiis*
Pausanias	*Descr.*	*Descriptio Graeciae*
Philo	*Opif.*	*De opificio mundi*
	Her.	*Quis rerum divinarum heres sit*
	Leg. 1, 2, 3	*Legum allegoriae I, II, III*
	Spec. 1, 2, 3, 4	*De specialibus legibus I, II, III, IV*
Plato	*Crat.*	*Cratylus*
	Gorg.	*Gorgias*
	Phaed.	*Phaedo*
	Resp.	*Respublica*
	Soph.	*Sophista*
	Symp.	*Symposium*
	Theaet.	*Theaetetus*
	Tim.	*Timaeus*
Plutarch	*Princ. Iner.*	*Ad principem ineruditum*
Socrates	*HE*	*Historia Ecclesiastica*
Suetonius	*Aug.*	*Divus Augustus*
Tertullian	*Marc.*	*Adversus Marcionem*

SECONDARY LITERATURE

ABD	Anchor Bible Dictionary
ACO	*Acta Conciliorum Oecumenicorum*
ANRW	Aufstieg und Niedergang der römischen Welt: Geschichte und Kultur Roms im Spiegel der neueren Forschung
BLE	*Bulletin de littérature ecclésiastique*
BM	*Benediktinische Monatsschrift zur Pflege religiösen und geistigen Lebens*
BSK	Beiträge zum Studium der Kirchenväter
BZAW	Beihefte zur Zeitschrift für die alttestamentliche Wissenschaft
BZNW	Beihefte zur Zeitschrift für die neutestamentliche Wissenschaft
CBAA	Catholic Biblical Association of America
CBQMS	Catholic Biblical Quarterly Monograph Series
CBOTS	Coniectanea Biblica Old Testament Series
CCSA	Corpus Christianorum Series Apocryphorum

CMC   Cambridge Medieval Classics
CRAI   *Comptes rendus de l'Académie des inscriptions et belles-Lettres*
CSR   *Christian Scholars Review*
DOP   *Dumbarton Oaks Papers*
GELS   A Greek-English Lexicon of the Septuagint
GOTR   *Greek Orthodox Theological Review*
GRBS   *Greek, Roman, and Byzantine Studies*
HTR   *Harvard Theological Review*
ITQ   *Irish Theological Quarterly*
JANER   *Journal of Ancient Near Eastern Religion*
JBL   *Journal of Biblical Literature*
JEA   *Journal of Egyptian Archaeology*
JECS   *Journal of Early Christian Studies*
JHP   *Journal of the History of Philosophy*
JJS   *Journal of Jewish Studies*
JSNT   *Journal for the Study of the New Testament*
JSOT   *Journal for the Study of the Old Testament*
JSP   *Journal for the Study of Pseudepigrapha*
JSPSS   *Journal for the Study of Pseudepigrapha Supplement Series*
JTS   *Journal of Theological Studies*
LCL   Loeb Classical Library
LSJ   Liddell, Scott and Jones' *A Greek-English Lexicon*
MIT   Massachusetts Institute of Technology
MSR   Mélanges de science religieuse
NETS   New English Translation of the Septuagint
NIGTC   The New International Greek Testament Commentary
NSBT   *New Studies in Biblical Theology*
NTS   *New Testament Studies*
NPNF   Nicene and Post-Nicene Fathers
OTL   Old Testament Library
OUP   Oxford University Press
PBR   *Patristic and Byzantine Review*
PG   Patrologia graeca [= Patrologiae cursus completus: Series graeca]. Edited by J.-P. Migne. 162 vols. Paris, 1857–1886
PGL   *Patristic Greek Lexicon*
PIOL   *Publications de l'Institut Orientaliste de Louvain*
PPS   Popular Patristics Series
PUF   Presses Universitaires de France
RAC   *Reallexikon für Antike und Christentum*

SC	Sources Chrétiennes
SGKA	Studien zur Geschichte und Kultur des Altertums
SJT	*Scottish Journal of Theology*
SVTP	Studia in Veteris Testamenti Pseudepigrapha
TB	*Tyndale Bulletin*
TFC	The Fathers of the Church
TLG	Thesaurus Linguae Graecae
TDNT	Theological Dictionary of the New Testament
VC	*Vigiliae Christianae*
SVTQ	*St. Vladimir's Theological Quarterly*
WBC	Word Biblical Commentary
ZAC	*Zeitschrift für Antikes Christentum*
ZAW	*Zeitschrift für die alttestamentliche Wissenschaft*

Introduction

The Council of Chalcedon bestowed the title 'Blessed Gregory, the Theologian' upon Saint Gregory of Nazianzus in AD 451.[1] Along with Saint John the Evangelist and Saint Symeon the 'New Theologian', Gregory is one of only three theologians on whom the title has been conferred in the Eastern Christian tradition. Born circa AD 329 to Gregory the Elder, Bishop of Nazianzus, Gregory's extensive education equipped him with the philosophical and rhetorical skills to theologise in a vast array of Greek literary forms. This led Gregory to become the most quoted author in Byzantine ecclesiastical literature, after the Bible.[2] His neologism 'theosis' continues to be applied in contemporary theology as the chief term used to describe deification.

Our theologian espouses a complex approach to the image of God, vis-à-vis the *imago Dei*, which spans his vast corpus of orations, poems and letters. Recognising the mystery of being an *imago Dei*, Gregory asks, 'Who was I at first? Moreover, who am I now? And, who shall I become? I don't know clearly.'[3] Despite Gregory's ambivalent response to his

---

[1] ACO 2.1.3, 473. For a full translation and commentary of the council, see Richard Price and Michael Gaddis, *The Acts of the Council of Chalcedon*, (Liverpool: Liverpool University Press, 2005). For Gregory's comments on the two natures of Christ cited by the council, see Or. 30.8 (SC 250, 240–42); Ep. 101.19 (SC 208, 44). N.B. SC assumes a different section numbering for the *Theological Epistles to Cledonius* from those found in PG and the modern translations.

[2] Jaques Norét, 'Grégoire de Nazianze, l'auteur le plus cité, après la Bible, dans la littérature ecclésiastique byzantine' in Justin Mossay (ed.), *Symposium Nazianzenum* 2 (Paderborn: Schöningh, 1983), 259–66.

[3] Carm. 1.2.14 (PG 37, 757, 17). In order to highlight the nuances in the texts, the translations are my own throughout the book, unless stated otherwise. See the Appendix for details of the editions and texts consulted.

rhetorical questions, a close reading of the texts reveals a cohesive narrative concerning humankind. Gregory's vision of the *imago Dei* differs from the predominant contemporary approach, which tends to view the *imago Dei* through a single lens, thereby reducing the *imago* to a single category of analysis. Traditionally, theologians have categorised the *imago Dei* as structural, relational, or functional, where 'structural' relates to the various capacities of the human person, for example, rationality or free will,[4] 'relational' considers the *imago Dei* in light of the relationship within the Trinity,[5] and 'functional' conveys how a human person achieves the task of being an *imago Dei*.[6] These interpretations are not satisfactory in themselves, since independently they cannot encapsulate the summation of human persons as they image God. Moreover, they are subject to critiques of exclusion, theological abstraction, and biblical errancy. In light of this, vociferous discussions continue in contemporary systematic theology, theological anthropology, and biblical studies. Over the past few decades, a number of theologians have responded, quite rightly, by emphasising the importance of viewing the *imago Dei* through a christological lens.[7] Added to this, those writing on the Christian doctrine of humanity have begun to attend to the need for a robust pneumatological account of the *imago Dei*.[8]

Gregory, on the other hand, not only incorporates all of these, but also describes the lived experience of being an *imago Dei*. His narrative offers contemporary theologians a fresh and comprehensive mode of discussing the *imago Dei*. Rather than viewing the *imago Dei* through a single lens,

---

[4] Alister E. McGrath, *Scientific Theology: Nature*, vol. 1 (Edinburgh: T&T Clark, 2002), 198–200. Following convention, I apply 'structural' and 'substantive' synonymously.

[5] Alistair I. McFadyen, *The Call to Personhood: A Christian Theory of the Individual in Social Relationships* (Cambridge: Cambridge University Press, 1990), 18; John Zizioulas, *Being as Communion: Studies in Personhood and the Church* (Crestwood, New York: St. Vladimir's Seminary Press, 1985), 15. For a critique of the relational approach, see Harriet A. Harris, 'Should We Say That Personhood Is Relational?', *SJT*, 51, no. 2 (1998), 214–34, 216–18.

[6] J. Richard Middleton, 'The Liberating Image? Interpreting the Imago Dei in Context', *CSR*, 24, no. 1 (1994), 8–25, 12. For a critique of the functional view, see G.C. Berkouwer, *Man: The Image of God, Studies in Dogmatics* (Grand Rapids: Eerdmans, 1962), 71.

[7] David Kelsey, *Eccentric Existence: A Theological Anthropology* (Louisville: Westminster John Knox, 2009), 8–9; John Behr, *The Mystery of Christ: Life in Death* (Crestwood, New York: St. Vladimir's Seminary Press, 2006); Kathryn Tanner, *Christ the Key* (Cambridge: Cambridge University Press, 2010).

[8] Marc Cortez, 'Idols, Images and a Spirit-ed Anthropology' in Myk Habets (ed.), *A Pneumatological Account of the Imago Dei* (Minneapolis: Fortress Press, 2016), 267–82.

Gregory offers a nuanced account, which resembles a richly coloured tapestry into which he has woven myriad threads.[9] He establishes his vision by narrating the *imago Dei* as a dynamic existence, which encompasses both the human person's life on earth and her telos. For Gregory, this relates to being and becoming a divine image (εἰκὼν θεία).[10] Moreover, Gregory situates the drama of human experience in the biblical narrative of creation, fall, and restoration, thus presenting a worldview where human persons inhabit a conceptual world consisting of good and evil spirits. He describes at length the numerous problems created by evil spirits, which result from the fallen angel Lucifer's banishment from heaven. Journeying towards God entails the free will of the *imago Dei*, which renders the human person vulnerable to the world, the flesh, and the devil, with her divinity constantly at risk.

Forthwith, I will generally use the transliteration *eikon* in order to create space for an interpretation which incorporates visibility and relays Gregory's broad interpretation as much as possible. The usual descriptions, 'divine image', 'image of God', or '*imago Dei*', do not necessarily suggest physicality; consequently, they may be interpreted in abstract terms. In some instances, Gregory uses shorthand to describe the human person simply as 'the *eikon*', rather than the '*eikon* of God'. I follow his usage throughout the book in order to remain as faithful as possible to the texts. The final point regarding ἡ εἰκὼν is that it is a feminine noun. To reflect this, from herein, I use the feminine pronoun or possessive adjective throughout the book when referring to the human *eikon*. I also make this move because we may assume a 'she' as much as a 'he' when describing an individual human person.

On some occasions, Gregory explicitly describes the *eikon* quite literally as a physical, visible *eikon*. He achieves this by conflating the creation narratives in Genesis 1 and 2:

… a mortal human (βροτός) was made from earth (χοῦς) and breath (πνόη), an *eikon* of the immortal One (ἀθανάτοιο εἰκών).[11]

We will explore the implications of this move through the course of the book. Observe how, on other occasions, Gregory likens the *eikon* to the soul (ψυχή) or spiritual intellect (νοῦς), as that which is invisible:

---

[9] For comment on Gregory's use of genre and rhetoric, see the Appendix.
[10] Carm. 2.1.50 (PG 37, 1389, 61–62).
[11] Carm. 1.1.8 (PG 37, 452, 74–75); 1.1.10 (PG 37, 469, 58); Or. 3.7 (SC 247, 250); 40.10 (SC 358, 218); 40.14 (SC 358, 226).

... even though the greatest feature in the nature of the human person is that she is [created] according to the *eikon* (εἰκών) and [possesses] the capacity of spiritual intellect (νοῦς).[12]

Above, at first glance, the *eikon* equates to the spiritual intellect. In light of this, commentators generally conclude that Gregory understands the *eikon* as the soul or the spiritual intellect.[13] On the one hand, this claim is correct since, following Origen,[14] Gregory refers to the divine image as either the spiritual intellect (νοῦς) or the soul (ψυχή) on numerous occasions.[15] This is important to note, since I am not contending that the secondary literature has, hitherto, misinterpreted Gregory's depiction of the human *eikon*; rather, scholars have not yet delineated the full breadth of Gregory's vision and the implications of his account.[16] Possibly this is

---

[12] Or. 22.13 (SC 270, 248). Contemporary English translations often translate νοῦς as 'mind', 'intellect', or 'rationality', all of which suggest 'reason'. For Gregory, νοῦς is that aspect of the soul through which human persons experience and perceive God; it relates to the spiritual realm. Thus, by translating νοῦς as 'spiritual intellect', I mean to move away from a kind of intellectual exercise and towards the idea that human persons yearn for and apprehend God to varying degrees through νοῦς.

[13] Manfred Kertsch, *Gregorio Nazianzeno: Sulla virtù, Carme giambico [I, 2, 10]* (Pisa: Edizioni Ets, 1995), 195; Michael Oberhaus and Martin Sicherl, *Gregor von Nazianz: Gegen den Zorn (Carmen I,2,25) Einleitung und Kommentar* (Paderborn: Ferdinand Schöningh, 1991), 75; Frederick W. Norris, 'Gregory Nazianzen's Doctrine of Jesus Christ' (Ph.D. Diss., Yale, 1970), 69; Kenneth Paul Wesche, '"Mind" and "Self" in the Christology of Saint Gregory the Theologian: Saint Gregory's Contribution to Christology and Christian Anthropology', *GOTR* 39, no. 1–2 (1994): 33–61, 51; Peter Gilbert, 'Person and Nature in the Theological Poems of St. Gregory of Nazianzus' (Ph.D. Diss., Catholic University of America, 1994), 290; Jostein Børtnes, 'Rhetoric and Mental Images in Gregory' in Jostein Børtnes and Tomas Hägg (ed.), *Gregory of Nazianzus: Images and Reflections* (Chicago: Museum Tusculanum, 2006), 37–57, 56; Heinz Althaus, *Die Heilslehre des heiligen Gregor von Nazianz* (Münster: Verlag Aschendorff, 1972), 72–74; Ben Fulford, *Divine Eloquence and Human Transformation: Rethinking Scripture and History through Gregory of Nazianzus and Hans Frei* (Minneapolis: Augsburg Fortress, 2013), 80–81; Hannah Hunt, *Clothed in the Body: Asceticism, the Body and the Spiritual in the Late Antique Era* (Surrey: Ashgate Publishing Limited, 2012), 194; Anca Vasiliu, *Eikôn* (Paris: PUF, 2010), 49; Hilarion Alfeyev, *La chantre de la Luminère: Introduction à la spiritualité de saint Grégoire de Nazianze* (Paris: Éditions du Cerf, 2006), 251; Kirsten Koonce, 'Agalma and Eikon', *American Journal of Philology*, 109, no. 1 (1988): 108–10; Anna S. Ellverson, *The Dual Nature of Man: A Study in the Theological Anthropology of Gregory of Nazianzus* (Stockholm: Uppsala, 1981), 25; Joseph Barbel, *Gregor von Nazianz. Die fünf theologischen Reden* (Düsseldorf: Patmos-Verlag, 1963), 284.

[14] Origen, *Homilies on Genesis and Exodus* 1.13, trans. Ronald Heine, TFC (WA, DC: Catholic University of America Press, 1982), 63.

[15] Or. 14.2 (PG 35, 860B–861A); 22.14 (SC 270, 248–49); 28.17 (SC 250, 134); 32.27 (SC 318, 142–44); Carm. 1.2.1 (PG 37, 529, 97).

[16] Gregory's anthropology incorporates both di- and tri-chotomist ideas, where the human person is presented both as body (σῶμα) and soul (ψυχή), and as dust (χοῦς), spiritual

because few full-length studies exist which consider in depth Gregory's approach; analyses on Gregory's account of the human *eikon* most often consist of a single chapter or paragraph in a study dedicated to broader aspects of Gregory's thought.[17] Exceptions to this are scholars such as Philippe Molac, who provides an extensive account of key words and concepts linked to the *eikon*. He demonstrates that Gregory's description of the spiritual intellect (νοῦς) is inseparably linked with flesh (σάρξ) through the soul (ψυχή). Molac develops this in light of Christology; here we aim to explore the breadth of what this may mean for the human person as an *eikon* of God.[18]

An apparent discrepancy exists between the *eikon* described as the invisible soul within the human person and the visible *eikon* as the whole human person, creating a problem for interpreters. We shall see that Gregory weaves various interpretations into his overall account, in order to depict the complexity of human existence. Whilst it is customary amongst theologians to ask, 'What *Is* the *eikon*?' Gregory appears not to be so concerned with this particular question. Rather, he pays more attention to describing the mystery of human experience and what it is like to *be* an *eikon*. Added to this, if we consider the occasions on which Gregory speaks about the human person as a mixture (μίξις) of dust and *eikon*, we may observe that the *eikon* transforms the dust and renders it spiritual, following the mixture of Christ. Therefore, when Gregory speaks about the *eikon* as the soul or the spiritual intellect, it is possible

---

intellect (νοῦς), and spirit (πνεῦμα). For example: body and soul: Or. 2.17 (SC 247, 112); 7.21 (SC 405, 232); 18.3 (PG 35, 988B–990A); flesh and spirit: Or. 7.23 (SC 405, 240); 40.2 (SC 358, 200); dust, spiritual intellect and spirit: Or. 32.9 (SC 318, 104). On the dual nature of Gregory's anthropology, see Ellverson, *The Dual Nature of Man*, passim.

[17] See for example, Børtnes, 'Rhetoric and Mental Images in Gregory', 56. The author comments on Gregory's approach to the human *eikon* with respect to Origen's anthropology, but does not develop the full breadth of Gregory's thought on the human *eikon*.

[18] Molac, Philippe, *Douleur et transfiguration. Une lecture du cheminement spirituel de saint Grégoire de Nazianze* (Paris: Les Éditions du Cerf, 2006). Also see Andreas Knecht, *Gregor von Nazianz: Gegen die Putzsucht der Frauen. Verbesserter griechischer Text mit Übersetzung, motivgeschichtlichem Überblick und Kommentar* (Heidelberg: Carl Winter Universitätsverlag, 1972), 71; Anne Richard, *Cosmologie et théologie chez Grégoire de Nazianze* (Paris: Institut d'Études Augustiniennes, 2003), 265; Jaroslav Pelikan, *Christianity and Classical Culture: The Metamorphosis of Natural Theology in the Christian Encounter with Hellenism* (New Haven; London: Yale University Press, 1993), 129. Whilst they observe the physicality of the *eikon*, their overall projects are not concerned with the implcations of this.

that he has in mind the whole human person as a visible *eikon* because the *eikon* transforms the dust and the two form a unity.

Throughout the course of this book, I shall argue that Gregory's vision is inspired to a great extent by biblical and extra-biblical literature, beginning with Gregory's description of Christ as the 'identical *Eikon*'.[19] To ascertain this, we will compare heuristically the biblical and extra-biblical narratives from which Gregory draws inspiration.[20] This is not to suggest that Gregory applies biblical concepts to the exclusivity of philosophical thought. I do not support a polarised approach, which posits early Christians as writing either biblically or philosophically.[21] The trend, which posits Greek philosophy as the enemy of Christianity, stems from the late nineteenth century. Adolf Harnack made a vociferous attack on the early church fathers, accusing them of infiltrating the gospel with Hellenism.[22] Harnack's Western post-Enlightenment worldview meant that he believed Scripture and philosophy to be incompatible. Ayres has critiqued this, offering a corrective view. He argues that whilst biblical texts provide the 'primary resource for the Christian imagination, [they] may be explicated through the use of whatever lies to hand and that may be persuasively adapted'.[23] Gregory speaks for himself when he refers to the Platonists as 'those who have thought best about God and are nearest to us'.[24] By making this claim, he acknowledges that there is a difference

---

[19] Or. 38.13 (SC 358, 132).

[20] Numerous scholars have challenged the use of terms such as 'extra-biblical', 'apocryphal', and 'pseudepigraphal' as they are too 'intimately linked' with heresy: Stephen J. Shoemaker, 'Early Christian Apocryphal Literature' in Susan A. Harvey and David G. Hunter (eds.), *The Oxford Handbook of Early Christian Studies* (Oxford: Oxford University Press, 2008), 521–48, 523; Evelyne Patlagean, 'Remarques sur la production et la diffusion des apocryphes dans le monde byzantin', *Apocrypha*, no. 2 (1991), 155–64. It is beyond the scope of this book to identify new terminology; therefore, I apply 'extra-biblical' interchangeably with 'pseudepigraphal', acknowledging that neither term is wholly adequate.

[21] A number of Western scholars have responded by attempting to distance Gregory from Greek philosophy; for example, Jean Plagnieux concludes that in Gregory, 'we are far from Plato, Philo, Plotinus and Origen'; *Saint Grégoire de Nazianze théologien* (Paris: Éditions Franciscaines, 1951), 427.

[22] Adolf Harnack, *History of Dogma*, trans. James Millar, vol. 3 (London: Williams & Norgate, 1897), 318. For a succinct overview of Harnack's criticisms, see William Rowe, 'Adolf Von Harnack and the Concept of Hellenization' in Wendy Helleman (eds.), *Hellenization Revisited: Shaping a Christian Response within the Greco-Roman World* (Lanham, MD: University Press of America, 1994), 69–97.

[23] Lewis Ayres, *Nicaea and Its Legacy: An Approach to Fourth-Century Trinitarian Theology* (Oxford: Oxford University Press, 2004), 392.

[24] Or. 31.5 (SC 250, 282–84).

between the Platonists and the Christians, whilst observing that the philosophers make an invaluable contribution to Christian theology.

Our theologian's dynamic approach to the *eikon*, which emphasises both divinity and vulnerability, unfolds throughout the following chapters. The book shadows closely the sequence of Gregory's own narrative in order to present his nuanced vision of the human *eikon*. Chapter 1 begins with a discussion of Gregory's hermeneutics, arguing that Gregory interprets the whole biblical narrative in light of Christ and the salvation story. Therefore, if we are to present as faithfully as possible Gregory's vision of the human *eikon*, we must begin with Christ, the 'identical *Eikon*'. We move on to establish the predominant biblical themes which feed into Gregory's multifaceted account of the human *eikon*. These include beliefs about the divine presence manifested through images and idols, ethics, and an interesting thread which concerns the spiritual warfare between the human *eikon* and the devil. The title 'devil' is used interchangeably with 'Satan' throughout the book; these are two of the many common epithets used by Gregory to denote the concept of 'powers of opposition' within the Christian tradition.

In Chapter 2, we will establish that Gregory considers anthropology within the theological framework of his doctrine of God, who is Father, Son, and Holy Spirit, and in particular the Son, who is the 'identical *Eikon*'. Gregory speaks of Christ as the *Eikon* in a way that denotes Christ's ontological imaging of the Father. Christ is a divine, living, and dynamic *Eikon*, which differentiates Christ from motionless images. Thus, for Gregory, *eikon* signifies 'likeness to' rather than 'difference from'. Secondly, Gregory goes to great lengths to argue that Christ is unified, which has significant implications on the way in which Gregory considers the physicality of the human *eikon*. Thirdly, Christ's kenosis makes possible the theosis of the human *eikon*. Finally, Christ battles with and defeats the devil, restoring the potential divinity of the *eikon* and securing the *eikon*'s victory over the devil.

Continuing the narrative of the existence of the *eikon*, Chapter 3 examines the creation of the human *eikon*, pointing to the significance of the materiality and visibility of the *eikon* when compared to the invisibility of angels. This relates to how Gregory depicts the *eikon* as divine. Due to his narration of how God mixes the spiritual *eikon* with the dust, and in light of the unity of the 'identical *Eikon*', I contend that Gregory portrays the *eikon* and the dust becoming a unity, thus a single, living human person. Drawing from Genesis 1, Gregory argues explicitly that God creates women and men equally as *eikones*. Moreover, he writes about the female *eikon* in a manner which demonstrates further his view of the *eikon* quite literally as a physical, living, and divine *eikon* of God.

Chapter 4 moves on to explore Gregory's re-telling of the fall against the backdrop of the 'garments of glory' tradition. After being persuaded by the devil to eat the fruit in paradise, the *eikon* is banished and clothed in garments of 'thick, dull flesh', which equates to the *eikon* being shrouded in sin. This renders the human person at greater risk from the devil. Here, we examine the way in which Gregory discusses the devil, arguing that Gregory attributes to the devil a diminishing existence. The battles with the spiritual powers of darkness form a primary strand in Gregory's narrative of the *eikon*'s existence, in which the devil hovers behind conversations of sin, the flesh, the world, and the passions.

Having followed the wounding of the *eikon* through the fall, the closing chapter attends to the *eikon*'s restoration and theosis which, Gregory stipulates, begins at baptism. The argument proceeds as follows: if we consider together (a) Gregory's theological anthropology in which God creates the human person specifically to be vulnerable or porous (borrowing these terms from Charles Taylor) to the spiritual realm, (b) Gregory's high pneumatology, (c) his ideas about the sacrament of baptism, and (d) the interaction between the *eikon* of God and the devil, we can interpret the divinity of the *eikon* literally and in the broadest terms, since it incorporates the ontological, functional, ethical, relational, and experiential aspects of being a divine *eikon*.[25]

Finally, I argue that Gregory's narrative of the human person as an *eikon* of God is summarised best as 'divine, yet vulnerable'. This reflects Gregory's multifaceted approach, which relates to both human nature and experience. My use of 'vulnerable' is not intended to suggest that God might wound the human *eikon* in any way; rather, it is applied to indicate a kind of openness which may be positive or negative. The *eikon* is positively vulnerable (or porous) to God, having been created with the purpose of becoming 'divine', but at the same time negatively vulnerable to 'the world, the flesh, and the devil'.

---

[25] I apply ontological to denote the first order of things from which the epistemological and moral stem, and as a means of describing the reality of the divinity of the *eikon*. In later chapters, when I refer to the transformation of the human *eikon* as ontological, I do not imply that she has crossed the gap (διάστημα) between herself and God. My argument is that the manner in which the *eikon* increases in divinity applies quantitatively and not qualitatively, since God alone is ontologically divine.

I

Being an Image of God

This chapter argues that Scripture forms the basis of Gregory's vision of the human *eikon*. As observed in the Introduction, the fourth century was a complex syncretism of philosophical trends and ideas; undoubtedly, Gregory absorbed a variety of beliefs. Gregory's work has been read traditionally in light of Plato,[1] Aristotle,[2] Stoicism,[3] Plotinus,[4] Philo,[5] and Origen.[6] Towards the turn of the last century, scholars began to explore more fully the way in which Gregory uses Scripture in order to make his claims about doctrine. Frances Young, Ben Fulford, Brian Matz, Paul Gallay, and Kristoffel Demoen provide a sample of those who have

---

[1] Henri Pinault, *Le Platonisme de Saint Grégoire de Nazianze: Essai sur le relations du Christianisme et de l'Hellénisme dans son oeuvre théologique* (La Roche-sur-Yon, France: G. Romain, 1925); Jan M. Szymusiak, *Éléments de théologie de l'homme selon saint Grégoire de Nazianze* (Rome: Pontificia Universitas Gregoriana, 1963), 29.

[2] Andrew O.P. Hofer, *Christ in the Life and Teaching of Gregory of Nazianzus* (Oxford: Oxford University Press, 2013), 124–51.

[3] Susanna Elm, 'Inscriptions and Conversions: Gregory of Nazianzus on Baptism (Or. 38–40)' in Kenneth Mills and Anthony Grafton (eds.), *Conversion in Late Antiquity and the Early Middle Ages* (New York: University of Rochester Press, 2003), 1–35; Althaus, *Die Heilslehre des heiligen*, 57–60; Boris Maslov, 'οἰκείωσις πρὸς θεόν: Gregory of Nazianzus and the Heteronomous Subject of Eastern Christian Penance', *ZAC*, 16 (2012), 311–43.

[4] Dayna Kalleres, 'Demons and Divine Illumination: A Consideration of Eight Prayers by Gregory of Nazianzus', *VC*, 61, no. 2 (2007), 157–88.

[5] Francesco Trisoglio, 'Filone Alessandrino e l'esegesi cristiana: contributo alla conoscenza dell'influsso esercitato da Filone sul IV secolo, specificatamente in Gregorio de Nazianzo', *ANRW II*, 21, no. 1 (1984), 588–730.

[6] Claudio Moreschini, 'Nuove considerazione sull'origenismo di Gregorio Nazianzo' in Mario Giradi and Marcello Marin (eds.), *Origene e l'alessandrinismo cappadoce (III-IV secolo)* (Bari: Edipuglia, 2002), 207–18.

brought to the fore different aspects of Gregory's exegesis and made clear the extent to which Gregory draws on Scripture to form his arguments.[7]

Beginning with a brief overview of Gregory's hermeneutics, we shall see that Gregory approaches the Bible primarily in light of Jesus Christ as the 'focal centre of God's ordering of all of history'.[8] Moving on from here, we explore the predominant biblical themes from which Gregory draws in order to form his vision of the human *eikon*. These entail Christ the visible *Eikon*, beliefs about images and idols in light of the creation narratives in Genesis, the ethical implications of being an *eikon*, and later pseudepigraphal interpretations which set the *eikon* in a cosmological battle with the devil. Like the church fathers before him, Gregory deploys *eikon* in a variety of ways, describing primarily the human person and Christ, but also referring to metaphors, paintings, and pagan statues.[9] Gregory's broad application reflects the fact that *eikon* plays a substantial role in patristic theology, occupying over five pages in Lampe's *Patristic Greek Lexicon*, compared with less than a page in Liddell, Scott, and Jones' *A Greek-English Lexicon*.[10] Deriving from εἴκω, which translates as 'to be like, to seem', εἰκών can mean 'likeness' in the sense of that which is physical, such as a picture or a statue, or that which is immaterial, for example, a phantom or semblance. We shall see that this melting pot of interpretations feed into Gregory's overall vision of the *eikon*. Although Christian iconography began to be discussed by Christians in the fourth century, we do not move on to discuss this since Gregory himself mentions only pagan images.[11]

---

[7] Frances M. Young, *Biblical Exegesis and the Formation of Christian Culture* (Cambridge: Cambridge University Press, 1997), 102–113; Fulford, *Divine Eloquence*; Brian Matz, *Gregory of Nazianzus* (Grand Rapids, MI: Baker Academic, 2016); Paul Gallay, 'La Bible dans l'oeuvre de Grégoire de Nazianze le Théologien' in Claude Mondésert (ed.), *Le monde greg ancien et la Bible* (Paris: Éditions Beauchesne, 1984), 313–34; Kristoffel Demoen, *Pagan and Biblical Exempla in Gregory Nazianzen: A Study in Rhetoric and Hermeneutics* (Turnhout: Brepols, 1996).

[8] Fulford, *Divine Eloquence*, 1; Mario Baghos, 'St Gregory the Theologian's Metanarrative of History', *Phronema*, 26, no. 2 (2011), 63–79, 75.

[9] For *eikon* being used to depict paintings, see Or. 2.11 (SC 247, 104); 4.65 (SC 309, 172); 4.80 (SC 309, 202); 11.2 (SC 405, 332); 14.32 (PG 35, 900D); 21.22 (SC 270, 156); *eikon* as metaphor: Carm. 1.2.24 (PG 37, 793, 37); *eikon* as pagan statues: Or. 11.5 (SC 405, 338); Carm. 1.2.27 (PG 37, 854, 8).

[10] Geoffrey W.H. Lampe, *PGL* (Oxford: Clarendon Press, 1961), 410–16; Henry George Liddell, Robert Scott, and Henry Stuart Jones, *A Greek-English Lexicon*, 9th with supplement ed. (Oxford: Clarendon Press, 1940; repr., 1973), 485.

[11] Also observed by Jostein Børtnes, 'Eikôn Theou: Meanings of Likeness in Gregory of Nazianzus' in Frances M. Young, Mark J. Edwards, and Paul Parvis (eds.), *Studia Patristica*, 41 (Leuven: Peeters, 2006), 287–91. For the beginnings of Christian worship

GREGORY'S HERMENEUTICS

Gregory makes explicit his view of the books which he considers to be 'divinely inspired' in a poem entitled *On the Genuine Books of Divinely Inspired Scripture*.[12] He states that all else is not genuine, although, as Demoen and Gallay have observed, this does not prevent him from citing and alluding to numerous extra-canonical books not included in this list.[13] For example, Gregory mentions by name the books of Wisdom and of Revelation, although they are excluded from his poem.[14]

As Daley has suggested, iconographers often depict Gregory holding a Bible because, for Gregory, Scripture could be said to be the 'doorway to divinization'.[15] When we consider the question of Gregory's biblical interpretation, we must remember that he approached the Bible as a priest and as a pastor, concerned both with his own purity and that of the Church. He wrote a prayer for praying prior to reading Scripture; in this he writes that the Bible is a book of 'holiness and purity' through which God may attend to the soul of God's servant.[16] He considers time spent dwelling in the written word to be the best use of time. This is indicated by the vast number of poems which comprise passages of the Bible put to verse, produced by Gregory for the purpose of easy memorisation.[17] Aside from poems, much of Gregory's biblical interpretation occurs in the context of festal orations, where language is sacramental, conveying 'the eternal meaning of the biblical events that are being celebrated'.[18] Gregory writes that only the one whose heart has been made to burn as she reads the Bible is fit to stand and speak about God, since the text itself is a means of illumination.[19] He counts himself among those who are

of images, see Ernst Kitzinger, 'The Cult of Images in the Age before Iconoclasm', *DOP*, 8 (1954), 83–150, 88–150.

[12] Carm. 1.1.12 (PG 37, 472–474). This poem is translated by Brian Dunkle, *Poems on Scripture: Saint Gregory of Nazianzus* (New York: St. Vladimir's Seminary Press, 2012), 37–39.

[13] Paul Gallay, 'La Bible dans l'oeuvre de Grégoire de Nazianze le Théologien', 318; for example, the Book of Judith is cited in Or. 45.15 (PG 36, 644B); Baruch 3.36 is cited in Or. 30.13 (SC 250, 252–54); Or. 1.6 (SC 247, 78–80) is reminiscent of Tobit 10.4.

[14] Or. 42.23 (SC 384, 100–02) denotes Solomon as the author of Wisdom.

[15] Brian Daley, 'Walking through the Word of God: Gregory of Nazianzus as a Biblical Interpreter' in J. Ross Wagner, Christopher Kavin Rowe, and A. Katherine Grieb (eds.), *The Word Leaps the Gap: Essays on Scripture and Theology in Honor of Richard B. Hays* (Grand Rapids: Eerdmans, 2008), 514–31, 523.

[16] Carm. 1.1.35 (PG 37, 517, 10).   [17] Carm. 1.1.15 (PG 37, 475–506).

[18] Frances M. Young, *Biblical Exegesis*, 143–44.

[19] Or. 2.71 (SC 247, 182–84); 2.96–97 (SC 247, 214–16); 40.37 (SC 358, 282–84).

illumined, since in *On the Holy Spirit*, Gregory bases his arguments for the deity of the Spirit solely on Scripture, thus demonstrating that he is able both to interpret the Bible and speak about God.[20] Whilst Gregory did not leave behind a plethora of exegetical commentaries, we should not conclude that the act of interpretation was of little consequence to him.[21] On the contrary, Gregory prizes not only the Bible itself, but also holds clear ideas about how it should be read and by whom it should be interpreted.[22] As Fulford argued, Gregory continued in Origen's understanding of Scripture, whilst 'formulating a hermeneutic of the biblical witness to Jesus Christ'.[23] Origen's three senses roughly correspond to the literal, moral, and spiritual readings representing body, soul, and spirit; above all, allegory is prized.[24] Our purpose does not concern the nuances of how Gregory follows Origen, other than to recognise that Gregory's overall approach to Scripture should not be simply categorised as 'typological', 'literal' or 'allegorical'.[25] Our focus here is on how Gregory interprets Scripture in light of salvation history.

A number of commentators have drawn attention to the idea that for Gregory, 'the Bible *is* Christ, because its every word brings us into the presence of the one who spoke it'.[26] This approach differs from the majority of contemporary Western biblical scholarship. For, when approaching the biblical narrative of the human story, and in particular the human *eikon*, Western scholars often read it in light of the 'creation, fall, redemption' narrative which runs from Genesis to Revelation. Gregory's narrative does not follow a strictly linear construction, where the incarnation is simply the next chapter in the story of salvation. This is evident when he speaks about the creation of humanity in writings

---

[20] For further discussion of Gregory's use of Scripture in the defence of the Spirit, see Thomas A. Noble, 'Gregory Nazianzen's Use of Scripture in Defence of the Deity of the Spirit', *TB*, 39 (1988), 101–23.

[21] Or. 37 (SC 318, 270–319) is Gregory's only exegetical oration, focusing on Matt 19:12.

[22] Or. 31:21–24 (SC 250, 314–22).

[23] Ben Fulford, 'Gregory of Nazianzus and Biblical Interpretation' in Christopher A. Beeley (ed.), *Re-Reading Gregory of Nazianzus* (Washington, DC: The Catholic University of America Press, 2012), 31–66, 31–32.

[24] For Origen's system of exegesis, see Karlfried Froehlich, *Biblical Interpretation in the Early Church* (Philadelphia: Fortress Press, 1984), 48–78.

[25] Fulford, 'Gregory of Nazianzus and Biblical Interpretation', 32.

[26] Paul Evdokimov, *Orthodoxy*, trans. Jeremy Hummerstone (New York: New City Press, 2011), 194; Charles Kannengiesser, *Handbook of Patristic Exegesis: The Bible in Ancient Christianity*, vol 1 (Leiden: Brill, 2003), 749.

concerned primarily with Christ, or the Christian lifestyle, for example, *On the Theophany*,[27] *On the Lights*,[28] *On New Sunday*,[29] *On Sacred Pascha*,[30] poems which occur in his *Arcana* and *In Praise of Virginity*.[31] Thus, Christ is not conceived as though he were at the middle of a straight line, where there is a 'before' and an 'after'.[32] Rather than two distinctive actions, creation and salvation should be understood as a continual process in light of Christ, 'bringing the creature ... to the stature of the Saviour, by whom and for whom all creation came into being'.[33] The principal implication of Gregory's view of the incarnation means that he reads Scripture as a unified whole, focusing on the narrative of salvation. For example, in *On Love for the Poor*, Gregory moves from the Old Testament through to the New Testament, highlighting all the various ways in God has demonstrated mercy through the ages.[34] This relates to the way in which Gregory views

... the convergence of humanity and divinity in Christ's person at the incarnation, the significance of which (as both a remedy to evil and as opening up the potential for deification) places Christ metaphorically at the centre of the historical process.[35]

This approach determines Gregory's use of intertextuality, which Hays rightly defines as the 'the embedding of fragments of an earlier text within a later one'.[36] An example of this lies in Gregory's first Easter oration, where he reads the escape from Egypt of the Israelites both in light of Christ's passion and resurrection, and the new life for those following Christ.[37]

Turning to the biblical themes upon which Gregory draws to inform his vision of the human *eikon*, let us begin with Christ.

---

[27] Or. 38 (SC 358, 104–38).   [28] Or. 39 (SC 358, 150–97).

[29] Or. 44 (PG 36, 608A–622A).

[30] Or. 45 (PG 36, 623A–664C). The creation of the human person in Oration 38 is repeated almost verbatim in Oration 45.

[31] Carm. 1.2.1 (PG 37, 521–78); Peter Bouteneff, *Beginnings: Ancient Christian Readings of the Biblical Creation Narratives* (Grand Rapids, MI: Baker Academic, 2008), 168.

[32] Or. 2.88 (SC 247, 202–04).

[33] John Behr, *The Mystery of Christ: Life in Death* (Crestwood, New York: St. Vladimir's Seminary Press, 2006), 86.

[34] Or. 14.27 (PG 35, 892D–896A); Carm. 1.1.9 (PG 37, 456–64).

[35] Baghos, 'Metanarrative of History', 75.

[36] Richard B. Hays, *Echoes of Scripture in the Letters of Paul* (New Haven: Yale University Press, 1989), 14.

[37] Or. 1.1–5 (SC 247, 72–94).

CHRIST, THE DYNAMIC IMAGE

Gregory's interpretation of Christ as *Eikon* originates from the Greek translation of the Hebrew in Genesis 1:26–27; ויאמר אלהים נעשה אדם בצלמנו כדמותנו.[38] The differences are minor: the Septuagint omits the second pronominal suffix 'our' and repeats the prefix 'according to' (καὶ εἶπεν ὁ θεὸς ποιήσωμεν ἄνθρωπον κατ' εἰκόνα ἡμετέραν καὶ καθ' ὁμοίωσιν).[39] Nevertheless, Philo explains that they are important. The early Christians preserved his work for generations; furthermore, he serves as the first overlap between Greek philosophical thought and Judaism. Although Gregory himself makes no direct reference to Philo in his surviving works, Trisoglio has demonstrated that Gregory is familiar with Philo's thought.[40] Regarding Genesis 1:26–27, Philo explains that moving from the Hebrew 'in' to the Greek 'according to' points towards the human person as an *eikon* of an *Eikon*.[41] From this position, he lays out a system of thought regarding the *eikon*, where the *eikon* is the Logos, through whom the world was made.[42] Origen builds on this by explaining that the Logos is 'in' the image of God, whereas humanity is 'according to' the image of God:

In addition a principle [beginning] is that in accordance with which something is, that is, in accordance with its form. So, if indeed the first-born of all creation is 'the image of the invisible God' (Col. 1:15), the Father is his principle. But similarly Christ is the form of those who have come to be in accordance with the image of God. Therefore, if men are created 'according to the image', the image itself is 'according to the Father'.[43]

Whilst Gregory does not offer a systemic explanation like Origen, he follows Philo, Paul, Origen, and later fathers by interpreting Christ as the *Eikon* according to whom human *eikones* are created, the implications of which we discuss in depth in the following chapter.

Two further traditions that feed into the concept of Christ as the *Eikon* of God run through the biblical narrative. First is Paul's Adam

---

[38] *Biblia Hebraica Stuttgartensia*, 2. Whilst Gen 1:26–28 are often read together, for our purposes we will be discussing Gen 1:26–27 throughout.

[39] From here on I cite LXX first, followed by Hebrew Bible references in parentheses on the occasions when the references are different.

[40] Trisoglio, 'Filone Alessandrino', 588–730.   [41] *Her.* 230–31.

[42] *Spec.* 3.81; *Spec.* 3.83; *Leg.* 3.96. John 1:1, 14 refers to Jesus Christ as the Logos.

[43] *Comm. Jn* 1.104; translation, Joseph W. Trigg, *Origen* (London: Routledge, 1998), 122.

Christology, where Christ is the second Adam, the true bearer of the divine *Eikon* in contrast to Adam.[44] Secondly, the portrayal of Wisdom as the *eikon* of God's goodness is found in Wisdom 7:26 and in Philo.[45] Paul's Adam Christology is the tradition that is most relevant to this study, since its soteriological emphasis is evident in Gregory's thought about the human *eikon*'s restoration, as I discuss in the following chapter. Paul argues that the believer is no longer affiliated to the 'first Adam', but rather the goal is to become the *eikon* of the 'heavenly man' (1 Cor. 15:49). Dragoş Giulea has coined this process '*Eikonic* soteriology' as it represents the 'transformation from being the *eikon* of Adam into the *eikon* of the glorious Jesus ... the *eikon* of the Heavenly Anthropos and the second Adam'.[46] Beginning at baptism (Rom 6:3–5), salvation is viewed through an eschatological lens, whereby humanity's transformation into Christ's *eikon* is understood to be a dynamic process, rather than a 'one-off' event. The follower of Christ is transformed by encountering the glory of the Lord through which believers 'are being transformed into the same *eikon* from one degree of glory (δόξα) to another' (2 Cor 3:18). This accounts for Gregory's dynamic approach to the human *eikon* which, as we shall discuss in Chapter 5, depicts the *eikon* becoming divine. Next, we look back to the creation chapters in Genesis. Here, we shall observe how Gregory weaves into his interpretation contemporary beliefs about pagan images and idols.

IMAGES AND IDOLS[47]

The depiction of the human person as God's *eikon* occurs first in Genesis 1:26–27, in which God's creation of humankind forms the climax of the

---

[44] 1 Cor 11:7, 15:49; 2 Cor 3:18, 4:4. George H. Van Kooten, 'Image, Form and Transformation. A Semantic Taxonomy of Paul's "Morphic" Language' in Rieuwerd Buitenwerf, Harm W. Hollander and Johannes Tromp (eds.), *Jesus, Paul, and Early Christianity: Studies in Honour of Henk Jan De Jonge* (Leiden: Brill, 2008), 213–42, 216.

[45] *Leg.* 1.43; see James D.G. Dunn, *The Epistles to the Colossians and to Philemon*, NIGTC (Grand Rapids: Eerdmans, 1996), 89; Friedrich-Wilhelm Eltester, *Eikon im Neuen Testament*, BZNW (Berlin: Topelmann, 1958), 76.

[46] Dragoş A. Giulea, *Pre-Nicene Christology in Paschal Contexts: The Case of the Divine Noetic Anthropos* (Leiden: Brill, 2014), 155.

[47] A version of this section of the chapter is published as an article; 'The Human Icon: Gregory of Nazianzus on Being an *Imago Dei*', *Scottish Journal of Theology*, 72, no. 2 (2019), 166–181.

creation account.[48] Since Gregory informs his readers that he does not know Hebrew, the following passage is translated from the Septuagint:[49]

And God said, 'Let us make the human being according to our *eikon* and likeness (καὶ εἶπεν ὁ θεός ποιήσωμεν ἄνθρωπον κατ' εἰκόνα ἡμετέραν καὶ καθ' ὁμοίωσιν), and let them rule over the fish of the sea, and over the flying creatures of heaven, and over the cattle and all the earth, and over all the reptiles that creep on the earth.' And God made humankind, according to the *eikon* of God he made it. Male and female he made them (καὶ ἐποίησεν ὁ θεός τὸν ἄνθρωπον, κατ' εἰκόνα θεοῦ ἐποίησεν αὐτόν, ἄρσεν καὶ θῆλυ ἐποίησεν αὐτούς).[50]

Since our primary concern is Gregory's interpretation of the human *eikon*, we shall discuss the interpretations which are relevant to Gregory's ideas, rather than attempting to resolve the disparities about which contemporary Hebrew Bible scholars debate.[51] In order to inform the interpretation of the *eikon* in Genesis 1:26–27, Hebrew Bible scholars have attended to the way in which צלם/εἰκών is employed throughout the Old Testament. On a number of occasions צלם/εἰκών describes a physical object, such as a statue or an idol (Wis. 2.23, Num 33:52, Ezek 7:20, Dan 3:1). This, alongside recent archaeological discoveries, has led certain scholars to re-examine ideas of the *eikon* in light of cultures

---

[48] Gerhard von Rad, *Genesis*, trans. John H. Marks, rev. ed., OTL (Philadelphia: Westminster, 1972), 57. Scholars generally agree that the redaction of Genesis 1 belongs to a Priestly source; Gordan J. Wenham, *Genesis 1–15*, WBC (Waco: Word, 1987), xxxvii–xlii. For a broad coverage of the history of the exegesis of Gen 1:26–28, see Claus Westermann, *Genesis 1–11: A Continental Commentary*, trans. John Scullion (Minneapolis: Fortress Press, 1994), 147–55; Gunnlaugur A. Jónsson, *The Image of God: Genesis 1:26–28 in a Century of Old Testament Research*, CBOTS (Stockholm: Almqvist & Wiksell, 1988).

[49] Carm. 2.1.39 (PG 37, 1335, 82–83). Gregory usually read the LXX, occasionally referring to Theodotion's translation; see Demoen, *Pagan and Biblical Exempla*, 235. For an overview of the development of the LXX, see Sarah A. Brayford, *Genesis* (Leiden: Brill, 2007), 1–31; John W. Wevers, *Text History of the Greek Genesis* (Göttingen: Vandenhoeck & Ruprecht, 1974).

[50] Gen 1:26–27. Translation amended from Sophie Cartwright, *The Theological Anthropology of Eustathius of Antioch* (Oxford: Oxford University Press, 2015), 142. Greek text from *Septuaginta*, Alfred Rahlfs (ed.) and emended by Robert Hanhart, rev. ed. (Stuggart, 2006), 2. צלם is translated consistently as εἰκών throughout the LXX; see Martin Rösel, *Übersetzung als Vollendung der Auslegung*, BZAW (Berlin: de Gruyter, 1994), 48.

[51] For views regarding ontology of the image of God, see Andreas Schüle, 'Made in the "Image of God": The Concepts of Divine Images in Gen 1–3', *ZAW*, 117, no. 1 (2005), 1–20, 5. For comments on structure, see Wenham, *Genesis 1–15*, 29–30. For the function of the *imago Dei*, see Middleton, 'Imago Dei in Context', 12.

contemporary to those of the Old Testament.[52] Research has demonstrated that the Ancient Near Eastern notion of an image (צלמ) involved a ritual process of transformation.[53] Once the ritual was completed, the image of the god was believed to embody the god so fully that the image became the god itself. Egyptian texts make clear that the craftsmen were not concerned primarily with representing what a god looked like. Instead, the image was the place where the god manifested itself; 'thus the presence of the god and the blessing that accompanied that presence were effected through the image'.[54] The images were considered to be living images embodying the divine presence, rather than being merely lifeless wood or bronze statues. In effect, through ritual, the images became the gods themselves and were considered to be 'divine'.

This research sheds light not only on aspects of Genesis 1:26–27, but also Genesis 2:7, in which the author depicts the human person as being formed from a mixture of earth and breath, akin to the formation of an *eikon* of a god:

And God formed a human being, dust from the earth, and breathed into [the human's] face a breath of life, and the human became a living being.[55]

Interpreted thus, the human person does not 'possess' the *eikon* within herself, but rather the human person herself is the *eikon*, manifesting the presence of her Creator. This relates to the New Testament claim that Christ is the *Eikon* of the invisible God, who manifests God's presence fully.

Since the Ancient Near Eastern background is located in a vastly different culture from Gregory's, we must establish an overlap in beliefs about images (whether statues or portraits) of gods and emperors in the Graeco–Roman world. Traditionally, scholars are sceptical regarding the belief that the Graeco–Roman gods were present in their statues. This is due to the lack of evidence of any ritual of animation in Ancient Greece, unlike in ancient Mesopotamia.[56] Furthermore, following a negative

---

[52] Edward M. Curtis, 'Image of God' in David N. Freeman (ed.) *ABD, H-J*, (New York: Doubleday, 1992), 389–91.

[53] Zainab Bahrani, *The Graven Image: Representation in Babylonia and Assyria* (Philadelphia: University of Pennsylvania Press, 2003), 121–48.

[54] Curtis, 'Image of God', 389; Ellen J. Van Wolde, 'The Text as an Eloquent Guide: Rhetorical, Linguistic and Literary Features in Genesis 1' in Craig A. Evans, Joel N. Lohr, and David L. Petersen (eds.), *The Book of Genesis: Composition, Reception, and Interpretation* (Leiden: Brill, 2012), 134–52.

[55] Gen 2:7. Translation adapted from NETS.

[56] Walter Burkert, *Greek Religion*, trans. John Raffan (Cambridge, MA: Harvard University Press, 1985), 91.

reading of Platonic mimesis, commentators on Plato have argued that the educated elite understood the *eikon* as merely a copy.[57] However, Plato's application of *eikon* is multifaceted, encompassing linguistic *eikones*, shadows, statues, and paintings.[58] Therefore, note that on occasion, *eikones* such as the sun, the cave, and soul provide us with 'models that give access to concepts derived from and participating in imperceptible truths'.[59] Whilst Plato does not depict the human as an *eikon*, he describes the cosmos as a sensible god made in the *eikon* of the intelligible.[60] This idea is associated with Plato's theory of Forms, where sensible objects are images of eternal models, in which images denote kinship rather than mere resemblance.[61] This occurs because the *eikon* proceeds from the model 'radiating from the Form', according to Plato.[62] For this reason, on occasion Plato speaks about an *eikon* as possessing great power; for example, Alcibiades declares that the *eikon* of Socrates is capable of making him feel ashamed.[63] Shortly, we shall observe that Gregory describes the effect of a particular portrait of Polemon in a similar manner.

Studies on images have challenged the view that *eikones* are simply copies by building on the 'popular' Graeco-Roman view, which accepted the presence of deities in *eikones*.[64] For example, Augustus banished Poseidon's statue because of bad weather; through this action it was believed that Augustus insulted Poseidon himself.[65] Also, an ambiguity in the Greek language means that '"Artemis" can imply either the goddess

---

[57] Verity J. Platt, *Facing the Gods: Epiphany and Representation in Greco-Roman Art, Literature and Religion* (Cambridge: Cambridge University Press, 2011), 204; Danielle S. Allen, *Why Plato Wrote* (Oxford: Wiley-Blackwell, 2010), 174–76.

[58] *Symp.* 215a; *Crat.* 432c; *Resp.* 515a. For a discussion on the impact of names on images, see Deborah Steiner, *Images in Mind: Statues in Archaic and Classical Greek Literature and Thought* (Princeton, NJ: Princeton University Press, 2001), 71–73.

[59] Allen, *Why Plato Wrote*, 153. For further discussion on participation, see ibid., 148–53.

[60] εἰκὼν τοῦ νοητοῦ θεὸς αἰσθητός; *Tim.* 92c.   [61] κοινωνία; *Phaed.* 100d–e.

[62] Alain Besançon, *The Forbidden Image: An Intellectual History of Iconoclasm* (Chicago, Ill.: University of Chicago Press, 2000), 28. On likeness and difference of images, see *Crat.* 432c; *Soph.* 236a.

[63] *Symp.* 216b.

[64] Christopher A. Faraone, *Talismans and Trojan Horses: Guardians and Statues in Ancient Greek Myth and Ritual* (Oxford: Oxford University Press, 1992), passim; Moshe Barasch, *Icon: Studies in the History of an Idea* (New York: New York University Press, 1992), 24; Hans Belting, *Likeness and Presence: A History of the Image Before the Era of Art*, trans. Edmund Jephcott (Chicago: University of Chicago Press, 1994), 37; Jaś Elsner, 'Iconoclasm as Discourse: From Antiquity to Byzantium', *Art Bulletin*, XCIV, no. 3 (2012), 368–84, 370.

[65] Suetonius, *Aug.* 16.

herself or an image of her'.[66] This explains why so much care had to be taken when handling statues; the 'ambiguity afforded an edge of danger, since incorrect treatment of a statue could be construed as an assault on the deity embodied in it'.[67] This notion of representation extends to ancient dream theory, where it makes no difference whether the dreamer sees the statue of a god or the god itself.[68] Images of Roman emperors are also pertinent to this discussion.[69] For instance, Theodosius made Maximus an emperor by erecting the latter's image, which he commanded the people to worship in place of their Alexandrian gods.[70] Furthermore, in Gregory's own lifetime, the images of the emperor Theodosius were smashed to pieces in the tax rebellion in AD 387, who was angry precisely because his imperial image 'embodied his own actual presence within the city'.[71] Thus, a statue of a god embodied the divine presence of the god; likewise *eikones* of emperors were perceived to embody the emperor's presence, functioning as a substitute for the emperor. On the subject of emperors and their *eikones,* in his first invective *Against Julian,* Gregory argues that it is acceptable to venerate an *eikon* of the emperor, but not if pagan gods also feature in the same picture.[72] This is because by the fourth century, Christians accepted the emperor cult; but for Gregory, bowing down before portraits or statues of pagan gods was a step too far. He offers no detail on the relationship between emperors and their *eikones,* unlike Basil, who, in *On the Holy Spirit,* writes,

Because it is said that there is a king and the image of the king, but not two kings, for the power is not divided and the glory is not portioned out ... On account of this the honour of the image passes over to the archetype.[73]

---

[66] Pausanias, *Descr.* 3.16.9; Matthew Dillon and Lynda Garland, *Ancient Greece: Social and Historical Documents from Archaic Times to the Death of Alexander* (London: Routledge, 2010), 240; Jaś Elsner, *Roman Eyes: Visuality & Subjectivity in Art & Text* (Princeton, NJ: Princeton University Press, 2007), 11; Robin Lane Fox, *Pagans and Christians* (Harmondsworth: Viking, 1986), 133.

[67] Elsner, *Roman Eyes*, 11; Pseudo-Lucian's *Amores*, 15–16.   [68] Barasch, *Icon*, 32–33.

[69] Plutarch wrote that the Roman emperor was considered to be an 'image of God, who orders all things'; *Princ. Iner.* 780E.

[70] Sabine MacCormack, *Art and Ceremony in Late Antiquity* (Berkeley: University of California Press, 1981), 67.

[71] Frederick G. McLeod, *The Image of God in the Antiochene Tradition* (WA, DC: Catholic University of America Press, 1999), 236.

[72] Or. 4.80–81 (SC 309, 202–06).

[73] *On the Holy Spirit* 18.45 (SC 17, 194). Translation, Stephen M. Hildebrand, PPS (Crestwood, New York: St. Vladimir's Seminary Press, 2011), 80–81. Børtnes has identified that John Damascene quoted extensively from all the Cappadocians in the florilegia to his *Treatises against the Iconoclasts;* see 'Rhetoric and Mental Images', 37.

Thus far, we have seen that pagan *eikones* are likenesses which have the potential to carry some presence or power of the figure represented, whether it is an emperor or a god. Pagan and Christian ideas about the power of certain portraits are also pertinent to this discussion. Recall Alcibiades' reaction to the *eikon* of Socrates, which made him feel ashamed. We see a similar idea at work in Gregory's second poem *On Virtue*.[74] In this poem, Gregory recounts the experience of a whore, who comes across an *eikon* of Polemon in the home of a dissolute youth.[75] Initially, Gregory informs his readers that Polemon was a man who was known for 'getting the better of the passions'. He moves on to suggest that whoever encounters the portrait of Polemon meets with the image of man who is said to be virtuous. Gregory describes the immense power of Polemon's gaze staring out from the portrait to such an extent that the woman was put to shame 'as if he were alive (ζῶν)'.[76] Gregory's description suggests that particular *eikones* bear a presence, or a power, which means that the person encountering them meets, in some way, the figure that the portrait is depicting. Gregory reinterprets a contemporary belief to serve a specific purpose in his corpus of poems, which relates to the practice of the Christian faith. I assume that Gregory is drawing upon the belief that pagan statues or portraits possessed the potential to gaze at their onlookers in a way that suggests the presence of 'magical powers'.[77] This relates, albeit indirectly, to the beliefs about images and idols manifesting the presence of the god or figure that they depict, which filter through a variety of ancient cultures.

Ideas such as these, i.e. pagan images and idols bearing the presence of the god or emperor which they embody, appear to have contributed to the interpretation of Genesis 1:26–27 in the work of theologians preceding Gregory; for example, Clement of Alexandria, living in the second-century. He asserts that human persons are rational sculptures of the Logos of God (*Prot.* I.5.4, I.6.4). As Laura Nasrallah argues, Clement 'engages and reverses the theological statements of statuary and images that repeated across the cityscapes of the Greek East'.[78] She goes as far as

---

[74] Carm. I.2.10 (PG 37, 680–754).

[75] For the identity of Polemon, see Wayne Meeks, *The Origins of Christian Morality: The First Two Centuries* (New Haven: Yale University Press, 1993), 22.

[76] Carm. I.2.10 (PG 37, 738, 807).

[77] Børtnes, 'Rhetoric and Mental Images in Gregory', 39.

[78] Laura Nasrallah, 'The Earthen Human, the Breathing Statue: The Sculptor God, Greco-Roman Statuary, and Clement of Alexandria' in Konrad Schmid and Christopher Riedweg (eds.), *Beyond Eden: The Biblical Story of Paradise [Genesis 2–3] and its*

to suggest that Clement's ideas about the image of God cannot be understood outside of second-century Alexandria, which is a landscape full of ideas about statues and idols:[79]

We must also take these statues seriously as *theological* statements. That is, even as Christians debate incarnation and *theosis*, so also these statues say something about human possibilities of becoming divine, and about the divine in human form.[80]

Clement is not the only theologian to consider the human *eikon* as a physical *eikon*; Irenaeus also emphasises the inclusion of the body when discussing the human *eikon*, resulting in the whole human person being, quite literally, an *eikon* of God.[81] Therefore, the human person could be said to be divine because she is an *eikon* of God, embodying the spirit of God.

Consider that for a human *eikon* to function like a pagan *eikon*, the concept of *eikon* must relate to the whole human person and not only to the spiritual intellect or the soul. This challenges the general view concerning Gregory's approach to the human *eikon*. As observed in the Introduction, scholars generally equate Gregory's understanding of the *eikon* with the soul or the spiritual intellect. This discussion is influenced by the approach of early theologians, such as Philo, who argued that the spiritual intellect (νοῦς) is the aspect of the human person which images God.[82] He came to this conclusion through his interpretation of the differing creation accounts in Genesis 1 and 2. Scholars are almost unanimous in believing that Philo regards the accounts as speaking of two different people; one earthly and one heavenly.[83] For Philo, it is the heavenly person alone who is made according to the *eikon* of God; this notion aligns itself with Philo's idea that the *eikon* is not corporeal, but relates only to the spiritual intellect. A few centuries later, Origen presents

---

Reception History (Tübingen: Mohr Siebeck, 2008), 110–40, 110. I am indebted to Crispin Fletcher-Louis for pointing me to Nasrallah's work.

[79] Nasrallah, 'The Earthen Human', 110.   [80] Nasrallah 122.

[81] *Dem.* 22; see John Behr, *St. Irenaeus of Lyons: The Apostolic Preaching* (Crestwood, New York: St Vladimir's Seminary Press, 1997); Matthew C. Steenberg, *Of God and Man: Theology as Anthropology from Irenaeus to Athanasius* (New York: T&T Clark, 2009), 17.

[82] *Spec.* 1.171; *Opif.* 134; translation David T. Runia, *Philo of Alexandria, On the Creation of the Cosmos according to Moses: Introduction, Translation and Commentary* (Leiden: Brill, 2001), 82. In making this move, Philo protects God from being understood as anthropomorphic, which is crucial to his theology; see *Leg.* 2.1.

[83] *Leg.* 1.31, 2.4. For an informative overview of the history of scholarly interpretation of this problem, see Thomas H. Tobin, *The Creation of Man: Philo and the History of Interpretation*, CBQMS (WA, DC: Catholic Biblical Association of America, 1983), 102–34.

the same view: 'The soul, not only for the first man, but of all men arose according to the image.'[84] Whilst Gregory undoubtedly interprets the human *eikon* as the spiritual intellect on numerous occasions, he also interprets the *eikon* quite literally as a physical *eikon*.

The belief that pagan statues and portraits are likenesses, which have the potential to bear some presence or power of the figure represented, informs Gregory's interpretation of Genesis 1:26–27. For our first example of how Gregory employs these ideas of contemporary statuary, we need look no further than *A Funeral Oration on the Great Basil*. Here, we observe Basil functioning in a manner similar to a pagan *eikon*, when Gregory likens him to a statue at the Epiphany Eucharist:

> With body and eyes and mind (διάνοιαν) unswerving, as though nothing new had occurred, but rather being fixed like a statue (ἀλλ' ἐστηλωμένον) so to speak, for God and the altar, while those around him stood in fear and reverence (τοὺς δὲ περὶ αὐτὸν ἐστηκότας ἐν φόβῳ τινὶ καὶ σεβάσματι).[85]

Like a stone or wooden *eikon*, Basil is perfectly still. In the same way that we would expect pagans to respond to a pagan *eikon* with fear and reverence, those around Basil respond likewise with 'fear and reverence'. In effect, Gregory treats Basil here as though he were a 'divine' *eikon*. If we bear in mind that *eikones* were often seen as being 'direct links back to their prototypes', it is logical that those around Basil would revere him, for in revering Basil as God's *eikon*, they revere God.[86]

Elsewhere, ideas about the pagan *eikon* as a bearer of divine presence shed light on the occasions when Gregory contrasts directly the human *eikon* with the pagan *eikon* or idol. Gregory seeks to undermine the power of the pagan *eikon*, by demonstrating the unique status of the human *eikon* when compared to pagan *eikones*. For the human person is the *eikon* who truly bears divine presence, as she alone is made alive through God's breath.[87] Gregory makes this point in his second poem on *Ignoble Ways of Nobility*:

---

[84] Homily 2.1; Origen, *Homilies on Jeremiah; Homily on 1 Kings 28*, trans. John Clark Smith, TFC (WA, DC: Catholic University of America Press, 1998), 23.

[85] Or. 43.52 (SC 384, 234).

[86] Peter Stewart, 'The Image of the Roman Emperor' in Rupert Shepherd and Robert Maniura (eds.), *Presence: The Inherence of the Prototype within Images and Other Objects* (Hants., UK: Ashgate, 2006), 245–58, 243–44; Suzanne Saïd, 'Deux noms de l'image en grec ancien: idole et icône', *CRAI*, 131, no. 2 (1987), 309–30, 323.

[87] Patricia Cox Miller, *The Corporeal Imagination: Signifying the Holy in Late Ancient Christianity* (Pennsylvania: University of Pennsylvania Press Incorporated, 2012), 133–42.

> For indeed the painted *eikon* (εἰκών) is not greater than the *eikon* of the
> breathing man, even though it shines (τῆς τοῦ πνέοντος ἀνδρὸς, εἰ καὶ
> λάμπεται).[88]

The notion of the breathing human *eikon* as superior to all other *eikones*
relates back to the way in which the human person was created. Conflating the creation accounts in both Genesis 1 and 2, Gregory depicts the
human *eikon* as animated through God's Spirit in his poem *On the Soul*:

> As [God] spoke, taking a portion of freshly made earth,
> with immortal hands God established my form and gave to it a share of
> [God's] own life.
> For into it [God] infused Spirit (πνεῦμα), a fragment of the hidden Godhead.
> From clay and breath a mortal *eikon* of the immortal One
> (βροτός ἀθανάτοιο εἰκών) was established . . .[89]

The example above is typical of how Gregory describes the creation of the
human *eikon*. She is unique amongst all *eikones* because she is created by
God and infused with God's Spirit. Before we continue to examine
Gregory's usage of contemporary beliefs relating to images and idols,
we must pause for a moment to note the significance of Gregory's
pneumatological anthropology, a theme to which we shall return in
Chapter 5. Above, Gregory describes the formation of the human *eikon*
as the earth infused with 'Spirit, a fragment of the hidden Godhead'.
Thus, for Gregory, the Spirit gives life to the *eikon* and therefore gives
meaning and purpose to the *eikon*. By being infused with Spirit, the *eikon*
is able to manifest the presence of God unlike any other kind of pagan
idol. By depicting the Spirit present in the creation of the *eikon*, Gregory
avoids a common oversight in theological anthropology. This oversight
has been observed by Mark Cortez, who has argued that a problem
occurs when theologians depict the Spirit as an 'eschatological addendum'.[90] By this, Cortez refers to the Holy Spirit being discussed only in
relation to the renewal and transformation of the human person, but not
viewed as present at the creation of the *eikon*.[91] Understood in this way,

---

[88] Carm. 1.2.27 (PG 37, 854, 8–9).   [89] Carm. 1.1.8 (PG 37, 452, 70–75).
[90] Marc Cortez, 'Idols, Images and a Spirit-ed Anthropology' in Myk Habets (ed.),
A Pneumatological Account of the Imago Dei (Minneapolis: Fortress Press, 2016),
267–82, 268.
[91] For example, see Stanley J. Grenz, *The Social God and the Relational Self: A Trinitarian
Theology of the Imago Dei* (Louisville, KY: Westminster John Knox Press, 2001),
225–28.

the Spirit makes an appearance halfway through the salvation story, but only after the fall and consequent need for renewal and healing. The Spirit, when depicted only as doing the work of transforming or renewing the *eikon*, is absent from the initial meaning and purpose of the *eikon*. Whereas Gregory positions the Spirit quite explicitly at the creation of the human *eikon*, before moving on to depict the Spirit's transformation of the *eikon* during and after baptism. By making this move, Gregory not only creates the space for understanding the Spirit's involvement in the creation of the *eikon* in terms of meaning and purpose (i.e. to bear the presence of God), but also he avoids locating the Spirit as an 'eschatological addendum'.

As we return to discuss the human *eikon* in light of other kinds of images, let us recall that as far as Gregory is concerned, the *eikon* is different precisely because she bears the Spirit of God and truly manifests divine presence. This becomes evident further through Gregory's use of language in his poem on the Ten Commandments, as they appear in Exodus 20:1–17 and Deuteronomy 5:6–22.[92] The second commandment in Exodus is relevant to this discussion:

You shall not make for yourself an idol (εἴδωλον) or likeness of anything whatever is in heaven above and whatever is in the earth beneath and whatever is in the waters beneath the earth (Ex 20:4).[93]

Gregory interprets this commandment as,

You shall not set up an empty likeness and a breathless *eikon* (οὐ στήσεις ἴνδαλμα κενὸν καὶ ἄπνοον εἰκώ).[94]

Whilst εἴδωλον occurs in both Exodus and Deuteronomy, Gregory exchanges it for εἰκών in his interpretation of the commandment. Since Gregory is famed for his rhetoric and chooses his words carefully, we should not assume that the alteration was either an oversight or merely used to fit with the metre of the poem. Rather, Gregory appears to recall that there is only one true *eikon* of God; namely, the human person. Frances Young offers a thesis which relates to Gregory's application of the ten commandments. She explores early church fathers' concepts of *eikon* in relation to Exodus 20:4 and idolatry; Colossians 1:15 and Christology; and Genesis 1:27 and anthropology, arguing that these three

---

[92] Carm. 1.1.12 (PG 37, 471–74).   [93] Translation from NETS.
[94] Carm. 1.1.15 (PG 37, 476).

passages are implicitly related in Athanasius, the Cappadocians, and Cyril of Jerusalem.[95] Young draws the three key texts together, arguing,

As the image of the Image of God human beings replace idols, all the more so as the corruption of sin is washed away and they are renewed after the Image in Christ so as to become more and more God-like.[96]

Young's thesis could be furthered by observing that Gregory's poetic reworking of the second commandment, cited above, is an explicit, not implicit, example of the human *eikon* replacing a pagan idol. Furthermore, a significant factor in how the human *eikon* functions on earth relates to where human *eikones* direct their worship. Gregory argues that it is not fitting for mortals to commit idolatry, precisely because they are *eikones* of God:

It is not right, it is not proper for a mortal to be born from God
   (οὐδ' ἐπέοικε θεοῦ βροτὸν ἐκγεγαῶτα)
A beautiful and imperishable *eikon* (ἄφθιτος εἰκών) of the Heavenly Word ...
To give way unlawfully to empty idols (εἴδωλα κενά)
Of things which live in the sea, the earth and that which flies in the air ...[97]

Above, Gregory argues that as an imperishable *eikon* the human person must not worship idols. The human person is the breathing *eikon* because she is filled with the breath of God, compared with idols which are empty; therefore she must not commit idolatry.

We will continue to explore this theme in Chapter 2, in which we see that Gregory also presents Christ as a physical *Eikon*; and Chapter 3, in which we will discuss how Gregory treats women literally as physical *eikones*. Together, these examples build a picture of how Gregory views the *eikon* literally as a visible *eikon* of God. I am not suggesting that what Gregory writes about *eikones* and idols is highly theorised; however, throughout his work, Gregory refers to physical *eikones* (whether two or three-dimensional) frequently enough to warrant considering how these concepts inform his overall idea of the human *eikon*.

BECOMING DIVINE

The designation of the double 'according to' (κατ 'εἰκόνα and καθ' ὁμοίωσιν) in the Septuagint translation of Genesis 1:26–27 led fathers, such as

---

[95] Frances M. Young, 'God's Image: The "Elephant in the Room" in the Fourth Century?' in Allen Brent and Markus Vinzent (eds.), *Studia Patristica*, 50 (Leuven: Peeters Publishers, 2011), 57–72.
[96] Ibid., 67.   [97] Carm. 2.2.7 (PG 37, 1555, 51–56).

Clement, Irenaeus, and Origen, to place a distinction between the *eikon* and the 'likeness'.[98] Interpreted thus, God gives the *eikon* to humanity at creation, whereas the 'likeness' is regarded as a process of transformation which reaches its completion at the eschaton. See Origen's explanation of this below:

> The highest good towards which every rational creature is hurrying, also called the end and goal of all things, ... is to become like God as much as possible ... this is indeed what Moses is pointing out above all when he describes the original creation of humankind ... thus when he said: 'In the image of God he created him' and said nothing more about the likeness, he is actually indicating that the human being did indeed receive the dignity of God's image in the first creation, and the dignity of his likeness is reserved for the consummation.[99]

Often scholars attribute this distinction between *eikon* and likeness to the adaptation of Platonic thought regarding progressive divinity.[100] Knowing God and becoming like God as far as possible (ὁμοίωσις θεῷ κατὰ τὸ δυνατόν) is the *telos* of Plato's philosophical system.[101] According to Van Kooten, this is 'the natural extension of the semantic-conceptual field of the image of God'.[102] Also, Andrew Louth writes,

> The verse from Genesis, to a Greek philosophical ear, suggested that the human was made in the image of God and that human destiny was assimilation to God, what the Greek Fathers, especially, came to call deification.[103]

Whilst Gregory speaks consistently about the *eikon* becoming divine, unlike Clement and Origen, he offers no explanation regarding the distinction between *eikon* and likeness. The closest he comes to describing

---

[98] *Strom.* 2.131.6; *Haer.* 5.6.1; *Princ.* 3.6.1.

[99] *Princ.* 3.6.1, trans. Hans Urs von Balthasar, *Origen, Spirit and Fire: A Thematic Anthology of His Writings*, trans. Robert J. Daly (Edinburgh: T&T Clark, 2001), 56. Also, see *Cels.* 4.30; Crouzel, *Théologie de l'image de Dieu chez Origène*, 217–45; Maximos Aghiorgoussis, 'Applications of the Theme "Eikon Theou" (Image of God) according to Saint Basil the Great', *GOTR*, 21, no. 3 (1976), 265–88, 276.

[100] Julia Annas, *Platonic Ethics, Old and New* (Ithaca: Cornell University Press, 1999), 52; David Sedley, 'The Ideal of Godlikeness' in Gail Fine (ed.), *Plato Volume 2: Ethics, Politics, Religion and the Soul* (Oxford: Oxford University Press, 1999), 309–28, 309; Daniel C. Russell, 'Virtue as "Likeness to God" in Plato and Seneca', *JHP*, 42, no. 3 (2004), 241–60.

[101] *Symp.* 207c–209e; *Theat.* 176e–177a; Sedley, 'The Ideal of Godlikeness', 309.

[102] George H. Van Kooten, *Paul's Anthropology in Context: The Image of God, Assimilation to God and Tripartite Man in Ancient Judaism, Ancient Philosophy and Early Christianity* (Tübingen: Mohr Siebeck, 2008), 125.

[103] Andrew Louth, 'The Fathers on Genesis' in Craig A. Evans, Joel N. Lohr, and David L. Petersen (eds.), *The Book of Genesis: Composition, Reception, and Interpretation* (Leiden: Brill, 2012), 561–78, 573.

this distinction is in Gorgonia's funeral oration. Gregory describes Gorgonia's real citizenship as being in heaven, drawing from Ephesians 2:17–22, Philipians 3:12–21, Galatians 4:25–26, and Hebrews 12:23. On Gorgonia, Gregory writes,

But if one is to explain her at a higher and more philosophical level, Gorgonia's native land was the 'Jerusalem above', the city not yet seen but known, the place of our common life, towards which we hasten – where Christ is citizen, and his fellow citizens the festal gathering and 'assembly of the first born whose names are written in heaven', where they celebrate their great founder by contemplating his glory, circling around him in a dance that will never come to an end. There, nobility consists in preserving his image and keeping one's likeness to the archetype (εὐγένεια δὲ ἡ τῆς εἰκόνος τήρησις καὶ ἡ πρὸς τὸ ἀρχέτυπον ἐξομοίωσις).[104]

Even here, Gregory does not echo Plato precisely in his approach to human *eikones* becoming divine. Gregory identifies Gorgonia's likeness to the archetype as that which is to be preserved, rather than obtained, and within the context of the followers of Christ being citizens in God's household. Thus, we cannot appreciate fully Gregory's beliefs about becoming divine without also turning to the biblical narrative. We shall return to explore this more fully in Chapter 5.

ETHICS AND THE IMAGE OF GOD

Being created as an *eikon* of God entails that all human life is precious and must be treated with care and respect. This is the interpretation offered in Genesis 9:6:

Whoever sheds the blood of a human, by a human shall that person's blood be shed; for by divine image I made humankind.[105]

This ethical interpretation of Genesis 1 continues to be prevalent throughout pseudepigraphal literature, Philo, and the early church fathers.[106]

---

[104] Translation Daley, *Gregory of Nazianzus*, 66; Or. 8.6 (SC 405, 256); ἐξομοίωσις in Or. 24.15 (SC 284, 74); 32.15 (SC 318, 116); ὁμοιώσεως in Or. 6.14 (SC 318, 156); Carm. 2.1.12 (PG 37, 1182, 221). Calvet-Sebasti (SC 405, 287) argues correctly that the archetype represents the Father.

[105] Translation from NETS.

[106] 2 Enoch 44; *Spec.* 3.83; *Comm. Jn.* 13.28.165. For further comments on ethics and the *eikon*, see Jacob Jervell, *Imago Dei: Gen 1,26f. im Spätjudentum, in der Gnosis und in den paulinischen Briefen* (Göttingen: Vandenhoeck and Ruprecht, 1960), 26–37.

Gregory follows the author of Genesis 9:6 and later interpreters in placing a high value upon the life of the human *eikon* precisely because she images God. Taken from an oration on theological discourse, the lines below exemplify this:

It is not the same thing to cut down a plant or a flower which blooms temporarily, and a human person (ἄνθρωπος). You are an *eikon* of God and you converse with an *eikon* of God.[107]

Above, Gregory demonstrates two ways in which he approaches the ethics of being an *eikon* of God; namely function and ontology.[108] Firstly, he argues that, in order to image God, the human *eikon* must imitate God's philanthropy towards other human *eikones*; this relates to the function of the *eikon*. Secondly, Gregory observes that human life is precious because human persons image God; this relates to her ontology. In a further oration, highlighting ethical concerns, Gregory states that the ruler must rule fairly because the ruler is an *eikon* of God. In making this move he argues that the divine function of the human *eikon* is to rule as God rules. Also, Gregory observes that the ruler should rule fairly because those over whom he rules are *eikones* of God.[109] Thus, the human *eikon* warrants fair treatment precisely because she is an *eikon* of God.

Observe this two-pronged approach regarding function and ontology in Gregory's treatment of philanthropy towards the poor.[110] Gregory argues that those who are poor and sick should be treated benevolently because they too are God's *eikones*.[111] Likewise, those who practise kindness toward the poor and the sick are most like God,[112] where practising philanthropy increases the divinity of the *eikon*.[113] Gregory's views on the relationship between poverty, wealth, and the *eikon* are consistent. They are scattered throughout his orations, poems, and

---

[107] Or. 32.30 (SC 318, 148).   [108] Or. 38.11 (SC 358, 124–26).

[109] Or. 17.9 (PG 35, 976B–D).

[110] Gregory recalls the creation of humankind as reason for providing relief for the needy in Or. 14.26 (PG 35, 892B–D); see Verna E. F. Harrison, 'Poverty, Social Involvement, and Life in Christ according to Saint Gregory the Theologian', *GOTR*, 39, no. 1–2 (1994), 151–64, 156.

[111] For a thorough critique of all of the literature pertaining to poverty relief by the Cappadocians, see Susan Holman, *The Hungry Are Dying: Beggars and Bishops in Roman Cappadocia* (Oxford: Oxford University Press, 2001), 1–29.

[112] Or. 14.22–23 (PG 35, 885B–888A); 14.27 (PG 35, 892D–893A).

[113] Or. 14.27 (PG 35, 892D–893A); 17.9 (PG 35, 976B–D).

letters,[114] occurring in abundance in *On Love for the Poor*.[115] Holman
has observed that Gregory exhorts his audience

to imitate the ἰσότης of God, which translators render equality, evenhandedness,
or 'the justice of God'. He also uses ἰσονομία, a Greek political term meaning
'equality of rights'.[116]

Thus, the purpose of the human *eikon* is to function like God in all ethical
concerns. The more she functions like God, the more the *eikon* becomes
like God, vis à vis 'divine'.

Gregory continues to develop the ethical implications of being an *eikon*
of God as a major theme regarding humankind throughout his writing.
Numerous scholars have observed that Gregory's high view of the human
eikon informs directly his ethics.[117] Exemplifying the scholarly opinion,
Mumford argues, 'the concept of the *eikon* functions for Gregory as it
does originally in *Genesis*, as a source of "normativity"'.[118]

THE DEVIL

Our final consideration of the biblical background to Gregory's account
of the human *eikon* concerns the interplay between the *eikon* and the
devil, which is a consistent theme in the Bible and a strong tradition in

---

[114] Or. 8.9 (SC 405, 262–64); 14 (PG 35, 858A–909C); 26.6 (SC 284, 138–40); 38.5 (SC
358, 110–12); 43.63 (SC 384, 262–64). There are similar themes in *Against Wealth*; see
Ulrich Beuckmann, *Gregor von Nazianz: Gegen die Habsucht (Carmen 1,2,28)
Einleitung und Kommentar*. SGKA. NF 2 (Paderborn: Ferdinand Schöningh,
1988), 12.

[115] Or. 14 (PG 35, 858A–909C).

[116] Susan R. Holman, 'Out of the Fitting Room: Rethinking Patristic Social Texts on "The
Common Good"' in Johan Leemans, Brian J. Matz, and Johan Verstraeten (eds.),
*Reading Patristic Texts on Social Ethics: Issues and Challenges for Twenty-First
Century Christian Social Thought* (WA DC, USA: Catholic University of America
Press, 2011), 103–23, 115.

[117] Or. 7.9 (SC 405, 202); 14.20 (PG 35, 881D–884B); 14.27 (PG 35, 892D–896A); 26.10
(SC 284, 248); Carm. 1.2.25 (PG 37, 824, 148–53); 2.2.6 (PG 37, 1549, 89). See
Pelikan, *Christianity and Classical Culture*, 123–24; Stanley S. Harakas,
'Presuppositions for Ethical Method in St. Gregory the Theologian's Five Theological
Orations', *GOTR*, 55, no. 1–4 (2010): 89–126, 120; Verna E.F. Harrison, 'Male and
Female in Cappadocian Theology', *JTS*, 41, no. 2 (1990), 441–71, 456; Tasos Sarris
Michopoulos, 'Mimisometha Nomon Theou: Gregory the Theologian's Ontology of
Compassion', *GOTR*, 39, no. 1–2 (1994), 109–21.

[118] James Mumford, *Ethics at the Beginning of Life: A Phenomenological Critique* (Oxford:
Oxford University Press, 2013), 188.

apocryphal and pseudepigraphal writings.[119] The dearth of research directed towards the devil, not only with reference to Gregory's work, but also more widely in theology, relates to the effect of the Enlightenment on Western culture.[120] Modernity ushered in scepticism towards transcendent beings, such as angels and demons. Consequently, when scholars of contemporary early Christian and biblical studies pay due attention to the devil, it is often to demythologise themes concerning evil powers.[121] However, we should not confuse the worldview of the pre-moderns with that which was largely adopted through modernity.

The tradition which attests to the enmity between the human *eikon* and the devil appears first in Wisdom 2:23–24, as an interpretation of the first three chapters of Genesis:

> ... for God created us for incorruption,
> and made us in the *eikon* of his own eternity,
> but through the devil's envy death entered the world
> (φθόνῳ δὲ διαβόλου θάνατος εἰσῆλθεν εἰς τὸν κόσμον),
> and those who belong to his company experience it.

Many scholars have observed that this theme of hostile angelic powers is also prevalent in the New Testament, particularly in Paul's letters.[122] The devil and his army of demons are seen as a threat to all that God has created, in particular, human persons.[123] Paul refers directly to the notion of evil powers, with reference to Christ as the *Eikon* in two ways. Firstly, Christ as God's *Eikon* has authority over the powers (Col 1:15–20, 2:10). The particular list of powers in Colossians 1:16 can also be found in

---

[119] John R. Levison, *Portraits of Adam in Early Judaism: From Sirach to 2 Baruch*, JSPSS (Sheffield: JSOT, 1988), 178.

[120] For a review of the Enlightenment reluctance to accept the reality of spirits, see Phillip Wiebe, *God and Other Spirits: Intimations of Transcendence in Christian Experience* (Oxford: Oxford University Press, 2004), 1–6.

[121] Hans Boersma, *Violence, Hospitality, and the Cross: Reappropriating the Atonement Tradition* (Grand Rapids, MI: Baker Academic, 2004), 194. Rudolf Bultmann was a key figure in this trend; Bultmann, 'New Testament and Mythology' in Hans Werner Bartsch (ed.), *Kerygma and Myth: A Theological Debate* (London: SPCK, 1964), 1–44; Walter Wink, *Unmasking the Powers: The Invisible Forces That Determine Human Existence* (Philadelphia: Fortress Press, 1986).

[122] Clint E. Arnold, *The Colossian Syncretism: The Interface Between Christianity and Folk Belief at Colossae* (Tübingen: Mohr Siebeck, 1995), 158; Peter T. O'Brien, *Colossians, Philemon*, WBC (Waco, TX: Word Books, 1982), 46.

[123] Dunn argues that Paul understood these powers to be real; see *Colossians and Philemon*, 93. For an argument against Dunn, see Wesley Carr, *Angels and Principalities* (Cambridge: Cambridge University Press, 1981), 48–52.

apocalyptic writings, which are concerned with the eschatological defeat of evil.[124] Secondly, Paul writes in reference to the notion that the

god of this world has blinded the minds of the unbelievers, to keep them from seeing the light of the gospel of the glory of Christ, who is the *Eikon* of God (2 Cor 4:4).

The 'god of this world' refers to a darkness which is 'cosmic, universal and demonic'.[125] Most scholars are agreed that this refers to the devil, since he is also named as a ruler in Ephesians 2:2, John 12:31, 14:30, and 16:11.[126] Whilst Paul does not give his readers a detailed description of what he thinks the evil powers are, it is clear that the notion of evil and the devil blur into one another as 'an existentially real power cohered in single focus'.[127]

Following Gregory, throughout the book, I identify 'the devil' with the biblical Satan, the fallen angel Lucifer, and the serpent in the Garden of Eden, referring to them interchangeably.[128] In linking the various titles, Gregory follows a common patristic reading of Isaiah 14:12, which understands Lucifer, the Morning Star, to be speaking of both Satan, who appears in Job, and the serpent in Genesis 3.[129] Ezekiel 28 also contributes to this tradition, having been read as linking a cosmic rebel and an earthly king.[130] In the New Testament, Revelation 12:9 draws together the serpent and the devil. This biblical basis is generally recognised to be the most likely source of the tradition, rather than the theory that the 'fall of Satan' myth originated from Zoroastrianism.[131] Throughout his work,

---

[124] 2 Enoch 20:1; 1 Enoch 41:9.

[125] Paul W. Barnett, *The Second Epistle to the Corinthians* (Grand Rapids: Eerdmans, 1997), 220.

[126] Murray J. Harris, *The Second Epistle to the Corinthians: A Commentary on the Greek Text* (Grand Rapids: Eerdmans, 2005), 328. For Paul's writing on 'powers', see Rom 8:38–39; 1 Cor 15:24; Col 1:16; Eph 1:20–21; Eph 6:12.

[127] Dunn, *Colossians and Philemon*, 109.

[128] For an overview of the tradition, see Jeffrey B. Russell, *Satan: The Early Christian Tradition* (New York: Cornell University Press, 1987); Henry Ansgar Kelly, *Satan: A Biography* (Cambridge: Cambridge University Press, 2006), 191–214.

[129] Justin Martyr was the Christian forerunner in equating Satan with the Serpent, *Dial. Tryph.* 45; also see Origen, *Princ.* 2.9.2.

[130] Neil Forsyth, *The Old Enemy: Satan and the Combat Myth* (Princeton, NJ: Princeton University Press, 1989), 139–44; Hector M. Patmore, *Adam, Satan, and the King of Tyre: The Interpretation of Ezekiel 28:11–19 in Late Antiquity* (Leiden: Brill, 2012), passim.

[131] Greg J. Riley, 'Devil' in Karen Van Der Toorn, Bob Beckling, and Peter W. Van Der Horst (eds.), *Dictionary of Deities and Demons in the Bible* (Leiden: Brill, 1999), 244–49, 246.

Gregory presents both the devil and the spiritual powers of darkness as enemies of the *eikon*. As Young's comment below indicates, Gregory's inspiration finds its origin in Jewish sources:

A lively sense of the reality of Satan had been inherited from the Jewish Apocalyptic tradition, which clearly had a considerable influence on New Testament and second-century Christianity.[132]

The prevalence of the struggle between the forces of evil and the human *eikon* is a theme which continues in the writing of the early church fathers. Origen, advancing a sophisticated demonology, identifies that demons are fallen angels. Unlike the view of pagan Greeks, who thought that some demons were good and others were bad, Origen states that all demons are evil.[133] They stand as powers behind the opposing political authorities, and their primary desire is to tempt human persons to sin.[134] Later, Athanasius writes about spiritual warfare in *Life of Anthony*, where the progressive holiness and divinity of the *eikon* encourage more attention from the envious 'enemy'. Athanasius stresses that it is the saints, having trained and placed themselves at the head of the battle, who struggle the most with the devil and his demons; however, they are far from helpless. Athanasius observes that in the Bible, demons hold no sway, even over the swine, since they must ask Christ's permission before they enter the swine. On the basis of this occurrence, he argues that demons hold even less sway over the person made as God's *eikon*, since she possesses greater authority over the powers of darkness than swine.[135]

Gregory develops this tradition by drawing even more prolifically on the biblical and pseudepigraphal theme of the devil and fallen angels, in order to describe the struggle of the *eikon*'s existence as she endeavours to draw closer to God. Gregory refers to Satan with a variety of metaphors and titles, most of which can be found in Scripture. The vast number of

---

[132] Frances M. Young, *The Making of the Creeds* (London: SCM Press, 1991), 88; Everett Ferguson, *Demonology of the Early Christian World* (New York: Edwin Mellen Press, 1984), 133.

[133] *Cels.* 5.5.

[134] *Princ.* 3.3.2; see Heinrich Schlier, *Principalities and Powers in the New Testament* (West Germany: Herder and Herder, 1961); George Caird, *Principalities and Powers* (Oxford: Clarendon Press, 1956).

[135] *Vit. Ant.* 29, (cf. Matt 8:31); see Athanasius, *The Life of Antony*, trans. Tim Vivian, Apostolos N. Athanassakis, and Rowan A. Greer (Kalamazoo, MI: Cistercian Publications, 2003), 126–27; David Brakke, 'Athanasius' in Philip F. Esler (ed.), *Early Christian World* (London: Taylor & Francis, 2002), 1102–27, 1122.

names and descriptions demonstrate Satan's significance to Gregory. They also serve to demonstrate the multitude of ways in which Gregory understands Satan as a threat. Many of the names exist as a list in the poem *Aversion of the Evil One and Invocation of Christ*:[136]

Thief, Serpent, Fire, Belial,[137] Vice, Death, Gulf, Dragon, Beast,[138] Night, Ambusher, Rage, Chaos, Slanderer and Murderer.[139]

Elsewhere, Gregory uses 'Satan',[140] 'Envy',[141] 'the Evil One',[142] 'the Devil',[143] 'the Adversary',[144] 'the Tempter',[145] 'the Enemy',[146] 'crooked',[147] 'ruler of the world',[148] and 'destroyer of the *eikon*'.[149] Since Gregory refers to Satan specifically as the 'destroyer of the *eikon*', it is clear that Satan represents a particular threat to the human *eikon* which she should not ignore. Below is a further example of Gregory's presentation of the devil's hatred of the *eikon*, which occurs in an extract from *On His Own Life*. In it, Gregory mourns the devil's constant attack on the

---

[136] Carm. 2.1.55 (PG 37, 1399–1401).

[137] Also see Carm. 1.2.1 (PG 37, 556, 457); Or. 24.15 (SC 284, 74). Belial is the name for Satan widely used in extra-biblical literature, where the name is given to a figure who is important as a deceiver; see S. David Sperling, 'Belial' in Karel Van Der Toorn, Bob Beckling, and Pieter W. Van Der Horst (eds.) *Dictionary of Deities and Demons in the Bible* (Leiden: Brill, 1999), 169–71, 170. It is also found in the form 'Beliar', which occurs only once in the New Testament: 2 Cor 6:15.

[138] Rev 12:9; Rev 13:1.

[139] Carm. 2.1.55 (PG 37, 1399, 4); cf. Matt 4:10; 12:26; 16:23; Mark 1:13; 3:23, 26; 4:15; Luke 13:16; 22:3.

[140] Or. 23.14 (SC 270, 310).

[141] Or. 6.10 (SC 405, 146); Carm. 1.1.7 (PG 37, 444, 66); 1.1.10 (PG 37, 466, 16); 1.2.1 (PG 37, 531, 120); 2.1.63 (PG 37, 1406, 4).

[142] ὁ πονηρός, Or. 2.88 (SC 247, 202); 6.10 (SC 405, 146); 28.15 (SC 250, 132); 30.6 (SC 250, 236–38); 37.10 (SC 318, 292); 37.12 (SC 318, 296); 38.14 (SC 358, 134); 40.10 (SC 358, 216), et al; cf. Matt 5:37; Eph 6:16; 2 Thess 3:3.

[143] ὁ διάβολος, Or. 2.62 (SC 247, 174); 35.3 (SC 318, 232); 38.12 (SC 358, 128); cf. Matt 4:1; 13:39; Luke 4:2–3, 6, 13.

[144] Or. 26.3 (SC 284, 230); 22.13 (SC 270, 248); 40.16 (SC 358, 230); see Francis X. Gokey, *The Terminology for the Devil and Evil Spirits in the Apostolic Fathers* (WA: AMS Press, 1961), 68–69; Jeffrey B. Russell, *Satan: The Early Christian Tradition* (New York: Cornell University Press, 1987), 34.

[145] Or. 30.6 (SC 250, 236); cf. Matt 4:3.

[146] Carm. 2.1.70 (PG 37, 1418, 4); 2.1.88 (PG 37, 1441, 168); cf. Luke 10:19.

[147] Carm. 1.1.7 (PG 37, 442, 41).

[148] Or. 1.4 (SC 247, 77); 8.12 (SC 405, 272); 11.4 (SC 405, 338); 14.21 (PG 35, 884C); 19.6 (PG 35, 1049C).

[149] ὁ φθορεὺς τῆς εἰκόνος, Carm. 2.1.65 (PG 37, 1407, 6); Or. 2.21 (SC 247, 118); 24.18 (SC 284, 80); 39.7 (SC 358, 162); 40.10 (SC 358, 218); Carm. 1.1.4 (PG 37, 419, 46–50); 1.1.9 (PG 37, 457, 9–12); 2.1.13 (PG 37, 1230, 43–50).

eikon. Note that here 'the corrupter' (ὁ φθορεύς) is one of the many epithets given to the devil:

> Excessively numerous are the paths which lead away from
> both the straight and settled road,
> they all lead to the pit of destruction.
> Into this the corrupter has torn down the *eikon*,
> in order that he might gain a way of slipping in,
> dividing doctrines, rather than tongues like God in ages past.[150]

The *eikon*'s encounter with demons continues to be a key theme in the work of theologians upon whom Gregory has exerted an influence, in particular Evagrius Ponticus. He was a protégé of Gregory, serving Gregory as a deacon in Constantinople. Constantinople, who produced a comprehensive demonology and method of combat in over five hundred types of demonic battles.[151] Brakke suggests that it is probable Evagrius 'learned from Gregory about the danger of demonic thoughts [λογισμοί], and the possibility of refuting them verbally with powerful words'.[152] In Chapter 4, we shall return to the problem of the devil's attacks on the human *eikon*, since we cannot properly interpret Gregory's understanding of the human *eikon* without discussing her relationship with the devil.

In this chapter, I have argued that Gregory interprets the experience of the human *eikon* in light of biblical themes and narratives. These include the creation narratives in Genesis; beliefs about images and idols; ideas about how the *eikon* might be perceived as 'divine'; ethics; and the *eikon*'s struggles with the spiritual powers of darkness. Whilst Gregory weaves into his vision of the human *eikon* a variety of biblical themes, his principal inspiration is Christ. With this in mind, we shall move on to discuss Gregory's depiction of Christ, the 'identical *Eikon*'.

---

[150] Carm. 2.1.11 (PG 37, 1107–8, 1146–51). In his critical edition of the text, Jungck corrected the aorist subjunctive passive λάβη to aorist optative active λάβοι, line 1150. For an alternative translation, see Caroline White, *Gregory of Nazianzus: Autobiographical Poems.* CMC (Cambridge: Cambridge University Press, 1996), 95.

[151] David Brakke, *Demons and the Making of the Monk: Spiritual Combat in Early Christianity* (Cambridge, MA: Harvard University Press, 2009), 49.

[152] David Brakke, *Talking Back: A Monastic Handbook for Combating Demons* (MN: Cistercian Publications, 2009), 19.

2

Jesus Christ, the Identical Image

Gregory provides the theological framework for the existence of the human *eikon* throughout his orations and poems. For example, observe that Gregory's *Arcana* begins with God and gradually progresses towards the creation of the human person. In order to reflect Gregory's sequence as closely as possible, the subsequent chapters follow the same pattern. We begin with Gregory's reflections on the close association between Christ and his human *eikon*:

Yesterday I was crucified with Christ, today I am glorified with him. Yesterday I was put to death with Christ, today I am made alive with him. Yesterday I was buried with Christ, today I am raised with him. But let us bear fruit for the one who died and rose on our behalf. Perhaps you think I speak about gold, or silver, or robes or stones of brilliance and value; earthly matter (ὕλη) which ebbs and flows, remaining below, of which the evil ones and slaves of things below and of the world-ruler (τοῦ κοσμοκράτορος) have more. Let us bear fruit ourselves, the most honourable possession belonging to God and the nearest to God. Let us give back to the *Eikon* that which is according to the *eikon* (ἀποδῶμεν τῇ εἰκόνι τὸ κατ᾽ εἰκόνα), let us recognise our worth, let us honour the archetype, and let us know the power of the mystery and on whose behalf Christ died.[1]

Above, Gregory identifies closely with Christ's death and, even more significantly, with Christ's resurrection. He states that Christ's actions demand a response: that human persons offer themselves to Christ, precisely because they are his *eikones*, the closest to God of all creation on

---

[1] Or. 1.4 (SC 247, 76–78). For a discussion on Christology and anthropology, see Goran Sekulovski, 'L'homme à l'image du Christ? Les fondements christologiques de l'anthropologie de Grégoire de Nazianze', *BLE*, CXV, no. 2 (2014), 231–42, 240.

earth. Interpreting the New Testament, Gregory refers to the Son as the 'identical *Eikon* (ἡ ἀπαράλλακτος εἰκών)'.[2] Commentators have paid considerable attention to Gregory's Christology, but not to the way in which Gregory speaks of Christ as the 'identical *Eikon*', and the relationship between this and the human person as an *eikon*. This may be due to the predominant focus in scholarship on the metaphysics of Gregory's Christology. However, at the heart of Gregory's theological anthropology is the belief that both Christ and humans are *eikones*. Exploring the title '*Eikon*' in relation to the Son reveals several important aspects concerning how the human person images God.

Firstly, Gregory employs *eikon* to denote Christ's ontological likeness to the Father. He explains that the Son is the kind of *eikon* which is identical to the Father in essence. This means that Christ is unique amongst *eikones* since he alone is 'identical' to God. Nevertheless, the fact that the human person shares this title with Christ points to how Gregory understands the likeness between the *eikon* and the prototype. Being 'κατ ᾿εἰκόνα', denotes the human person's affiliation to, rather than distance from, God.

Secondly, both Christ and the human *eikon* are living and dynamic *eikones* (ζῶντες), differentiating them both from motionless *eikones*. This conjures up the notion of *Eikon* as a verb, rather than a noun; it is dynamic, rather than static.

Thirdly, Christ is a unified person: Gregory applies the title '*Eikon*' to both the transcendent Logos and the incarnate Christ and does not consider *Eikon* reserved for the Son before he is incarnate.[3] This is key to my argument in Chapter 3, in which we explore the similarity between Gregory's writing about the unity of Christ and the composition of the human person. We have observed that commentators frequently draw attention to the occasions upon which Gregory depicts the *eikon* as the spiritual intellect or the soul. In response to this, I argued that the *eikon* transforms the dust to form a whole human person; consequently, *eikon* may refer to both the soul and the whole human person. This argument is strengthened in light of the unity of Christ. The way in which Gregory depicts Christ's unity mirrors his description of the human person who is formed from a mixture of *eikon* and dust. Therefore, as *Eikon* refers to the transcendent Logos and the incarnate Christ, likewise *eikon* denotes the whole human person, body and soul.

---

[2] Col 1:15; Or. 38.13 (SC 358, 132).
[3] Or. 38.13 (SC 358, 130–34); 29.17 (SC 250, 112–14).

Fourthly, *Eikon* relates to the dynamic pattern of Christ's kenosis, which secures the human *eikon's* theosis. Christ realises this through uniting the whole human person to God and thereby restoring the human *eikon* to her created potential of becoming divine.

The final point of correlation between Christ and his human *eikon* relates to the struggle with spiritual powers of darkness. Developing the biblical narrative, Gregory portrays Christ as battling with and constantly defeating the devil during his life on earth and through his passion. Christ achieved what Adam and Eve did not: he conquered the devil.[4] Through this, the healing of the human *eikon* is enacted and she is set back on her path towards becoming divine. Added to this, she is provided with the means of resisting and conquering evil.

THEOLOGICAL CONTEXT

As with all thought about God, ancient and current, Gregory's doctrine does not develop in a vacuum; his context is one of bitter discussions over Christology and Pneumatology, during which he develops his theology in response to several other competing cosmologies. Since a plethora of scholarship already exists concerning the various doctrinal controversies in which Gregory was involved, we will not discuss in depth the particular groups to which Gregory was responding.[5] Nor will we attempt to resolve disparities between contemporary commentators on these groups or those leaders around whom they formed.[6] From what we read in his orations, there were a number of key doctrinal issues which Gregory was concerned to defend, for example, the deity of the *Logos*.[7] In addition to arguing for Christ's divinity and equality with God, he also worked to defend Christ's humanity against Apollinarianism, which denied that Christ possessed a

---

[4] Or. 38.13–14 (SC 358, 134–38); 37.1 (SC 318, 270–72).

[5] For an excellent overview of the various shifts through the fourth century, see Christopher Beeley, *Gregory of Nazianzus on the Trinity and the Knowledge of God: In Your Light We Shall See Light* (Oxford: Oxford University Press, 2008), 16–34.

[6] For example, on Arius being a 'literal minded conservative', see Frances M. Young, *From Nicaea to Chalcedon: A Guide to the Literature and Its Background* (London: SCM Press, 1983), 64. This contrasts with the view that the Arian debate involved sophisticated arguments about metaphysics; see Rowan Williams, *Arius: Heresy and Tradition* (London: SCM Press, 2001), passim. For a deconstruction of Ariansim, see Ayres, *Nicaea and Its Legacy*, 1–126.

[7] Or. 2.37 (SC 247, 138); 20.5 (SC 270, 68); 31.30 (SC 250, 338); 33.16 (SC 318, 194); 37.22 (SC 318, 316); Carm. 2.1.2 (PG 37, 887–907).

human soul and was finally condemned in the Council of Constantinople in AD 381.[8]

Groups guilty of compressing 'the three' into 'one', thus denying the persons within the Godhead, caused further difficulties for Gregory.[9] Eunomius and Aetius also created dissension for Gregory and his fellow Cappadocians, since they refused to acknowledge the likeness of the *Logos* to the Father and denounced the Spirit's deity.[10] In arguing for the Spirit's deity, Gregory opposed not only Eunomius, but also groups referred to as the 'Pneumatomachians'.[11] Gregory understood himself to be willing to take the arguments for the deity of the Spirit further than his friend Basil who, according to Gregory, compromised on the language concerning the Spirit.[12] Throughout his orations, Gregory employs his best rhetorical skills in order to show the flaws in the arguments of his various opponents.[13] In spite of this, as far as Gregory is concerned, he lost his battle in declaring that the Holy Spirit is consubstantial to God.[14] Gregory informs

---

[8] Or. 30.5 (SC 250, 234); Ep. 101.1–101.11 (SC 208, 36–40); Ep. 102.3 (SC 208, 70–72); see John N.D. Kelly, *Early Christian Doctrines* (New York: Continuum, 1977), 289–95; Christopher A. Beeley, 'The Early Christological Controversy: Apollinarius, Diodore, and Gregory Nazianzen', *VC*, 65, no. 4 (2011), 376–407, 405. In this article, Beeley argues that Gregory is far more opposed to Diodore than Apollinarius, and that it is Nyssen who is the most aggressive opponent of Apollinarius.

[9] Or. 20.5 (SC 270, 66); 31.30 (SC 250, 338); 33.16 (SC 318, 194); 37.22 (SC 318, 316).

[10] Robert Letham, *The Holy Trinity: In Scripture, History, Theology, and Worship* (Phillipsburg, NJ: P&R Publishing, 2004), 146. Gregory followed Athanasius (*Ep. Serap.* 1.27) in referring to the Spirit 'as consubstantial with the Father'; for a comprehensive discussion of this issue, see Michael A. Haykin, *The Spirit of God: The Exegesis of 1 and 2 Corinthians in the Pneumatomachian Controversy of the Fourth Century* (Leiden: Brill, 1993), 170–85.

[11] The commonly used term 'Macedonians' is a misnomer as there is little historical evidence to associate Macedonius with those who renounced the deity of the Spirit; Richard P.C. Hanson, *The Search for the Christian Doctrine of God: The Arian Controversy 318–381* (Edinburgh: T&T Clark, 1988), 760.

[12] Ep. 58.7, Gallay *Lettres 1*, 75; Boris Bobrinskoy, *The Mystery of the Trinity: Trinitarian Experience and Vision in the Biblical and Patristic Tradition* (Crestwood, New York: St. Vladimir's Seminary Press, 1999), 246.

[13] Basil Studer, *Trinity and Incarnation: The Faith of the Early Church* (Edinburgh: T&T Clark, 1993), 141. For more on Gregory's rhetoric, see the Appendix.

[14] The creed of Constantinople was put forward as a statement of faith which would be acceptable to all parties; see Adolf-Martin Ritter, *Das Konzil von Konstantinopel und sein Symbol* (Göttingen: Vandenhoeck & Ruprecht, 1965), 182–208. Also, the council is 'circumspect in what it affirms of the Spirit'; see John Behr, *The Nicene Faith*, vol. 2 (Crestwood, N.Y.: St. Vladimir's Seminary Press, 2004), 374. Contra Kelly, who mistakenly writes that Gregory won the debate about the consubstantiality of the Spirit and that it was formally endorsed; see *Early Christian Doctrines*, 263.

his readers of this in the poem, *On His Own Life*, in which he makes bitter complaints about the ambiguity of the faith of the bishops.[15]

Whilst Gregory attends to the doctrine of the Trinity in many orations, poems, and letters, his so-called *Theological Orations* were written during AD 379-381, while in Constantinople. Whilst he did not achieve the success he longed for during his lifetime, Gregory's five *Theological Orations* received great endorsement decades later at the Council of Chalcedon. In the first of these our theologian teaches on how to know God, whilst ultimately he believes that complete knowledge of God is impossible. This is because, as Gregory informs us in a further oration, God is boundless like the sea.[16]

At the beginning of his second theological oration, *On the Doctrine of God*, Gregory puts himself in the place of Moses, ascending the heights of Mount Sinai, and on reaching the top of the mountain he enters the cloud. Gregory's purpose in penetrating the cloud is to contemplate God. Whilst sheltering in the rock, which is Christ, however, Gregory explains that he can only see God in the way that one sees 'shadowy reflections of the Sun in water'.[17] As close as Gregory comes to God, ultimately, he finds that God is unknowable, from which he concludes: 'to tell of God is not possible ... but to know him is even less possible'.[18] However, one can know that 'God' is 'Father, Son and Holy Spirit'[19] and 'one divinity and power'.[20] This summarises Gregory's approach to the Christian faith, according to which God is both 'One' and 'Trinity'. Beeley has demonstrated that in speaking about the unity of God,[21] Gregory's language varies between One (μόνας, ἕν),[22] God (θεός),[23] Divinity (θεότης),[24] being (οὐσία),[25] and nature (φύσις).[26] When he speaks about the threeness of God, Gregory usually refers to hypostases (ὑποστάσεις),[27] persons (πρόσωπα),[28] or three (τρία).[29]

---

[15] Carm. 2.1.2 (PG 37, 1506–19).   [16] Or. 38.7 (SC 358, 114).

[17] Or. 28.3 (SC 250, 76); St. Gregory of Nazianzus, *On God and Christ: The Five Theological Orations and Two Letters of Cledonius*, trans. Lionel Wickham and Frederick Williams, PPS (Crestwood, New York: St. Vladimir's Seminary Press, 2002), 39.

[18] Or. 28.4 (SC 250, 78–80), trans. *On God and Christ*, 40.   [19] Or. 38.8 (SC 358, 118).

[20] Or. 1.7 (SC 247, 80).

[21] Beeley, *Trinity and the Knowledge of God*, 221–22; Robert W. Jenson, *The Triune Identity: God According to the Gospel* (Philadelphia: Fortress Press, 1982), 105–14.

[22] Or. 6.22 (SC 405, 176); Carm. 1.1.3 (PG 37, 413, 60–71).   [23] Or. 20.7 (SC 270, 70).

[24] Or. 21.13 (SC 270, 136); 31.14 (SC 250, 302); Carm. 1.1.3 (PG 37, 409, 10).

[25] Or. 6.13 (SC 405, 154); 31.28 (SC 250, 330); 34.13 (SC 318, 220).

[26] Or. 33.16 (SC 318, 194); 34.15 (SC 318, 224); 42.15 (SC 384, 82).

[27] Or. 20.7 (SC 270, 70); 34.15 (SC 318, 226).

[28] Or. 31.30 (SC 250, 338); 37.22 (SC 318, 316).   [29] Or. 6.22 (SC 405, 176).

The plethora of debate about Gregory's Trinitarian doctrine remains outside of our primary field of enquiry.[30] Much of the discussion centres on Gregory's depiction of the monarchy and causality of the Father.[31] In response to this, both Beeley and Ayres have offered persuasive arguments. Beeley argues that if one reads all of Gregory's orations, it is evident that whilst Gregory does present the Father as the cause of the Godhead, he does not understand the Son and the Spirit to be subordinate to the Father. Likewise, Ayres defends Gregory's approach, arguing that the generation between the three is reciprocal.[32]

THE IDENTICAL IMAGE OF GOD

And this was the very Word of God, the eternal, the invisible, the incomprehensible, the incorporeal, the beginning from the beginning, the light from the light,[33] the source of life and immortality,[34] the impression of the beautiful Archetype (τὸ ἐκμαγεῖον τοῦ ἀρχετύπου κάλλους),[35] the immovable seal,[36] the identical *Eikon* (ἡ ἀπαράλλακτος εἰκών), the definition and explanation of the Father. He proceeds to his own *eikon* and bears flesh on behalf of flesh and mingles with a spiritual soul for the sake of my soul, purifying like with like (ἐπὶ τὴν ἰδίαν εἰκόνα χωρεῖ καὶ σάρκα φορεῖ διὰ τὴν σάρκα καὶ ψυχῇ νοερᾷ διὰ τὴν ἐμὴν ψυχὴν μίγνυται, ὁμοίῳ τό ὅμοιον ἀνακαθαίρων).[37]

Gregory interprets Paul in presenting Christ as the 'truest' *Eikon* on no less than twenty occasions.[38] This evidence challenges assertions made by

---

[30] For a comprehensive bibliography concerning Gregory's Trinitarian doctrine, see John A. McGuckin, '"Perceiving Light from Light in Light" (Oration 31.3): The Trinitarian Theology of Saint Gregory the Theologian', *GOTR*, 39, no. 1–2 (1994), 7–32, 7–8. For a critique of Gregory's Trinitarian doctrine, see Vladimir Lossky, *The Vision of God*, 2nd ed. (Crestwood, New York: St. Vladimir's Seminary Press, 1983), 69; Rowan Williams, *The Wound of Knowledge: Christian Spirituality from the New Testament to St. John of the Cross*, 2nd ed. (London: Darton, Longman and Todd, 1991), 74.

[31] Thomas F. Torrance, *Trinitarian Faith: The Evangelical Theology of the Ancient Catholic Faith* (Edinburgh: T&T Clark, 1998), 238; Najeeb G. Awad, 'Between Subordination and Koinonia: Toward a New Reading of the Cappadocian Theology', *Modern Theology*, 23, no. 2 (2007), 181–204.

[32] Christopher A. Beeley, 'Divine Causality and the Monarchy of God the Father in Gregory of Nazianzus', *HTR*, 100, no. 2 (2007), 199–214, 213; Ayres, *Nicaea and Its Legacy*, 245–50.

[33] John 8:12.   [34] John 1:14.   [35] Heb 1:3.   [36] John 6:27.

[37] Or. 38.13 (SC 358, 132).

[38] Col. 1:15; ἡ ἀπαράλλακτος εἰκών, Or. 38.13 (SC 358, 132); 1.4 (SC 247, 76); 2.98 (SC 247, 216); 4.78 (SC 309, 200); 14.2 (PG 35, 860C); 14.7 (PG 35, 865C); 29.17 (SC 250, 212); 30.3 (SC 250, 230); 30.20 (SC 250, 268); 45.9 (PG 36, 633C); Carm. 1.1.2 (PG 37, 402,

Richard and Harrison, who both argue that Gregory portrays the human *eikon* as the *eikon* of the Trinity.[39] Richard suggests that there is a distance between Gregory and the Alexandrian tradition of reserving the function of the *Eikon* for the Son. In making her case, she neglects the number of occasions on which Gregory refers to Christ as God's *Eikon*. It may be that Richard and Harrison are influenced by contemporary trends which posit the *imago Dei* as imaging the Trinity.[40] Whilst this approach is appealing due to its emphasis on relationality and inclusivity, it does not reflect the New Testament, which understands Christ to be the true *Eikon* of God. As John Behr has argued, the result is that the focus is taken off Christ 'except insofar as he is one of the persons in communion in heaven'.[41] There is no doubt that Gregory focuses first on Christ as *Eikon*, since in addition to naming Christ 'identical *Eikon*', he refers to the human person explicitly as the '*eikon* of Christ (Χριστοῦ εἰκών)', but he does not infer that the human person is the *eikon* of the Trinity.[42] I do not highlight this to detract from the way in which the Spirit gives life to the human *eikon* and deifies the *eikon*, but rather to argue that in order to learn about the human *eikon*, Gregory points first to Christ.

Following the biblical depiction of Christ as *Eikon* raises challenges for Gregory, in light of defending the Nicene theology against forms of 'Arianism'.[43] In order to establish that Christ is God, Gregory emphasises that Christ is a unique form of *eikon*, because he is not only reflecting or mirroring the Father's glory, but is also of the same substance as his prototype. This explains why, when Gregory applies *eikon* to the Son, he is consistent in using it to denote the Son's similarity to the Father, rather than his difference.[44] Gregory emphasises this through his use of

8–10); 1.2.1 (PG 37, 533, 145); 1.2.14 (PG 37, 762, 92); 2.1.1 (PG 37, 1016, 628); 2.1.38 (PG 37, 1326, 7); 2.1.45 (PG 37, 1356, 32); Ep. 101.32 (SC 208, 50); Ep. 102.11 (SC 208, 76).

[39] Richard, *Cosmologie et théologie*, 464; Verna E.F. Harrison, 'Illumined From All Sides By the Trinity' in Christopher A. Beeley (ed.), *Re-Reading Gregory of Nazianzus: Essays on History, Theology, and Culture* (WA, DC: Catholic University of America Press, 2012), 13–30.

[40] Dominic Robinson, *Understanding the 'Imago Dei': The Thought of Barth, von Balthasar and Moltmann* (Surrey: Ashgate Publishing Limited, 2011); Grenz, *The Social God and the Relational Self*, passim.

[41] Behr, *Mystery of Christ*, 176.   [42] Carm. 1.2.29 (PG 37, 893, 126).

[43] I use 'Arianism' lightly, since, as Lewis Ayres has argued, the fourth-century theological context was much more complicated than simply adopting Arius' views; see *Nicea and Its Legacy*, 99.

[44] Or. 29.17 (SC 250, 212); 38.13 (SC 358, 176); 45.9 (PG 36, 633C); Carm. 2.1.38 (PG 37, 1326, 7).

adjectives; Christ is not 'made according to the *eikon* (κατ᾽ εἰκών)', but is the identical *eikon* (ἡ ἀπαράλλακτος εἰκών).[45] Furthermore, in *On the Son*, Gregory's use of 'equal nature' alongside *eikon* demonstrates that when discussing the Son, our theologian understands *eikon* to be denoting an equal nature to the Father:

> The Word of the great God sprang from the Father, eternal Son,
> *Eikon* of the original, nature equal to the one who begot him
> (εἰκὼν ἀρχετύποιο, φύσις γεννήτορι ἴση).[46]

In Chapter 1, we saw that the human *eikon* in Genesis may be interpreted in light of contemporary approaches to pagan images, both portraits and statues. These bear the presence of the figure they image, in a manner which ontologically affiliates them with their prototype. Thus, they are considered 'divine' and could be described as being of the same nature as their prototype. With this idea of *eikones* in mind, it is possible to see how Gregory holds the apparently paradoxical belief that Christ is both *Eikon* and the same nature as his Father, especially if we bear in mind that pagan *eikones* were regarded as genuine substitutes for their prototypes. For Gregory, Christ is far closer to the Father than any other *eikon*; thus Gregory marries Pauline and Nicene theology.

Further to this, in his oration *On the Son*, Gregory takes care to explain that the Son's titles have always existed as the Son has always existed. For Gregory, Christ being an *Eikon* of God means that Christ is eternally begotten:

> Clearly, these are speaking about the Son, and others which are of the same meaning, not being newly acquired, nor became attached later to the Son, or to the Spirit, any more than to the Father himself. For perfection does not stem from that which is added.[47]

If we are in any doubt that Gregory's use of *Eikon* in relation to Christ implies anything less than full participation in the Godhead, Gregory

---

[45] Or. 38.13 (SC 358, 132).

[46] Carm. 1.1.2 (PG 37, 402, 7–8); cf. Carm. 2.1.1 (PG 37, 1016). The poem is a defence against Eunomius; for a full background, see Claudio Moreschini and Donald Sykes, *St Gregory of Nazianzus: Poemata Arcana* (Oxford: Clarendon Press, 1997), 96. *Eikon* of the Archetype (εἰκὼν ἀρχετύποιο) does not occur in the Bible; however, it is used by Philo. For comment on *Eikon* being used to distinguish the Son from the Father, see Philippe Molac, '"A-t-il commis une faute en étant pour toi miséricordieux? Pour moi, c'est très admirable!" la Christologie dans le deuxième poème dogmatique de Grégoire de Nazianze', *BLE*, 109, no. 4 (2008), 307–38, 316.

[47] Or. 29.17 (SC 250, 214); 2.98 (SC 247, 216).

makes this explicit in his second oration, *On the Son*. Gregory works his way through some of the titles given to the Son in the New Testament, offering a brief explanation of why each particular label was given. Beginning with 'Son' (Υἱός),[48] Gregory elaborates upon, 'Only-begotten' (Μονογενής),[49] 'Word' (Λόγος),[50] 'Wisdom' (Σοφία),[51] and 'Power' (Δύναμις).[52] After these, he moves onto 'Truth' ('Αλήθεια), the elucidation of which appears in full below:

And he is called 'Truth', because He is one (ἕν), not many by His nature (τῇ φύσει), for truth itself is one, while falsehood is fragmented in multiple ways; and because He is the pure seal of the Father (ὡς καθαρὰ τοῦ Πατρὸς σφραγίς), and the most faithful impress (χαρακτὴρ ἀψευδέστατος).[53]

In order to explain why Christ should be called 'Truth', Gregory employs χαρακτήρ, which has an extensive semantic field including impress, stamp, and *eikon*.[54] The wide range of meanings is reflected in Gregory's work, despite the term only appearing in fifteen occasions throughout his corpus.[55] He uses it both positively and negatively to depict *eikones* which accurately represent their archetypes and those which do not.[56] Above, when applying it to Christ, he supplies the adjective 'most faithful (ἀψευδέστατος)' as a means of qualifying that Christ is different from other impressions.[57] With the need to re-interpret and clarify what kind of 'faithful impress' is Christ, we might ask why Gregory uses this description. As with Gregory's use of *eikon*, the answer lies in Scripture. On this occasion, Gregory is drawing from Hebrews, which conveys that the Son is the same substance as the Father:[58]

---

[48] Or. 30.20 (SC 250, 266).   [49] John 1:18.   [50] John 1:1.

[51] Or. 30.20 (SC 250, 268); 1 Cor. 1:30.   [52] Eph 5:9.

[53] Or. 30.20 (SC 250, 268); Heb 1:3.

[54] Paul Ellingworth, *The Epistle to the Hebrews: A Commentary on the Greek Text* (Grand Rapids: Eerdmans, 1993), 99; Luke Timothy Johnson, *Hebrews: A Commentary* (Louisville, KY: Westminster John Knox Press, 2006), 69; Ulrich Wilckens, 'χαρακτήρ' in Gerhard Kittel and Gerhard Freidrich (eds.), *Φ-Ω TDNT*, vol 9 (Grand Rapids: Eerdmans, 1974), 418-23, 421-23; *PGL*, 1513. Scholars generally agree on the semantic field of χαρακτήρ being the same as εἰκών; see David J. MacLeod, 'The Finality of Christ: An Exposition of Hebrews 1:1-4', *Bibliotheca Sacra*, 162, no. 646 (2005), 210-30, 229; Harold W. Attridge, *The Epistle to the Hebrews*, Hermeneia (Philadelphia: Fortress Press, 1989), 43-44.

[55] Or. 2.15 (SC 247, 108); 2.43 (SC 247, 146); 6.11 (SC 405, 150); 20.1 (SC 270, 56); 23.7 (SC 270, 296); 32.27 (SC 318, 144); 40.27 (SC 358, 258); 42.18 (SC 384, 88); et al.

[56] Or. 40.27 (SC 358, 258); 11.4 (SC 405, 338).   [57] Or. 40.26 (SC 358, 258).

[58] χαρακτήρ appears once in the New Testament, although Philo applies it on fifty-one occasions; William L. Lane, *Hebrews 1-8*, WBC (Dallas, Texas: Word Books, 1991), 12-13.

He is the reflection of God's glory and the exact imprint of God's very being (ὃς ὢν ἀπαύγασμα τῆς δόξης καὶ χαρακτὴρ τῆς ὑποστάσεως αὐτοῦ), and he sustains all things by his powerful word.[59]

Like Colossians 1:15–20, which uses εἰκών to describe Christ, Hebrews 1 denotes Christ as one through whom the world was created (Heb 1:1), who sustains all things (Heb 1:3), and to whom all powers are subject (Heb 1:13). In the collection of letters attributed to Basil, the author of *Epistula 38* connects Hebrews 1:3 to John 14:9, Colossians 1:15, and Wisdom 7:26, with the purpose of explaining that in relation to Christ, both χαρακτήρ and εἰκών express Christ's likeness to the Father.[60]

After explaining why the Son is called 'Truth', Gregory continues his list of Christ's titles with εἰκών, appearing to use it synonymously with χαρακτήρ. Here Gregory provides his reader with a rare explanation of what he intends by εἰκών when it is applied to Christ:

And He is called '*Eikon*' (Εἰκών)[61] because he is consubstantial (ὁμοούσιον), since he comes from the Father, but the Father does not come from Him. For the nature of an *eikon* is to be a representation (μίμημα) of the archetype, and to be given its name. But there is more to be said than this: for an *eikon* is motionless (ἀκίνητος), representing a being set in motion; however here is one living (ζῶν), also imaging a living being and possessing a more precise similarity than that of Seth to Adam and all those born from parents. For this is the nature of those who are simple (ἡ τῶν ἁπλῶν φύσις), there is neither likeness nor unlikeness, but they are the whole impression of the whole, and the same rather than similar (ἀλλ᾽ ὅλον ὅλου τύπον εἶναι, καὶ ταὐτὸν μᾶλλον ἢ ἀφομοίωμα).[62]

In the passage above, Gregory leaves his reader in no doubt about what he means when he describes the Son as *Eikon*.[63] Gregory's use of terms such as ἁπλοῦς purports a clear message: the Son images in a way that means he is identical in substance to the Father. Here, Gregory presents a description of εἰκών which is radically different from the one offered by Eunomius, who, in *Apology 24*, argues that likeness does not refer to likeness in substance but only in operation (οὐ πρὸς τὴν οὐσίαν φέροι ἂν ἡ

---

[59] Heb 1:3.
[60] On the authorship of the letter and other texts where Basil and Nyssen have connected Christ to χαρακτήρ and εἰκών, see Alessandro Capone, 'Apollonaris, Basil and Gregory of Nyssa', ZAC, 17, no. 2 (2013), 315–31. For further discussions of the close relationship between χαρακτήρ, εἰκών, and δόξα, see Karl Prüum, 'Reflexiones theologicae et historicae ad usum Paulinum termini "eikon"', *Verbum Domini* XL (1962), 232–57, 236–37.
[61] Col. 1:15.   [62] Or. 30.20 (SC 250, 268).
[63] For a study arguing that Paul and a number of early church fathers used *eikon* to denote similarity, see Sebastián Bartina, '"Cristo imagen del Dios invisible" según los papiros', *Studia Papyrologica*, 2 (1963), 13–34, 22ff.

εἰκὼν τὴν ὁμοιότητα, πρὸς δὲ τὴν ἐνέργειαν).[64] Thus, Gregory is both specific and clear in his notion of *eikon*, using it in a way that is different from his opponents to denote the ontological likeness of the Son to the Father. Whilst Gregory is explicit that the human *eikon* is not consubstantial with God's substance, his consistent appraisal of *eikon* as a concept which closes the gap should be taken seriously when considering the human *eikon*, since she is the *eikon* of the Son and follows his pattern.[65]

A further title, which Christ and the human *eikon* share in the passage cited above, identifies them each as a living *eikon* (ζῶν), rather than as one who is motionless (ἀκίνητος).[66] Gregory's inspiration for this comes from John 14:6, where Christ is depicted as saying, 'I am the way and the truth and the life' (ἐγώ εἰμι ἡ ὁδὸς καὶ ἡ ἀλήθεια καὶ ἡ ζωή).[67] This shared notion of Christ and human persons as living *eikones* has significant implications on how humans image God.[68] Gregory offers his reader a vision of a human *eikon* which denotes a 'lived' existence. If she were not God's *eikon*, the human would be like a breathless statue, unable to resemble her prototype in any real sense. This is why it is unhelpful to consider the *eikon* only in terms of static metaphysical categories, concerned singularly with the questions about which internal part of the human person is denoted by the *eikon*. Approaching the *eikon* as the capacity or category of the human person means that we miss Gregory's crucial point about being the *eikon* of God: the *eikon* exists principally as a living being imaging a living being.

IMAGE OF GOD: LOGOS OR INCARNATE CHRIST?

Gregory refers to Christ as the 'identical *Eikon*' and does not appeal to this phrase to distinguish between 'the transcendent Logos' and 'the incarnate Christ'. Nevertheless, during the first five centuries, views about

---

[64] Frederick W. Norris, *Faith Gives Fullness to Reasoning: The Five Theological Orations of Gregory Nazianzen* (Leiden: Brill, 1990), 180. From Eunomius' argument, it is clear that εἰκών is both varied in meaning and controversial, which is why it requires such careful attention.

[65] Or. 42.17 (SC 384, 86).

[66] In the LLX, ζωή is applied in opposition to death; see Deut 30.15; likewise, everlasting life, Dan 12:12; life itself, Gen 2:7; Takamitsu Muraoka, *GELS* (Leuven: Peeters, 2009), 315. In the New Testament, it is the only term for life which is applied to God; Frederick W. Danker and Walter Bauer, *A Greek-English Lexicon of the New Testament and Other Early Christian Literature*, 3rd ed. (Chicago: University of Chicago Press, 2000), 430–31. Many early church fathers, such as Clement, used ζωή as a synonym for God; *PGL*, 594–96.

[67] Or. 29.17 (SC 250, 212).   [68] Or. 38.11 (SC 358, 126).

Christ's unity were still evolving, with differences occurring over whether the *Eikon* of God was the transcendent Logos or the incarnate Christ.[69] We should recall that significant discussions of Christology had not yet occurred at this time, but take place in the run-up to the councils of Ephesus (AD 431) and Chalcedon (AD 451). Preceding Gregory, Origen, for example, designates the transcendent Logos as the true *Eikon* as he intends to prevent anthropomorphic views of God: 'as the Father is invisible by nature, he has begotten an *eikon* that is also invisible'.[70] Whilst it is universally recognised that Origen's thought influenced Gregory, note that Gregory emphasises that the visible Christ, rather than the invisible Logos, is God's *Eikon*.[71]

Gregory is explicit that he sees Christ and the Logos as a unity, thus rendering Christ as *Eikon*.[72] At first, it may appear as though Gregory follows Origen's thesis regarding the *Eikon* being invisible when he writes in a poem entitled *Oaths of Gregory*,

> I swore on the Logos himself, who to me is greatest God,
> source from source, from the eternal Father,
> *Eikon* of the archetype, a nature (φύσις) equal to his begetter,
> who came from heaven even into a mortal life.[73]

However, Gregory identifies Christ with the Logos from several different angles. Firstly, Gregory's use of 'Logos' when speaking about Christ indicates that he considers the Logos and Christ as 'One'. Secondly, Gregory is explicit in describing Christ as 'One' Son and not 'two' sons, since his approach to soteriology necessitates that the Logos assumes the human soul within the concept of a single self, thus transforming

---

[69] The two concepts of Christ would not be fully reconciled until the time of Cyril of Alexandria, followed by the council of Chalcedon.

[70] *Princ.* 1.2.6, Origen, *On First Principles*, trans. George W. Butterworth (London: SPCK, 1936), 19. Also, see *Hom. Gen.* 1.13; *Cels.* 6.63. For more on Origen's belief that *Eikon* describes transcendent Logos but not the incarnate Christ, see Frances M. Young, *God's Presence: A Contemporary Recapitulation of Early Christianity* (Cambridge: Cambridge University Press, 2013), 162.

[71] Trigg, 'Knowing God', 83; Hanson, *Christian Doctrine of God*, 782; Claudio Moreschini, *Filosofia e letteratura in Gregorio di Nazianzo* (Milan: Vita e Pensiero, 1997), 309.

[72] For a discussion on Logos language in Gregory's work, see Petrus J. Maritz, 'Logos Articulation in Gregory of Nazianzus' in Hendrick F. Stander (ed.), *Acta Patristica et Byzantina* (Pretoria: University of Pretoria, Department of Ancient Languages, 1995), 99–108.

[73] *Carm.* 2.1.2 (PG 37, 1017, 1–4).

humanity. Finally, Gregory refers specifically to Christ's flesh as *Eikon*, denoting that Christ images God in the fullness of his being.

Gregory states that Christ is the 'Power of God' and the 'Wisdom of God', observing that these are titles attributed to the Son.[74] In his poem entitled *Hymn to Christ after the Silence at Pascha*, Gregory begins by addressing 'Lord Christ' and moves on to praising him in the following manner:

> Light of the Father, Logos of the Great Spiritual Intellect, mightier than myth,
> High Light of the Highest Light, Only Child,
> *Eikon* of the Immortal Father and seal of eternity
> (εἰκὼν ἀθανάτοιο πατρὸς, καὶ σφραγὶς ἀνάρχοι).[75]

Gregory continues his poem by praising Christ as the 'giver of Life' and as the 'Demiurge of being and being to come'.[76] His understanding of the incarnate Christ as the pre-existent Logos means that it is possible for Gregory to conceive of Christ as creator, the role which Paul assigns to the *Eikon* of God in Colossians 1.[77] It is not suggested here that Gregory conceives of the incarnate Christ as existing in human form before creation; however, his language does reveal the identification of Christ 'as the eternal son of God' which reflects the New Testament custom of not regarding the two as separate identities.[78] Below is explicit support for this:

> Not that he became two (δύο), but that he was upheld to be one (ἕν) from two ... two natures meeting in one, not two sons.[79]

Beeley, who has written extensively on the unity of Christ in Gregory's theology, explains the importance of this when he writes, 'the central principle and ultimate focus of Gregory's Christology is the union of God and human existence in the person of Jesus'.[80]

---

[74] Or. 29.17 (SC 250, 212).   [75] Carm. 1.2.38 (PG 37, 1325, 12–1326, 2).

[76] Carm. 1.2.38 (PG 37, 1326, 6–7).

[77] Also, see Or. 40.2 (SC 358, 200). A key discussion amongst New Testament scholars concerns whether the *eikon* language implies the pre-existence of Christ in Paul's thought. Considering Col 1, 'there can be little doubt that a role in the original creation of the cosmos is attributed to God's Son the Christ'; James D.G. Dunn, *The Theology of Paul the Apostle* (Edinburgh: T&T Clark, 1998), 269.

[78] Christopher A. Beeley, 'Gregory of Nazianzus on the Unity of Christ' in Peter William Martens (ed.), *In the Shadow of the Incarnation: Essays on Jesus Christ in the Early Church in Honor of Brian E. Daley, S.J.* (Notre Dame, IN: University of Notre Dame Press, 2008), 97–120, 98.

[79] Or. 37.2 (SC 318, 274).

[80] Christopher A. Beeley, *The Unity of Christ: Continuity and Conflict in Patristic Tradition* (New Haven: Yale University Press, 2012), 184; Kenneth Paul Wesche, 'The Union of

Gregory's particular approach to soteriology advances fourth-century views on Christ's unity. It is universally agreed that Gregory's famed phrase, 'For that which is unassumed is unhealed (τὸ γὰρ ἀπρόσληπτον, ἀθεράπευτον)', encapsulates his soteriology and thus his Christology.[81] According to Gregory, for the Son to assume all that is human, it is crucial that the Son assumes the human soul, because of the soul's role as mediator between divine and human:

For this reason, God was united with the flesh through the mediating soul, and the separate realities were combined well (ἀνεκράθη) by the affinity towards both of that which it was mediating.[82]

Gregory posits the co-existence of the human soul and the Logos within the concept of a single 'self', which accommodates both divine and human natures.[83] Below, as Hofer has argued extensively, when Gregory discusses the mixture of the divine and human, he does this in a manner which expresses predominance of the stronger over the weaker, thus unifying the whole:

He bears all of me, with all that is mine, in himself (ἐν ἑαυτῷ) so that he may consume in himself that which is inferior, in the same way that fire consumes wax or as the sun consumes mist on the ground, so that I may partake of that which is his through the blending (διὰ σύγκρασιν).[84]

God and Man in Jesus Christ in the Thought of Gregory of Nazianzus', *SVTQ*, 28, no. 2 (1984): 83–98; Peter Bouteneff, 'St Gregory Nazianzen and Two-Nature Christology', *SVTQ*, 38, no. 3 (1994), 255–70; Hofer, *Christ in the Life of Gregory of Nazianzus*, passim.

[81] Ep. 101.32 (SC 208, 50); Brian Daley, '"Heavenly Man" and "Eternal Christ": Apollinarius and Gregory of Nyssa on the Personal Identity of the Savior', *JECS*, 10, no. 4 (2002), 469–88, 479; Donald L. Gelpi, *The Firstborn of Many: Synoptic Narrative Christology*, vol. 1 (Marquette: Marquette University Press, 2001), 117. In applying this dictum, Gregory was building on Irenaeus, *Haer.*, preface to book 5, and Origen, *Dial.*, 136.

[82] Or. 2.23 (SC 247, 120).

[83] Or. 30.6 (SC 250, 236); 33.15 (SC 318, 194). For the importance of self to Gregory's Christology, see Wesche, 'Union of God and Man', 95. Scholars debate whether Gregory emphasises Christ's divinity over his humanity; Alois Grillmeier, *Christ in Christian Tradition: From the Apostolic Age to Chalcedon (451)*, vol. 1; trans. John S. Bowden, 2nd revised ed., (London: Mowbray, 1965), 369. Grillmeier criticises Gregory for being Antiochene in his Christology, whereas others argue that Gregory is more akin to the Alexandrian tradition; Boris Bobrinskoy, 'The Indwelling of the Spirit in Christ: "Pneumatic Christology" in the Cappadocian Fathers', *SVTQ*, 28, no. 1 (1984), 49–65, 64. I suggest that Gregory does not fall neatly into either category and is best read on his own terms.

[84] Or. 30.6 (SC 250, 236); Hofer, *Christ in the Life of Gregory of Nazianzus*, 91–120.

To appreciate Gregory's statement above, we must turn to his pronounce-
ment of the incarnation as 'O, new mixture! O, paradoxical blending!'[85]
How does Gregory understand this 'new mixture'? Do divine and human
co-exist, but remain separate, like beans and grains of wheat, or are they
fully blended to the extent where there could be no easy identification of
each component, or does Gregory take some other approach?[86] The
response depends somewhat on the question of Gregory's philosophical
influences with regards to the concept of mixture. Generally, scholars
suggest that Gregory is most influenced by Stoic thought on this issue.[87]
For example, Sykes states confidently that the Stoic influence upon Gregory leads him to

> stress the reality of the union of the elements without losing the individuality of the
> constituent elements and their retention of their specific characteristics.[88]

This is the view expressed by philosophers such as Chryssipus, for whom
κρᾶσις occurs when two elements co-exist but remain separate.[89]
Recently, Hofer has challenged this by surveying different philosophical
approaches. He reviews Stoic and Neoplatonic philosophers with respect
to the discussion of mixing.[90] Building on work by Wolfson in the mid-
twentieth century, Hofer discusses an Aristotelian notion of μίξις and
κρᾶσις, where one component transforms the other.[91] In relation to this,

---

[85] Or. 38.13 (SC 358, 134); cf. 2.23 (SC 247, 120); 14.15 (PG 37, 876B); 30.6 (SC
250, 236).
[86] Compare the description of Chryssipus' theories of blending by Alexander in Robert
B. Todd, *Alexander of Aphrodisias on Stoic Physics: A Study of the De Mexitione with
Preliminary Essays, Text, Translation and Commentary* (Leiden: Brill, 1976), 116–17.
[87] Moreschini, SC 358, 56; Franz Xaver Portmann, *Die göttliche Paidagogia bei Gregor von
Nazianz: eine dogmengeschichtliche Studie* (St. Ottilien: EOS Verlag der Erzabtei
St. Ottilien, 1954), 64; Norris, 'Doctrine of Jesus Christ', 85; Susanna Elm,
'"O Paradoxical Fusion!" Gregory of Nazianzus on Baptism and Cosmology (Orations
38–40)' in Annette Yoshiko Reed and Ra'anan S. Boustan (eds.), *Heavenly Realms and
Earthly Realities in Late Antique Religions* (New York: Cambridge University Press,
2004), 296–316, 300, n11; Althaus, *Die Heilslehre des heiligen*, 57–60; Bouteneff,
Beginnings, 148; Sigurd Bergmann, *Creation Set Free: The Spirit as Liberator of Nature*
(Grand Rapids: Eerdmans, 2005), 87. For these and other references, see Hofer, *Christ in
the Life of Gregory of Nazianzus*, 96. For an overview of mixture in Stoic philosophical
thought, see Anthony A. Long and David N. Sedley, *The Hellenistic Philosophers:
Volume 1, Translations of the Principal Sources with Philosophical Commentary*
(Cambridge; New York: Cambridge University Press, 1987), 290–93.
[88] Moreschini and Sykes, *Poemata Arcana*, 242.   [89] Todd, *Stoic Physics*, 116–17.
[90] Hofer, *Christ in the Life of Gregory of Nazianzus*, 96–106.
[91] Hofer departs from Wolfson because the latter argues that predominance is evident in the
Fathers' explanation of the 'unity of person in Jesus', but not the union of soul and body;

Aristotle writes, 'mixture is the union of things mixable, which have been altered'.[92] Hofer describes this approach to mixture as 'predominance'.[93] This leaves a significant difference in approach between Aristotle and the Stoics:

For Aristotle, there is a sort of transformation so that the stronger overpowers the weaker, while for the Stoics, that which is little is preserved intact when it comes into contact with that which is greater.[94]

Hofer argues that Gregory leans more towards the Aristotelian model of mixture, whilst maintaining his own approach. Hofer achieves this by pointing to Gregory's choice of images to describe the mixing that has taken place in Christ. The result of this mixing is that the Word transforms the meaner element in the same way that fire transforms wax.[95] Since mixture is key to the way in which Gregory speaks of the human person, we will return once more to Gregory's understanding of mixture during our discussion of the creation of the human *eikon* in the following chapter.[96]

Finally, let us turn to *Against Apollinarius*, where Gregory depicts Christ's flesh as God's *Eikon*:

But since God is unmingled (ἄμικτος) with flesh (σαρκίῳ),
and the soul (ψυχή) and spiritual intellect (νοῦς) [are] such a thing as is in the middle,
the flesh, then, is both God's housemate and [God's] icon:
(σαρκὸς μέν, ὡς σύνοικος, ὡς δ'εἰκὼν θεοῦ).
God's nature (φύσις) mingles (μιγεῖσα) with its kin,
and from there it has communion with the dull, thick flesh (πάχους).[97]

At the heart of Gregory's defence against Apollinarius is the notion that Christ possesses a human soul. Through the soul, God is able to be in

---

see Harry A. Wolfson, *The Philosophy of the Church Fathers; Faith, Trinity and Incarnation*, vol. 1 (Cambridge, MA: Harvard University Press, 1956), 386.

[92] Hofer, *Christ in the Life of Gregory of Nazianzus*, 99; *On Generation and Corruption* 1.10, 328b.

[93] In his unpublished Ph.D. thesis, Peter Gilbert also suggests that Gregory leans towards an understanding of mixture which closely resembles Aristotle; see 'Person and Nature', 285.

[94] Hofer, *Christ in the Life of Gregory of Nazianzus*, 101.   [95] Or. 30.6 (SC 250, 236).

[96] For discussions of perichoresis as the basis for Christology, see Nonna Verna Harrison, 'Perichoresis in the Greek Fathers', *SVTQ*, 35, no. 1 (1991), 53–65, 55; Peter Stemmer, 'Perichorese. Zur Geschichte eines Begriffs', *Archiv für Begriffsgeschichte*, 27 (1983), 9–55.

[97] Carm. 1.1.10 (PG 37, 469, 56–60). Translation adapted from Peter Gilbert, *On God and Man: The Theological Poetry of St. Gregory of Nazianzus* (Crestwood, New York: St. Vladimir's Seminary Press, 2001), 83.

communion with the flesh, which means that in this poem the flesh is considered as God's *Eikon* through its identification with the soul. This sheds further light on how we interpret Gregory's approach to the human *eikon*. In view of what Gregory writes about Christ as a complete, unified, and living *Eikon*, which includes his flesh, it is not surprising that the human person follows the same pattern since she is the *eikon* of Christ.

Thus far, I have argued that we may understand Gregory's intention regarding the unity of the human *eikon* if we turn first to Christ as *Eikon*. We continue to learn how Gregory thinks about the human *eikon* as we turn to his writing on soteriology, particularly where he draws on Philippians 2:7 to discuss the implications of Christ's kenosis.

KENOSIS AND THEOSIS

Through his soteriology, Gregory presents Christ as restoring the potential for human persons to become divine, vis à vis, theosis. This is a key thread running through Gregory's beliefs about the human *eikon*, which we will explore more fully in Chapter 5. In part, Gregory's views on kenosis stem from the premise stated in his soteriological dictum to which we pointed to earlier:

That which is unassumed is unhealed, but that which has been united to God (ἥνωται τῷ θεῷ) is also being saved.[98]

In other words, Christ must become human for the human *eikon* to be restored, uniting the Logos to humanity through the soul.[99] As a means of describing the particular way through which Christ becomes incarnate, Gregory draws from Philippians 2:7, where Paul writes of Christ emptying himself and taking on the form of a slave (ἀλλὰ ἑαυτὸν ἐκένωσεν μορφὴν δούλου λαβών).[100] Paul's proclamation appears in a hymn about Christ, which has attracted much attention from New Testament scholars due to its complex theology.[101] Whilst the hymn itself does not mention *eikon*, a number of Pauline scholars have argued that form (μορφή) and *eikon*

---

[98] Ep. 101.32 (SC 208, 50).   [99] Or. 38.13 (SC 358, 130–34).

[100] Or. 4.78 (SC 309, 200); 30.3 (SC 250, 230); 38.13 (SC 358, 134); 45.9 (PG 36, 633B–636A); Carm. 1.2.1 (PG 37, 533, 144–48); 2.1.14 (PG 37, 762, 90–92); 2.1.45 (PG 37, 1355, 28–30). According to Matz, Gregory cites Phil 2:7 on 44 occasions, either as a direct quote or as an allusion; see Brian J. Matz, 'Philippians 2:7 as Pastoral Example in Gregory Nazianzen's Oration 12', *GOTR*, 49, no. 3–4 (2004), 270–90, 282.

[101] For a historical review of how the verses in Philippians have been read, see David Brown, *Divine Humanity: Kenosis Explored and Defended* (London: SCM Press, 2010), 1–33.

(εἰκών) fall in the same semantic field, thus contrasting Christ with Adam as God's *eikon*.[102] In a passage from his oration *On the Son,* in which he argues that Christ is God, Gregory himself contrasts the form (μορφή) of a slave and the divinity of the *eikon* (εἰκών) explicitly:

And what about 'the bending of every knee'?[103] 'The emptying' for our sakes, and the divine *'Eikon'* blending with the 'form of a slave'?[104]

Gregory draws together 'form (μορφή)' and *'eikon* (εἰκών)' by arguing that the divine *Eikon* and form of a slave are blended, which points to how he interprets the act of Christ's kenosis. Christ, as the divine *Eikon*, blends with the form of a slave, but does not stop being God; on the contrary, as John Behr has argued, Christ's taking the form of a servant actually 'manifests his true divinity' rather than diminishes it.[105] Observe below how this belief is also evident in Gregory's poetry:

Christ, on seeing as great a heavenly share as he placed in the mortal body
being devoured by heart-gnawing (θυμοβόροιο δαπτόμενον) evil
and the crooked dragon (σκολιὸν δράκοντα) ruling over mortals,
in order that he might raise his portion
he did not send towards the disease other forms of help,
(for a little cure is of no use to great sufferings). But having emptied
      (κενώσας) his glory,
the heavenly and the eternal *Eikon* of heaven,
assumed flesh in the holy womb of an unwed woman
with laws that are human and not mortal (ἀνδρομέοις τε καὶ οὐ βροτέοισι
      νόμοισι) . . .[106]

Above, Gregory describes Christ, the *Eikon*, as eternal; therefore, Christ's kenosis does not mean that he, the *Eikon,* ceases to be God, but rather that he ceases to live in the glory of heaven for a time. Christ's kenosis and assumption of humanity points towards the nature of his existence as at once divine and vulnerable, where his vulnerability is chosen and temporary; it does not belong to the Godhead. Whilst Tsirpanlis and Matz have discussed Gregory's approach to Christ's kenosis in depth, they have not

---

[102] Van Kooten, 'Image, Form and Transformation', 213–42. For arguments against synonymy, see Larry W. Hurtado, *Lord Jesus Christ: Devotion to Jesus in Earliest Christianity* (Grand Rapids: Eerdmans, 2005), 121–23; David Steenberg, 'The Case Against the Synonymity of Morphe and Eikon', *JSNT*, 34 (1988), 77–86; Markus Bockmuehl, '"The Form of God" (Phil. 2: 6). Variations on a Theme of Jewish Mysticism', *JTS*, 48, no. 1 (1997), 1–23.
[103] Phil. 2:10.   [104] Or. 30.20 (SC 250, 230).   [105] Behr, *Mystery of Christ,* 35.
[106] Carm. 1.2.1 (PG 37, 533, 139–47).

observed this key point.[107] Tsirpanlis argues that Christ's kenosis is the basis of the Christian life; whilst this is correct, it denotes only part of Gregory's intention. Matz discusses broader concerns, arguing correctly that kenosis itself performs more than one function in Gregory's writing; namely, it denotes both the full deity and humanity of Christ, and is used as a language for salvation and as an example for believers to 'follow Christ's example of humility'.[108]

In light of the passages cited above, it appears that Gregory views Christ's kenosis as far more than simply an ethical example of how humans are supposed to live; rather, through kenosis, Gregory points both to an ontological uniting of divinity to humanity. It is precisely the uniting of divine and human through kenosis which procures the theosis of the human person. For Gregory, this is more than simply a rhetorical play on words, but rather it is a further means of expressing the 'exchange formula' described by Irenaeus: Christ became human so that humans could become like him.[109] We shall return to this and to theosis in Chapter 5; here, let us conclude our brief discussion of kenosis by observing that Christ's divine, yet vulnerable existence is encapsulated in Gregory's declaration, 'God crucified':[110]

... lest you leave off the argument, on hearing about the blood of God, his passion and his death (μήπου τὸν λογισμὸν ὀκλάσῃς, αἷμα θεοῦ, καὶ πάθος ἀκούων, καὶ θάνατον) ...[111]

---

[107] Constantine N. Tsirpanlis, 'The Doctrine of Katharsis: Contemplation and Kenosis in St Gregory of Nazianzus', *PBR*, 3 (1984), 5–17; Matz, 'Philippians 2:7', 270–90.

[108] Ibid., 284.

[109] *Haer.* 5, Praef. Whilst the 'kenosis-theosis' pattern is a key theme for Gregory, Norris exaggerates somewhat when he writes, 'It could almost be said that in Gregory's view, all of theology could be included under the kenosis-theosis pattern'; *Doctrine of Jesus Christ*, 62. For discussions of kenosis-theosis in the Pauline works, see Ben C. Blackwell, *Christosis: Pauline Soteriology in Light of Deification in Irenaeus and Cyril of Alexandria* (Tübingen: Mohr Siebeck, 2011), passim; Michael J. Gorman, *Inhabiting the Cruciform God: Kenosis, Justification, and Theosis in Paul's Narrative Soteriology* (Grand Rapids: Eerdmans, 2009); David Litwa, *We Are Being Transformed: Deification in Paul's Soteriology* (Berlin & New York: Walter de Gruyter, 2012).

[110] Or. 45.29 (PG 36, 661D). For God as passible, see Or. 30.1 (SC 250, 226). Gregory Nyssen charged Apollinarius with violating divine impassibility on the basis of his claim that God had died. Whilst Beeley (*Unity of Christ*, 221) infers that Gregory Nazianzen was moving towards being guilty of the same charge, there are also occasions on which Gregory depicts Christ as the conqueror with no hint of impassibility, as we shall see shortly.

[111] Or. 45.19 (PG 36, 649C); 26.12 (SC 284, 254); 43.64 (SC 384, 266–68); 45.28–29 (PG 36, 661B–663A).

Since elsewhere Gregory is equally specific that God is impassible and incapable of suffering in God's own being, it appears that Gregory views the passion itself as a paradox.[112] Gregory does not merely refer to Christ's passion in such extreme terms for the sake of paradox, but rather as a means of highlighting the complexity of salvation. Moreover, when he depicts Christ's vulnerability, it is in light of the promise of the resurrection, in which Christ beats death, the devil, sin, and the flesh, as we shall see shortly. Gregory holds in tension Christ's vulnerability with Christ's being a divine conqueror of evil. A significant consequence of Christ's becoming incarnate involves his encounters with the devil and demonic powers. Gregory is explicit that only the identical *Eikon* is able to resist and conquer the devil. Through his resistance, Christ provides a way for the human *eikon* to achieve the victory over the devil, which she was unable to accomplish on her own behalf.[113]

CONQUERING EVIL

In spite of the attention paid to Gregory's Christology and soteriology, commentators pass over Christ's interactions with the devil as though they are of little consequence, or pass over Christ's defeat of evil altogether.[114] As we have already discussed, this is possibly due to the effect of the Enlightenment, which renders discussions of the devil unpopular, except in cases where scholars seek to demythologise spiritual beings. Gregory writes that when Christ became incarnate, Satan was ruling over human persons, meaning that evil was devouring their hearts. The situation was so dire that only the identical *Eikon* could rescue the human *eikon*.[115] Unlike the human *eikon*, Christ does not succumb to the devil's schemes; rather he takes authority over the devil. As a means of

---

[112] Or. 30.5 (SC 250, 234). For a convincing defence of paradox as a necessary means of discussing God, see John Milbank, 'The Double Glory, or Paradox versus Dialectics: On Not Quite Agreeing with Slavoj Žižek', in Creston Davis (eds.), *The Monstrosity of Christ* (MA: MIT, 2009), 110–233. Milbank highlights that the 'both/and' of paradox is 'in no way static, because the likeness to the other shown through the different identity of the first thing acts to ensure that the first thing reaches further out toward that alterity, yet only by further realising its own distinctiveness', 171.

[113] Or. 39.13 (SC 358, 178).

[114] The exception is Althaus, who observes that Gregory connects the cross with the defeat of the devil; see *Die Heilslehre des heiligen Gregor von Nazianz*, 126–27.

[115] Carm. 1.2.1 (PG 37, 533, 139–47); 1.1.10 (PG 37, 465, 5–9); Or. 1.4 (SC 247, 76); 7.23 (SC 405, 240); 29.17 (SC 250, 212–14); 30.21 (SC 250, 274); 44.4 (PG 36, 612B).

revealing Christ's authority over the devil, Gregory draws on gospel accounts in which Christ drives out demons.[116] Gregory also presents Christ's life as one of wisdom and self-control, in which Christ not only discerns the temptations of the devil but also resists him.[117] Christ's ultimate victory over the devil occurs on the cross, as seen below in the passage taken from an oration in praise of Saint Cyprian:

Thus, in this way, there are many means available to us for the purpose of guiding us towards that which is greater, and many means of educating us in virtue; reason, law, prophets, apostles, the very sufferings of Christ (αὐτῶν τῶν Χριστοῦ παθημάτων), the first martyr who went up on the cross, also gathering me in, so that he might put a nail through my sin (ἵνα προσηλώσῃ τὴν ἐμὴν ἁμαρτίαν) and triumph over the serpent and sanctify the tree and conquer pleasure and heal Adam and restore the fallen *eikon* (τὴν εἰκόνα πεσοῦσαν ἀνακαλέσηται).[118]

Above, Gregory draws together Christ's victory over the serpent and the restoration of the fallen *eikon*. Gregory does not explain how Christ's crucifixion means that the devil is beaten, other than the comments that he makes in *On the Baptism of Christ*. In this oration, Gregory explains that humankind is separated from God through the envy of the devil and the taste of sin.[119] The separated and wounded human *eikon* is able to receive healing only through the incarnation, death, and resurrection of Christ. After succeeding in his temptation of the first humans, the devil attempts to trick Christ. Thinking of himself as invincible, the devil is tricked into believing that he is attacking Adam, when in fact he is attacking God.[120] Gregory appears to give little thought to God's morality in tricking the devil, as he makes no further comment other than that death was put to death by flesh.[121]

[116] Or. 29.20 (SC 250, 220); 38.16 (SC 358, 142).
[117] Or. 14.3 (PG 35, 861B); 40.10 (SC 358, 216–18).
[118] Or. 24.4 (SC 284, 46); Carm. 1.1.9 (PG 37, 459, 34–40); 1.2.1 (PG 37, 535, 162–69); 1.2.45 (PG 37, 1355–56). On this theme, also see Judith L. Kovacs, '"Now Shall the Ruler of This World Be Driven Out": Jesus' Death as Cosmic Battle in John 12:20–36', *JBL*, 114, no. 2 (1995), 227–47.
[119] Or. 39.13 (SC 358, 176–78); 30.1 (SC 250, 226); 33.9 (SC 318, 174–76); 33.14 (SC 318, 186–88); 43.64 (SC 384, 266–68); 45.22 (PG 36, 653A–C).
[120] Or. 39.13 (SC 358, 178).
[121] Or. 39.13 (SC 358, 178). For a discussion which links the deceit to Gregory's concept of ransom, see John P. Egan, 'The Deceit of the Devil According to Gregory Nazianzen' in Elizabeth A. Livingstone (ed.), *Studia Patristica*, 22 (Leuven: Peeters Press, 1989), 8–13. This loosely follows Althaus, *Die Heilslehre des heiligen*, 133–34.

In presenting Christ as the conqueror of evil powers, Gregory inter-weaves a theme prevalent in Irenaeus, who views atonement as conquest, or who sees conquest in the atonement.[122] In the twentieth century, Gustaf Aulén coined this theme 'Christus Victor'. Commenting on Irenaeus, Aulén writes, 'The work of Christ is first and foremost a victory over the powers which hold mankind in bondage: sin, death and the devil.'[123] Ben Myers provides one of the most recent critiques of Aulén's theory, arguing that it is not present in patristic literature.[124] Aulén's overall thesis is indeed overstated; however, it could not be argued that Christ's defeat of the devil is a minor strand in Gregory's writing on the human *eikon*.[125] We shall continue to observe in the following chapters that Gregory is consistent in his description of Christ's conquering powers of opposition; unlike Aulén's suggestion, Gregory achieves his account without resorting to dualism.

It is important to note that for Gregory, like Irenaeus and Origen before him, the victory is won on the cross through non-violent means, since it is won through Christ's sacrifice.[126] Encompassed in Christ's sacrifice is the theme of ransom, which Gregory addresses rather unsatis-factorily, concluding that it could not have been paid to the devil, nor to the Father because he 'neither requested nor required it'. Instead, Gregory suggests that it is part of the plan (οἰκονομία) where the human person needs to be sanctified by God, who 'prevailed over the tyrant by might (τοῦ τυράννου βίᾳ κρατήσας)'.[127] Whilst Gregory places the *eikon* in a cosmological battle with the devil, the overall picture is not pessimistic, since Christ has won the victory for the human *eikon*.

We began this chapter by arguing that Gregory follows the New Testament witness, which speaks of the Son as the *Eikon* of God. In making this move, Gregory applies consistently *eikon* to denote Christ's likeness to the Father, rather than the difference. As I shall demonstrate in the following chapters, Gregory applies *eikon* as a term denoting human

---

[122] *Haer.* 3.18.7; see Hendrickus Berkhof, *Christ and the Powers* (Scottdale: Herald, 1962), 31.

[123] Gustaf Aulén, *Christus Victor: An Historical Study of the Three Main Types of the Idea of Atonement*, trans. A.G. Herbert (London: SPCK, 1965), 20.

[124] Ben Myers, 'Atonement and the Image of God' in *Los Angeles Theology Conference* (15–16 January 2015).

[125] For a further contemporary summary and critique of 'Christus Victor'; see Boersma, *Violence, Hospitality, and the Cross*, 181–201. The 'Christus Victor' view of atonement can only function to a certain extent within cosmic dualism, although this does not need to be ultimate or eternal.

[126] *Or.* 4.78 (SC 309, 200).   [127] *Or.* 45.22 (PG 36, 653B).

likeness to God, following his treatment of Christ. Whilst the human *eikon* does not exist eternally, in all other ways *eikon* situates her ontology, function, and relationship to God as categories that express radical likeness to her Creator. This likeness is realised through both Christ and the human *eikon* being described as 'living beings', which leads me to suggest that *eikon* is more clearly expressed as that which is dynamic rather than static. Added to this, we have observed that the title '*Eikon*' refers to the transcendent Logos and the incarnate Christ, rather than being reserved for the former. The implications upon the human *eikon* are significant because we are prevented from adopting the view that the *eikon* equates to the spiritual intellect or the soul alone; rather, *eikon* speaks of the whole human person, including the flesh.

3

Creation of the Image of God

Having established that Christ, the identical *Eikon*, informs how Gregory construes the human *eikon*, we continue to follow Gregory's own sequence by moving on to explore his account of creation. Observe below how Gregory adopts an interrogative practice when considering the creation of the *eikon*, like the psalmist before him:

What are human beings that you are mindful of them, mortals that you care for them? (Psalm 8:5; 8:4)[1]

What are human beings that you are mindful of them? What is this new mystery about me?[2]

As we pursue questions concerning the created identity of the human *eikon*, we recall that Gregory appears not to be as concerned with the answer to the particular question, 'what is the *eikon*?' Rather, he pays more attention to describing the mystery of human experience and what it is like to *be* an *eikon*. Throughout the book, we see that this approach enables Gregory to weave into a cohesive account myriad threads, which, on occasion, appear to be related somewhat disparately.

In Chapter 2, we established that Gregory presents Christ, the identical *Eikon* who, as a unified, living *eikon*, is different from pagan *eikones*. Here, we explore how the human *eikon* follows Christ in this manner, as in many others. I shall argue the importance of visibility and materiality to the human *eikon* through the close consideration of (a) angels, (b)

---

[1] For the sake of inclusivity, here I have translated ἄνθρωπος, which occurs both in Psalm 8 and Oration 7, as 'human beings'.

[2] Or. 7.23 (SC 405, 238–40).

Gregory's interpretation of the creation of the *eikon* in light of biblical and extra-biblical themes and (c) female *eikones*. We observe that Gregory plays on beliefs about images and idols, revealing once again his vision of the human *eikon* as a kind of divine, living statue who images visibly God.

CREATIO EX NIHILO

In order to clarify further my interpretation of Gregory's use of 'divine' in relation to the human *eikon*, we begin by determining how *creatio ex nihilo* is intrinsic to Gregory's doctrine of God and to his theological anthropology. For Gregory, the implications of *creatio ex nihilo* are that only God exists eternally and, consequently, the human *eikon* is a creature. Therefore, when Gregory speaks of the human *eikon* as 'divine', her divinity is conferred, since divinity belongs to God alone in the proper sense.

The way in which Gregory writes about theology and economy suggests that he does not distinguish between them, other than for clarification of the terms themselves; rather, he writes in such a way that they are one and the same.[3] Observe this in Gregory's second theological oration, *On the Doctrine of God,* in which Gregory ruminates at some length on the wonders of cosmology and creation. During his wondering, Gregory observes that God alone is the creator and sustainer of the world:

For how could also this universe have been caused to subsist (ὑπέστη), or set together (συνέστη) if God had not given being (οὐσιώσαντος) and sustained all things?[4]

Gregory's belief that God is both the cause (αἴτιος) and source (ἀρχή) of all being relates to his understanding of the doctrine *creatio ex nihilo.*[5] By the fourth century, during which Gregory was writing, *creatio ex nihilo* was a normative Christian doctrine, which he accepted.[6] For Gregory, *creatio*

---

[3] Or. 38.8 (SC 358, 118).

[4] Or. 28.6 (SC 250, 110). The philosophy attributed to Gregory's doctrine of creation is dealt with thoroughly in Moreschini and Sykes, *Poemata Arcana*, 143–51; Portmann, *Die göttliche Paidagogia bei Gregor von Nazianz,* 53–62.

[5] Or. 28.6 (SC 250, 110); 20.7 (SC 270, 72).

[6] By the early third century, theologians such as Clement of Alexandria and Origen did not question *creatio ex nihilo*. Considered by numerous scholars to derive from Genesis, the earliest alleged example of *creatio ex nihilo* occurs in 2 Maccabees 7:28. According to May, the doctrine appeared in its fullest sense in the Christian climate, stemming from Christian thinkers such as Theophilus of Antioch; Gerhard May, *Creatio Ex Nihilo*

ex nihilo is significant, since it is key to his concept of monotheism, in which God is One.[7] Further to this, Gregory employs *creatio ex nihilo* as a means of confirming the sovereignty of God and denying the eternity of matter (ἡ ὕλη). In making this move, Gregory follows Wisdom and Job in their depiction of matter as formless:[8]

> Come now and let us celebrate the creation of great God,
> contesting against false opinions.
> God is One (εἶς θεός); but matter and forms, things thought by
>   the wisest of the Greeks to be eternal, are a feeble story.
> . . . but if these things were mixed,
> how is it that they were mixed? Who mixed them other than God?
>   If it is God who mixed them,
> then accept him as the Creator of everything as well
>   (τοῦτον καὶ κτίστορα δέχνυσο πάντων).[9]

Gregory reasons that only God is without beginning and, since God created everything, all things are contingent on God. Elm has discussed how Gregory integrated the creation account in Genesis into a variety of Platonic and Neo-Platonic cosmological traditions; however his adherence to the Christian doctrine of *creatio ex nihilo* suggests that Gregory approached his doctrine the opposite way.[10] Furthermore, in *On Pentecost*, Gregory follows the sequence laid out in Genesis without alteration:

But, there is no doubt that in six days God gave substance to matter (ἡ ὕλη). God both shaped and arrayed it with varied and complex forms and created this world which we see now.[11]

(New York: T&T Clark, 2004). Scholars have critiqued May's thesis, arguing that there is evidence of *creatio ex nihilo* in the Septuagint; see Russell R. Reno, *Genesis* (London: SCM Press, 2010). Also, see Paul Copan, 'Is Creatio Ex Nihilo a Post-Biblical Invention? An Examination of Gerhard May's Proposal', *Trinity Journal*, 17, no. 1 (1996), 77–93. Copan's thesis discusses the whole biblical narrative and is widely supported; see Frank F. Bruce, *The Epistle to the Hebrews* (Grand Rapids: Eerdmans, 1964), 281; Richard J. Clifford, *Creation Accounts in the Ancient Near East and in the Bible* (Washington, D.C.: CBAA, 1994), 199.

[7] Or. 7.19 (SC 405, 226); 24.7 (SC 284, 52); 32.7 (SC 318, 98); Carm. 1.1.4 (PG 37, 415–17).

[8] Wis. 11:17; Job 19:29; see Muraoka, *GELS*, 694.

[9] Carm. 1.1.4 (PG 37, 415–16, 1–15); 1.1.6 (PG 37, 430, 1–11); Or. 24.7 (SC 284, 52); 25.8 (SC 284, 174–76); 28.8 (SC 250, 114–16); 32.10 (SC 318, 104–06). For Athanasius and Irenaeus, *creatio ex nihilo* entails that creatures are ontologically different from God, which also applies to Gregory; see Paul Gavrilyuk, 'Creation in Early Christian Polemical Literature: Irenaeus against the Gnostics and Athanasius against the Arians', *Modern Theology*, 29, no. 2 (2013), 22–32, 30.

[10] Elm, 'O Paradoxical Fusion!', 297.

[11] Or. 41.2 (SC 358, 314–16); 43.67 (SC 384, 272–74).

Gregory's following of the Christian doctrine *creatio ex nihilo* is significant to his account of the human *eikon*, since it informs Gregory's perception of the divinity of the *eikon*. For Gregory, a clear distinction exists between God and God's *eikon,* relating to the fact that the human *eikon* receives her existence as a gift from God. Therefore, when he speaks of the human *eikon* as divine, Gregory does not imply that she is God's ontological equal. This becomes apparent further through Gregory's discussion of angels, whom he also describes as 'divine', but in a manner which suggests a difference from God, as we shall see in the following section.

INVISIBLE REALM OF ANGELS

Gregory depicts God creating the world as two realms, invisible and visible, respectively, which form a single whole. Following Gregory's sequence, we will explore the invisible realm first, which is the home of the angels. Since in his writings Gregory describes the human *eikon* as 'another kind of angel (ἄγγελος ἄλλος)', a discussion of these 'invisible spirits' is vital to build a finer picture of the human *eikon*.[12] Note that, following Genesis 1, Gregory does not name angels as *eikones* of God; as we shall see below, human persons alone image God. This is significant as it points towards the uniqueness of the human as God's *eikon*. Key to Gregory's description of humans is the belief that they are a mixture of the material and spiritual realms; their materiality means that they are visible, unlike angels, whom Gregory describes as invisible and simple. Thus, their materiality means that humans are able to function quite literally as visible, breathing *eikones* of God, as proposed in Chapter 1.

Angels hold a substantial place in Gregory's worldview, occurring in every poem in the *Arcana*, and many other poems and orations.[13] From his discussions of angels, it is clear that Gregory, in line with his patristic Christian tradition, 'accepted the reality of the spiritual world'.[14] However, despite the fact that Gregory refers to the angelic realm frequently, his name appears rarely in the secondary scholarship concerned with

---

[12] Or. 38.11 (SC 358, 126); 45.7 (PG 36, 635C); Carm. 1.2.1 (PG 37, 529, 90); 1.2.15 (PG 37, 777, 155).

[13] See *On Spiritual Beings*; Carm. 1.1.7 (PG 37, 438–46), which Gregory dedicates to the subject of angels.

[14] Ferguson, *Demonology*, 133.

angels in Byzantium.[15] This may be because Gregory is often associated with his work on Christology and the Trinity. These subjects themselves receive more attention than angelology in contemporary scholarship; consequently, scholars rarely draw attention to the centrality of angels to Gregory's thinking. To date, Rousse has paid the most detailed attention to Gregory's angelology.[16] Concerning Gregory's sources, Rousse suggests a combination of Scripture, Plato, Origen, and possibly Clement, who suggested that a treatise should be written about angels, although if he did write one it is nowhere to be found.[17] Added to this, note that Gregory lived following an age where the importance of angels had increased significantly through the influence of mystical Judaism and extra-biblical traditions.[18]

When Gregory writes about angels, he clarifies that such matters are really too great for him to fully comprehend.[19] This follows the patristic tradition, since the early church fathers generally perceived angels as being beyond human understanding. Should we incline towards questioning Gregory's authority on the glory of angels, he informs us that the Spirit has given the information to him.[20] In claiming that he has heard directly from the Spirit, Gregory is drawing attention to his own authority, and stands alongside a Christian tradition 'of a Jewish esotericism that existed at the time of the Apostles', where particular Christians were given visions and insights into the mysteries of heaven.[21] In spite of his 'hesitation' in speaking about such matters, Gregory is sure of certain aspects of the angelic realm. Angels are closest to God, since their realm was created first:

---

[15] Gregory is mentioned once in Glenn Peers, *Subtle Bodies: Representing Angels in Byzantium* (California: University of California Press, 2001). Only a brief consideration is given to Gregory's 'innovative ideas' in Ellen Muehlberger, *Angels in the Religious Imagination of Late Antiquity* (IN: Indiana University, 2008). In a recent systematic review of angels, Gregory is overlooked in favour of Origen; see Oliver Dürr, *Der Engel Mächte: Systematisch-theologische Untersuchung: Angelologie* (Stuttgart: Verlag W. Kohlhammer, 2009), 50. For the exception to this pattern, see Jean Daniélou, *The Angels and Their Mission: According to the Fathers of the Church*, trans. David Heimann (Westminster, MD: Christian Classics, Inc., 1982), 34, 40, 51, 58, 59, 66, 86, 87.

[16] Jacques Rousse, 'Les anges et leur ministère selon Saint Grégoire de Nazianze', *MSR*, 22 (1965), 133–52.

[17] Ibid., 152. See *Strom.* 6.3.

[18] David Flusser, *Judaism of the Second Temple Period: The Jewish Sages and Their Literature*, trans. Azzan Yadin (Grand Rapids: Eerdmans, 2009), 40.

[19] Or. 38.10 (SC 384, 122–24); 28.31 (SC 250, 172).   [20] Carm. 1.1.7 (PG 37, 446, 96).

[21] Jean Daniélou, 'Les traditions secrètes des Apôtres', *Eranos Jahrbuch*, 31 (1962), 199–215, 214.

First, while [God] conceived the angelic and heavenly powers, this thought was an action, attained by the *Logos* and perfected by the Spirit. And in this way the secondary splendours (λαμπρότητες δεύτεραι) came about, servants (λειτουργοὶ) of the first Splendour; one must consider them as intellectual spirits (νοερὰ πνεύματα) or fire as such immaterial and incorporeal, or as another nature, which is closest to that of which has been spoken.[22]

Gregory's depiction of angels as spirits and fire follows Psalm 103:4 (104:4) and Hebrews 1:7.[23] This idea is also common in Jewish Apocalyptic texts, such as 2 Enoch 29:13 and 2 Baruch 21:6.[24] Gregory refers to angels as 'second lights', observing that they receive blessings from God.[25] They are an order separate from human persons, who, as we shall see, are the 'third lights'.

Angels have multiple functions, each in a particular rank, according to their brilliance.[26] They serve the Trinity by praising God and executing God's commands in heaven, continuing on earth as Christ's entourage.[27] Furthermore, angels are characterised as co-workers alongside human persons, active in the life of the Church and present at baptism.[28] Gregory's concept of priestly ministry incorporates angels, since he stands with them at the Eucharist.[29] As Daniélou notes, 'the mysteries of Christ are celebrated by the heavenly powers at the same time as they are celebrated by the Church on earth'.[30] This is important to remember when considering the heavenly and the earthly realms since, for Gregory, they function simultaneously in the life of the Church.[31]

Humans require protection from the devil's schemes, which we will explore in depth in Chapter 4. Consequently, angels assume the role of

---

[22] Or. 38.9 (SC 358, 120); 6.12 (SC 405, 152); 28.3 (SC 250, 106); 28.31 (SC 250, 172); 38.10 (SC 384, 122); 40.5 (SC 358, 204); 41.11 (SC 358, 258); 44.3 (PG 36, 609B); 45.5 (PG 36, 629A); Carm. 1.1.7 (PG 37, 439–40, 6–15); 1.2.1 (PG 37, 524, 30–34).

[23] Or. 28.31 (SC 250, 170).

[24] Harold Barnes Kuhn, 'The Angelology of the Non-Canonical Jewish Apocalypses', *JBL*, 67, no. 3 (1948), 217–32, 119. The notion that angels were somehow composed of intellectual fire and spirit was usual from the second century, appearing to stem from Theodotus; see Peers, *Subtle Bodies*, 2–3.

[25] Or. 22.14 (SC 270, 252).

[26] Or. 28.31 (SC 250, 170–74); Carm. 1.1.7 (PG 37, 440, 22–26); 1.2.10 (PG 37, 688, 103).

[27] Or. 38.14 (SC 358, 136); 45.25 (PG 36, 657B).   [28] Or. 40.36 (SC 358, 280).

[29] Or. 40.4 (SC 358, 204); 2.73 (SC 247, 186).

[30] Daniélou, *Angels and their Mission*, 66.

[31] Gregory expresses a vision of heaven with angels endlessly singing praise to God, which would later be developed even more fully in Dionysius the Areopagite's *Celestial Hierarchy*.

guardians, both of churches and of people.[32] Indeed, Gregory speaks about his own angel when he is ill, and asks the angel to come to his aid.[33] Gregory's personal experience with angels extends to a vision of 'one like an angel', where he situates himself alongside the great Habakkuk.[34] Bocur and Mueller explore this vision in relation to later iconography that depicts this scene. They conclude that 'the angel offers an image of what the human herald of the Good News should be'.[35]

Having established the prevalence of angels in Gregory's worldview, we draw to a close our brief tour of the heavenly realm with an extract from *On Spiritual Beings*. This serves as a summary of Gregory's high regard for the fiery spirits:

> Radiant angels, without visible form,
> going about the great throne, since they are nimble spiritual intellects,
> fire and divine spirits (πνεύματα θεῖα) flying swiftly through the air,
> hurrying, they obey God's great commands
> being both simple and spiritual intellects (ἁπλοῖ τε, νοεροί τε)...[36]

Gregory's esteem for angels, both in the passage above and elsewhere, presents us with some questions. It may have been that Gregory was aware of the various complexities of his argument, which is why he provides the disclaimer that these intellectual spirits are really too great for him to comprehend. We will consider how angels become demons in Chapter 4, where we shall see that Gregory admits he cannot understand how Lucifer chose to move away from God. Nevertheless, in spite of the fact that some angels do fall from heaven, observe that Gregory presents angels as superior to human persons since, in some respects, he describes angels as 'closest to God'. Furthermore, Gregory exhorts human persons to imitate the angelic way of life in service of God, by practising virginity and in growing in likeness to God.[37]

---

[32] Or. 42.9 (SC 384, 70).   [33] Carm. 2.1.89 (PG 37, 1443, 8).

[34] Or. 45.1 (PG 36, 624A).

[35] Bogdan G. Bucur and Elijah N. Mueller, 'Gregory Nazianzen's Reading of Habakkuk 3:2 and its Reception: A Lesson from Byzantine Scripture Exegesis', *Pro Ecclesia*, 20, no. 1 (2011), 86–103, 102. For a print and description of the icon, see Leslie Brubaker, *Vision and Meaning in Ninth-Century Byzantium: Image as Exegesis in the Homilies of Gregory of Nazianzus* (Cambridge: Cambridge University Press, 1999), 284–85.

[36] Carm. 1.1.7 (PG 37, 439–40, 13–17).

[37] Or. 37.10–11 (SC 318, 292–96); Carm. 1.2.3 (PG 37, 633, 2–6). See Karl S. Frank, *Angelikos bios. Begriffsanalytische und begriffsgeschichtliche Untersuchung zum 'engelgleichen Leben' im frühen Mönchtum* (Münster: Aschendorff, 1964), passim.

The problem I wish to raise here concerns the titles that Gregory bestows upon angels and human persons. Above, Gregory describes angels as 'divine', a title that is shared with human *eikones*. Gregory does not state how angels are divine, other than to imply it is by virtue of their proximity to God. However, in spite of their shared divinity, Gregory does not bestow upon angels the gift of being God's *eikon*, but rather follows Genesis by reserving God's *eikon* as a privilege for human persons alone. If angels are closer to God and more like God than human *eikones*, then it is surprising that Gregory does not consider them to image God. In response to this, I suggest that Gregory is doing something more profound than simply echoing biblical titles and descriptions for being human. Rather, it is possible that Gregory is making sense of his own materiality. By preserving *eikon* as a means of describing the human person, Gregory points towards the fact that an aspect of imaging God concerns visibility, as we have observed. Humans are visible, whereas angels are invisible, which means that they cannot visibly image God.[38] Moreover, Christ is the identical *Eikon*, through which Gregory affirms the significance of the incarnation, by preserving the title *eikon* for the human. Before we discuss this further, let us explore briefly Gregory's description of the creation of the cosmos, in which the invisible and visible realms form a 'praiseworthy', single world. The harmony of creation is echoed in the human person, as we shall see shortly.

VISIBLE REALM OF THE IMAGE OF GOD

And since the first things seemed good to God, [God] had in mind a second material (ὑλικός) and visible realm, and this is the structure and compound of heaven and earth and of the things in between; praiseworthy according to each good natural part, but even more laudable because of the suitability and harmony of everything, one bearing up well with another, and all parts (drawing) towards the whole, into completion of a single world (εἰς ἑνὸς κόσμου συμπλήρωσιν), in order that he might show not only his own nature to himself, but also that he was able to give substance to that which is completely strange (to Godself).[39]

---

[38] Angels may appear in human form, for example, as Gabriel does in the annunciation to the Virgin Mary; however, they do not generally share the same bodily form as humans.

[39] Or. 38.10 (SC 358, 122–24). Gregory's doctrine of creation cannot be found in its entirety in any of his predecessors; Donald F. Winslow, *The Dynamics of Salvation: A Study in Gregory of Nazianzus* (Cambridge, MA: Philadelphia Patristic Foundation, 1979), 46–47.

Together the two realms make a 'single world', which is harmonious, beautiful and ordered.[40] Observe that Gregory presents the material, visible realm as wholly good. Following Genesis, where the ordering of creation is important, Gregory's ideas concerning the created order connect together in various orations. For example, he explains that there is order in the body of Christ, the Church, because God purposed creation itself in an ordered fashion.[41] Furthermore, Gregory frequently cites Psalm 8 to suggest that our only exact knowledge concerning creation is that it is ordered.[42] Next, we shall see that the order and harmony continue to be fundamental to God's creation of the human *eikon*.

The Mixed Human Eikon

And there was not yet a mixture (τὸ κρᾶμα) from both,[43] nor yet a particular mingling (ἡ μίξις) of opposites...[44] the Creator-Logos, wanting to exhibit this, [makes] a single living being from both (ζῷον ἓν ἐξ ἀμφοτέρων), by which I mean from the invisible and visible nature, fashioned the human person (δημιουργεῖ τὸν ἄνθρωπον). While taking the body from the existing matter (ἡ ὕλη), God blew in the breath of himself, which Scripture knew to be the spiritual, intellectual soul (νοερὰ ψυχή) and an *eikon* of God.[45]

Above, Gregory combines the creation narratives found in Genesis 1 and 2, depicting the human *eikon* as the breath of God mixing with matter.[46] Throughout his work, Gregory varies between describing God as mixing the *eikon* with matter (ἡ ὕλη), clay (ἡ πηλός, ἡ ὕλις), and dust/earth (ὁ χοῦς), respectively.[47] As demonstrated earlier, Gregory argues

---

[40] Or. 6.14 (SC 405, 156); 28.27–29 (SC 250, 158–68); Carm. 1.2.34 (PG 37, 954, 115–19).

[41] Or. 32.10 (SC 318, 104).

[42] Or. 20.11 (SC 270, 80); 28.5 (SC 250, 108–10); 32.27 (SC 318, 142).

[43] Or. 20.11 (SC 270, 80); 14.7 (PG 35, 865). See Song of Songs 7:2, where it is used to describe a mixture of wine and water, and *Paed.* 2.2, where Clement discusses the union of soul and body. Also see *PGL*, 774.

[44] Or. 38.11 (SC 358, 124); 2.23 (SC 247, 120); 2.54 (SC 247, 162); 4.49 (SC 309, 152); 6.2 (SC 405, 124); 21.23 (SC 270, 156); 45.9 (PG 36, 633B–636A); Carm. 1.1.4 (PG 37, 423, 92); 1.1.8 (PG 37, 453, 79–86); et al.

[45] Or. 38.11 (SC 358, 124).

[46] Or. 14.2 (PG 35, 860B–D); 20.11 (SC 270, 80); 32.27 (SC 318, 142); Carm. 1.1.8 (PG 37, 452, 70–74); 1.2.1 (PG 37, 552, 395–97).

[47] For examples of the *eikon* mixed with the following, see matter (ἡ ὕλη), Or. 38.11 (SC 358, 124); clay (ἡ πηλός), Or. 14.6 (PG 35, 865A); dust/earth (ὁ χοῦς), Or. 14.2 (PG 35, 860B–D); Carm. 1.2.1 (PG 37, 529, 97); 2.1.45 (PG 37, 1362, 119).

that God creates matter; key to Gregory's concept of creation is that neither matter nor forms are eternal. The additional materials used in the creation of the human person; namely, clay and dust, both appear in the Septuagint, which depicts God as a potter.[48] The most frequent terminology that Gregory applies for the mixing of the *eikon* with dust or matter is μίξις, which he uses in conjunction with κρᾶσις, appearing to apply them indiscriminately and in a variety of ways.[49]

If we were to read Gregory's description of the *eikon* found above, without taking into account his view of how the invisible and visible realms are mixed, we might conclude that Gregory considers the *eikon* only to be the breath of God, vis à vis the intellectual soul. Rather, Gregory understands the complexity and mystery of human existence, which is reflected in his different approaches to being a human *eikon*. Thus, whilst Gregory applies *eikon* to the soul or the spiritual intellect on some occasions, he does so in such a way that the *eikon* transforms the dust and renders it spiritual. This results in the human *eikon* becoming a unified, dynamic being, which is a broader concept than that proposed by a categorical approach, as emphasised throughout the book.

For insight into the transformation of dust by the *eikon*, we turn back to Gregory's writing about Christ, the identical *Eikon*. In Chapter 2, we established that Gregory incorporated Christ's flesh into his views about Christ, the identical *Eikon*.[50] This allows humanity and divinity to come together in a unique way in Christ, such that he remains a unified hypostasis or person.[51] If we consider Gregory's writing about the human person, we may see that a similar process ensues. Gregory approaches God's mixing of *eikon* and matter as a unification, where the *eikon* bestows upon the dust its proper end, which is to be made spiritual. This is evident in Gregory's short poem entitled *Concerning Human Life*, in which the dust is made spiritual by the *eikon*:

---

[48] For examples of the potter using clay, see Is. 29:16; Jer. 18:6; Muraoka, *GELS*, 556. For the human person as a mixture of God's breath and dust, see Gen 2:7.

[49] Gregory also speaks of mixing in relation to the elements of the universe; see Or. 2.29 (SC 247, 128); 2.54 (SC 247, 162); 6.2 (SC 405, 124); 6.15 (SC 405, 160); 38.13 (SC 358, 134). Also, drawing on Paul, Gregory applies the terms rhetorically when he states that ideally, one should approach the congregation with a mixture of strictness and gentleness; see Or. 2.54 (SC 247, 162). Lastly, Gregory speaks of his tears mingled with joy; see Or. 4.49 (SC 309, 152).

[50] Carm. 1.1.10 (PG 37, 469, 56–60).

[51] Hofer, *Christ in the Life of Gregory of Nazianzus*, 92–120.

> And now peeping out, just like from some depth,
> the dust, made spiritual by the divine *eikon* (ὁ χοῦς ὁ θεία
> πνευματωθεὶς εἰκόνι) cries out the earthly tragedies ...[52]

It is this transformation of the dust that allows Gregory to refer to the whole human person as God's *eikon*:

> I am a human person, a model (πλάσμα) and an *eikon* of God.[53]

Therefore, when Gregory speaks about the *eikon* as the soul or the spiritual intellect, it is possible that he also implies the whole human person because the *eikon* transforms the dust and thus the two form a unity together. The creation of the human person as a unified, mixed *eikon* is essential to her theosis, which we will examine further in Chapter 5. Let us observe one final point about the transformation of dust: in order for the transformation of dust or matter to occur, and for a dynamic human person to be formed, the material realm must be vulnerable (or porous) to the divine, spiritual realm. Thus, material vulnerability to God is a necessary aspect of being a human *eikon*. Certainly, as Gregory depicts the creation of the human person, her vulnerability to God is wholly positive. Understood in this way, vulnerability is not related to being wounded, but rather depicts the concept of porosity, as I observed in the Introduction.

In order to appreciate more fully Gregory's view of the human *eikon*, in which the human person is vulnerable to the spiritual realm, let us explore briefly the work of Catholic philosopher, Charles Taylor. He identifies a significant difference between the worldview of those living in the premodern era and contemporary times, which explains how in the premodern era, human persons maintained porous boundaries.

'Porous Self'

In his seminal work, *A Secular Age*, Charles Taylor charts the move away from the position held in pre-modern societies, in which it is almost 'impossible not to believe in God', to the position in which belief in

---

[52] Carm. 1.2.18 (PG 37, 787, 13–14); 1.1.8 (PG 37, 452, 74–75); 1.1.10 (PG 37, 469, 58); Or. 3.7 (SC 247, 250); 40.10 (SC 358, 218); 40.14 (SC 358, 226). Gregory is not very far from Methodius who envisaged that 'the soul infuses the body with the image ... the soul makes the body more truly the body, more truly the image of God'; Cartwright, *Theological Anthropology of Eustathius*, 161.

[53] Carm. 1.2.34 (PG 37, 947, 20).

God is 'no longer axiomatic'.[54] Since his overall project is complex, we will discuss the aspects relevant to our argument, and only in the broadest terms. In his earlier work, *Sources of the Self*, Taylor explains that the shifts following pre-modernity come to bear in the way we view

> our thoughts, ideas, or feelings as being 'within' us, while the objects in the world which these mental states bear on are 'without'. ... [This] is a function of a historically limited mode of self-interpretation, one which has become dominant in the modern West.[55]

According to Taylor, this is radically different from the interpretation of the self in the pre-modern world, which he characterises as 'porous'.[56] He explains that the ancient and medieval philosophical life meant befriending the highest things to the extent that there was little differentiation between internal and external forces.[57] Said another way, the pre-modern self was characterised by 'porous' boundaries between the self and external forces, rather than being surrounded by boundaries which are demarcated firmly.

Taylor summarises this pre-modern world as one of 'enchantment'.[58] By applying this term, like Taylor, I do not intend to invoke images of fairies and elves; rather, 'the world of spirits, demons and moral forces'.[59] In the enchanted world, the human person is 'open and porous and vulnerable to a world of spirits and powers'.[60] This is a view with which Classical scholars concur:

> 'To the ancients, the line of demarcation between god and man was not as constant and sharp, or the interval as wide, as we might naturally think'.[61]

Thus, disenchantment constitutes the opposite of this; it forms the condition in which we live today, whereby the only place for thoughts or feelings is firmly within the boundaries of the 'mind'.[62] Through modernity and the rise of humanism, the 'porous self' was displaced by a 'disenchanted' view of the world and by the 'buffered self'.[63] Taylor

---

[54] Charles Taylor, *A Secular Age* (Cambridge, MA: Harvard University Press, 2007), 3.
[55] Charles Taylor, *Sources of the Self: The Making of the Modern Identity* (New York: Cambridge University Press, 1989), 111.
[56] Taylor, *A Secular Age*, 27.
[57] For a concise summary and critique of Taylor's thesis, see Samuel Kimbriel, *Friendship as Sacred Knowing* (Oxford: Oxford University Press, 2014), 10–34.
[58] 'Enchantment is an antonym to Weber's application of "disenchantment" as a means of describing our modern condition'; Taylor, *A Secular Age*, 446.
[59] Ibid., 29.   [60] Ibid., 27.   [61] Nock, 'Notes on Ruler-Cult I-IV', 145.
[62] Taylor, *A Secular Age*, 30.   [63] Ibid., 27.

explains that the 'buffered self feels invulnerable before the world of spirits and magic forces'.[64] The buffered self represents 'a very different existential condition... For the modern, buffered self, the possibility exists of taking a distance from, disengaging from everything outside the mind'.[65]

It is difficult to conceive how, writing in a pre-modern age, Gregory would have understood himself as a 'porous self' or a 'vulnerable' self, the description which I have been applying to the human *eikon* throughout this book. The 'porous self' signifies that the human person is so permeable or porous that when God breathes life into her, the *eikon* can be described as a 'god' or 'divine'. Therefore, it is possible for human persons to share in God's life due to their propensity to permeability.[66] In Gregory's case, this permeability is possible for a human person precisely because she is made according to the *eikon* of God. This becomes crucial to how we understand Gregory's description of theosis in Chapter 5, where we will argue that Gregory understands literally the divinity of the *eikon*, precisely because of her porosity to the Holy Spirit.

Let us turn back now to Gregory's depiction of the human *eikon* at creation and move next to discuss the different titles which Gregory applies to the first human *eikon*. We continue to observe that Gregory draws his principal inspiration from Scripture; furthermore, we shall see that the titles relate to the visibility of the *eikon*:

God placed upon the earth a kind of second world, great in miniature, another angel, a mixed worshipper, overseer of visible creation, an initiate of the spiritual (creation), king of that which is on earth, being governed from above, earthly and heavenly, transient and immortal, visible and spiritual, mid-way between magnitude and lowliness. (οἷόν τινα κόσμον δεύτερον, ἐν μικρῷ μέγαν, ἐπὶ τῆς γῆς ἵστησιν, ἄγγελον ἄλλον, προσκυνητὴν μικτόν, ἐπόπτην τῆς ὁρατῆς κτίσεως, μύστην τῆς νοουμένης, βασιλέα τῶν ἐπὶ γῆς, βασιλευόμενον ἄνωθεν, ἐπίγειον καὶ οὐράνοιον, πρόσκαιρον καὶ ἀθάνατον, ὁρατὸν καὶ νοούμενον, μέσον μεγέθους καὶ ταπεινότητος). ... A living being, provided for here and being transferred elsewhere, and, to cap the mystery off, being made god (θεούμενον) by her inclination towards God.[67]

---

[64] Ibid., 548.   [65] Ibid., 38.

[66] Paul Gavrilyuk, 'The Retrieval of Deification: How a Once-Despised Archaism Became an Ecumenical Desideratum', *Modern Theology*, 25, no. 4 (2009), 647–59, 649.

[67] Or. 38.11 (SC 358, 124–26).

Microcosm

Above, Gregory 'depicts creation as brought to unity within the human microcosm'.[68] In doing this, he draws on a tradition which includes theologians such as Philo, Origen, and Basil, who incorporate this theme into their writings.[69] The concept is related to the Old Testament, which presents the temple as the microcosm of the world.[70] Paul develops this idea in the New Testament, where he depicts the people of God as temples of the Holy Spirit.[71] Macaskill has argued that early Christians promoted the idea of the human person as a microcosm, because the concept 'acquired a distinct connection with redemptive Christology'.[72] He draws this conclusion from reading the works of Irenaeus, who developed the idea of Christ initiating a new creation, known as 'recapitulation'. Christ, whom the New Testament represents as the new/second Adam, redeems God's whole creation:

... therefore does the Lord profess himself to be the Son of Man, recapitulating in himself that original man out of whom woman was fashioned, in order that, as our race went down to death through a vanquished man, so we may ascend to life again through a victorious one, and as through a man death received the palm [of victory] against us, so again, by a man we may receive the palm against death.[73]

The redemptive theme of recapitulation is evident in Gregory's work, as we shall see next. As demonstrated in Chapter 2, for Gregory, Christ's battle and victory over sin and Satan is cosmic.[74] Throughout his orations and poems, Gregory presents the unity and harmony bestowed on

---

[68] Doru Costache, 'Seeking Out the Antecedents of the Maximian Theory of Everything: St Gregory the Theologian's Oration 38' in Doru Costache and Philip Kariatlis (eds.), *The Cappadocian Legacy: A Critical Appraisal* (Redfern, NSW: St Andrew's Orthodox Press, 2013), 225–42, 233. For further attention to Gregory's microcosm, see Tomáš Špidlík, *Grégoire de Nazianze* (Roma: Pont. Institutum Studiorum Orientalium, 1971), 104–07; Bernhard Wyß, 'Gregor von Nazianz: ein griechisch-christlicher Denker des vierten Jahrhunderts', *Museum Helveticum* 6 (1949), 177–210.

[69] *Her.* 31.155; *Cels.* 6.63; *Hex. Hom.* 11.14.

[70] Gregory K. Beale, *The Temple and the Church's Mission: A Biblical Theology of the Dwelling Place of God*, NSBT (Leicester: Apollos, 2004), passim; Scott W. Hahn and David Scott, *Temple and Contemplation: God's Presence in the Cosmos, Church, and Human Heart* (Steubenville, Ohio: St Paul Center for Biblical Theology, 2008), 336.

[71] *Or.* 2.97 (SC 247, 216).

[72] Grant Macaskill, 'Adam Octipartite/Septipartite' in Richard Bauckham, James R. Davila and Alexander Panayotov (eds.), *Old Testament Pseudepigrapha: More Noncanonical Scriptures* (Grand Rapids: Eerdmans, 2013), 3–21, 11.

[73] *Haer.* 5.21.1; translation John Behr, *Irenaeus of Lyons: Identifying Christianity* (Oxford: Oxford University Press, 2013), 169.

[74] *Or.* 44.4 (PG 36, 609D–612C); 38.13 (SC 358, 130–34); *Ep.* 101.19 (SC 208, 44).

humanity as constantly under threat. Satan's attacks on the human *eikon* are often with a view to destroying her harmony. In a poem in which Gregory laments that the Evil One has plagued him with disease, he describes vividly that the intent of Satan is to disturb the harmony with which he was first created.[75] Thus, when Gregory describes the human *eikon* as a microcosm, he incorporates the idea of Christ's restoration of humanity. Furthermore, he reminds the reader of the harmonious mixture of material and spiritual realms. This is also pertinent to his depiction of the human person as 'another angel'.

Another Angel

Moreschini argues that Gregory appeals to the human person as 'another angel', simply because she serves and adores God, and because her soul is of the same spiritual nature as the angels.[76] Whilst his arguments are correct in part, I believe that Moreschini misses the full significance of Gregory's intention when he refers to the human person as 'another angel'. Earlier in this chapter, whilst discussing Gregory's approach to angels, we saw that Gregory describes the angelic realm as that which is closest to God. Therefore, in referring to the human *eikon* as 'another angel', Gregory demonstrates his high regard for her. Added to this, Gregory departs somewhat from Origen by likening humans to angels at creation. Origen, on the other hand, compares humans to angels at their telos.[77] By comparing humans to angels at creation, Gregory presents humans as 'angelomorphic', a term which Mueller defines as 'someone or something [who] is depicted as angelic'.[78] Scholars have traced this tradition back to Ezekiel and his apocalyptic vision of the angelomorphic or anthropomorphic figure on the throne, the early Christian interpretation of which was that Ezekiel saw the pre-incarnate Christ, the Logos.[79] Interest in angelology increased in the last few centuries before Christ,

---

[75] Carm. 1.2.50 (PG 37, 1385, 5–10).   [76] Moreschini (SC 358, 126, n1).

[77] *Cels.* 4.29; Benjamin P. Blosser, *Become Like the Angels* (WA, DC: Catholic University of America Press, 2012), 2; Mark J. Edwards, *Origen Against Plato* (Aldershot: Ashgate, 2002), 100–02.

[78] Elijah N. Mueller, 'Temple and Angel: An Outline of Apocalyptic Themes in John of Damascene' in Robert J. Daly (ed.), *Apocalyptic Thought in Early Christianity*, n6 (Grand Rapids, Michigan: Baker Publishing Group, 2009), 240–49, 241.

[79] Jarl E. Fossum, *The Image of the Invisible God: Essays on the Influence of Jewish Mysticism on Early Christology* (Freiburg, Schweiz: Universitätsverlag Freiburg, 1995), 7–8.

which is evident in the translation of the Septuagint.[80] Golitzin argues that the glory bestowed on the first human persons in paradise and the representation of humans as angels are predominant themes shared by fourth-century Christian writings and extra-biblical literature of the Second Temple period.[81] This is true for Gregory's work, since his description of the human person as another angel at creation is also found in 2 Enoch 30:12, alongside his designation of her as a mixture of invisible and visible realms, an *eikon* of God, microcosm, and a ruler. These parallels suggest that Gregory could have come into contact with 2 Enoch, if indeed it existed in Greek, and was written before the fourth century.[82] Gregory and 2 Enoch share a similar vision of the human person as 'divine' at creation, encompassed in the idea of being 'another angel'.[83] Both apply the notion of the human person as angelic, in order to indicate her brilliance and likeness to God.

Moving on from Gregory's inspiration, we shall see that Gregory is consistent in comparing humans to angels. For example, he describes people of high moral character, such as Athanasius, as being angelic in appearance and mind.[84] Gregory depicts humans as angels not only at the beginning and during their lives, but also at their death. In the funeral oration for his father, he writes that his father is now closer to God, being worthy of angelic rank and confidence.[85] Gregory also appeals to the argument of a human person attaining angelic rank when he lays out his ideas about who should be permitted to theologise.[86] Added to this, he refers to his own role as that of an angel hymning praise:

---

[80] Deut. 32:8; 33:2; Ps. 8:6 (8:5); see Richard N. Longenecker, *Biblical Exegesis in the Apostolic Period* (Grand Rapids: Eerdmans, 1999), 7.

[81] 1 Enoch 71.11; 2 Enoch 30.11; T. Levi 4.2; Alexander Golitzin, 'Recovering the "Glory of Adam": "Divine Light" Traditions in the Dead Sea Scrolls and the Christian Ascetical Literature of Fourth-Century Syro-Mesopotamia' in James R. Davila (ed.), *The Dead Sea Scrolls as Background to Postbiblical Judaism and Early Christianity: Papers from an International Conference at St. Andrews in 2001* (Leiden: Brill, 2003), 275–308; Bogdan G. Bucur, 'From Jewish Apocalypticism to Orthodox Mysticism' in Augustine Casiday (ed.), *The Orthodox Christian World* (Oxford; New York: Routledge, 2012), 466–80, 475.

[82] On this question, Mueller argues 'Gregory Nazianzus the elder was originally part of a Judeao-Pagan cult, which could easily have had similar scriptures'; 'Temple and Angel', 244. This does not account for the particular parallels found in 2 Enoch 30.12.

[83] Crispin H.T. Fletcher-Louis, '2 Enoch and the New Perspective on Apocalyptic' in Andrei Orlov, Gabriele Boccaccini, and Jason Zurawski (eds.), *New Perspectives on 2 Enoch: No Longer Slavonic Only* (Leiden: Brill, 2012), 127–48, 136.

[84] Or. 21.9 (SC 270, 128).

[85] Carm. 1.2.1 (PG 37, 529, 89–91); 1.2.2 (PG 37, 577, 720–24).

[86] Or. 28.3 (SC 250, 106); cf. Exod. 7:1.

Mortal man is your glory anew (σὸν βροτὸς αὖ κλέος ἐστιν),
whom you placed here as an angel,
composing songs of praise of your splendour, O Light.[87]

One way of translating the lines from the poems above would be, as Abrams has done, to translate ἄγγελος as 'messenger'. However, I suggest that 'angel' is more suitable, since the preceding lines speak of angels singing around the Trinity.[88] Also, at the end of the poem, Gregory sings like an angel himself; therefore, it is less likely that he would have had 'messenger' in mind when angels are a prevalent theme all through the poem.[89] The angelic practice of singing celebratory songs is not only possible for Gregory; rather, it is open to all human persons, especially virgins.[90] Praising God in song comprises one of the chief purposes in human existence.[91] However, if we were inclined to think that life on earth as 'another angel' is easy, Gregory corrects us. When he writes about singing as an angel to the Trinity, Envy, a frequent epithet for Satan, makes an appearance, always watching Gregory's speech.[92] Through drawing attention to Envy, Gregory makes it clear that for a mortal, angelic life is always under attack, which we will discuss in Chaper 4.

Contrary to Winslow's statement that Gregory does not equate 'either pre-lapsarian or redeemed humanity with angels', we have reviewed evidence enough to suggest that Gregory depicts intentionally the human person as 'a new kind of angel'.[93] She is like an angel in the way that she performs similar functions to angels, such as singing praises to God. Her 'newness' or 'otherness' lies in Gregory's belief that the human *eikon* is both spiritual and material; she is 'mixed' and, more significantly, she alone images God. Recall Chapter 1, in which I argued that Gregory portrays humans as breathing *eikones* of God, in contrast to pagan statues and paintings, which are not living. Humans are the only created beings able to function as God's visible *eikones*, precisely because they are a mixture of spiritual and material realms. Therefore, the human person is a 'different kind of angel', because she visibly images God on earth, in a manner that angels cannot because they are invisible. We shall explore further implications of Gregory's comparisons between human *eikones* and angels in Chapter 4, when we discuss his use of the 'garments of glory' tradition.

---

[87] Carm. 2.1.38 (PG 37, 1327, 25–26).
[88] Suzanne Abrams Rebillard, 'Speaking for Salvation: Gregory of Nazianzus as Poet and Priest in His Autobiographical Poems' (Ph.D. Diss., Brown University, 2003), 343.
[89] Carm. 2.1.38 (PG 37, 1325–329, 1–52).   [90] Or. 18.4 (PG 35, 989B).
[91] Or. 44.10–11 (PG 36, 617A–621C).   [92] Carm. 2.1.34 (PG 37, 1321–22).
[93] Winslow, *Dynamics of Salvation*, 49.

King

Let us move on to explore the significance of the human *eikon* as 'king over that which is on earth'. Gregory applies consistently the concept of kingship as a further metaphor which denotes the uniqueness of the human *eikon*. In a sermon that is addressed to the 'anxious citizens of Nazianzus and the angry ruler', Gregory explores the theme of ruling in connection with the *eikon* of God, as we observed in Chapter 1. Gregory directs his remarks to the prefect, whom he identifies as the *eikon* of God.[94] In the passage below, Gregory reveals that every single human person images God:

You rule with Christ and you govern with Christ, the sword is from him to you, not for use, but for threats. May you keep it as a purified offering to the one who has given it to you. You are an *eikon* of God, and you lead the *eikon* by the hand, governing here and being transferred towards another life (ἐνταῦθα οἰκονομουμένην, καὶ πρὸς βίον ἄλλον μεθισταμένην).[95]

Like the author of Genesis thousands of years before him, Gregory observes provocatively in this passage that not only prefects and leaders image God, but rather this is the privilege of every human person. Gregory is consistent in propounding this belief throughout his writing, and maintaining the connection between being an *eikon* and being a king. In *On New Sunday*, where he reflects upon being created as God's *eikon*, Gregory argues that the earth was created for human *eikones* in the same way that a palace is built for a king:

Nor is it surprising that a human person was the last creature to be brought forth, yet even so received the distinction of God's *eikon* and the touch of his hand: quite properly, for when a palace destined for a king is under construction (ἔδει γὰρ, ὥσπερ βασιλεῖ, προυποστῆναι τὰ βασίλεα) it must be completed before a king is escorted to it, his retinue already in full attendance.[96]

Two features concerning the passage above require attention. Firstly, Gregory applies *eikon* as a term which suggests magnificence and a

---

[94] Or. 17.8 (PG 35, 976A–B).   [95] Or. 17.9 (PG 35, 976B–D).

[96] Or. 44.4 (PG 36, 609D–612B); Carm. 1.1.8 (PG 37, 451, 60); 1.1.4 (PG 37, 423, 99); 1.2.1 (PG 37, 528, 82). Also see Wis. 13.5; Rom. 1.20. Gregory Nyssen writes in a similar manner: *Op. Hom.* 4, PG 44, 136C, 'For as, in ordinary human use, those who make images of rulers both mould the figure of their form, and represent along with this the royal rank by the vesture of purple, and the image is commonly called a king, so human nature, too, as it was made to rule the rest, was, by its likeness to the King of all, made as if it were a living image, sharing with the archetype in both rank and name ...'; unpublished translation kindly shared by Fr. Andrew Louth.

likeness to God, for it is only through being God's *eikon* that the human person is compared to a king. Secondly, the concept of the human *eikon* as a king on earth relates to the idea of humans ruling on earth as God rules in heaven.[97] This follows a tradition of reading Genesis 1:26–27 in light of Psalm 8:3–9 (8:2–8), where the psalmist writes:

> Out of mouths of infants and nurslings
> > you furnished praise for yourself,
> for the sake of your enemies,
> > to put down enemy and avenger,
> because I will observe the heavens, works of your fingers—
> > moon and stars—things you alone founded.
> What are human beings that you are mindful of them
> > or son of man that you attend to him?[98]
> You diminished human beings a little in comparison with angels;
> > with glory and honor you crowned them.
> And you set them over the works of your hands;
> > you subjected all under their feet,
> sheep and cattle, all together,
> > and further the beasts of the plain,
> the birds of the air and the fish of the sea
> > —the things that pass through paths of seas.[99]

The metaphor of kingship, royalty, and dominion has also long been discussed in relation to the God who creates in Genesis 1:1–2:3, alongside the Ancient Near Eastern tradition whereby the *eikon* of God is associated with the king.[100] This is followed in the New Testament, which refers to Jesus, the *Eikon*, as Lord and ruler.[101] Writing on Genesis 1, Wenham

---

[97] This has been a predominant view in Old Testament research since the 1960s; see Stephen L. Herring, 'A "Transubstantiated" Humanity: The Relationship between the Divine Image and the Presence of God in Gen. I 26f.', *Vetus Testamentum* 58 (2008), 1–15, 1; Prüum, 'eikon', 248. For a review of the relevant literature, see Wayne Sibley Towner, *Genesis* (Louisville: Westminster John Knox Press, 2001), 28.

[98] I have retained the exclusive language here in order to maintain the unity with the New Testament, in which Christ refers to himself as the 'Son of Man'; see, for example, Mark 2:10; 8:31.

[99] Translation adapted from NETS.

[100] W. Randell Garr, *In His Own Image and Likeness: Humanity, Divinity, and Monotheism* (Leiden, The Netherlands: Brill, 2003), 191–200; J. Richard Middleton, *The Liberating Image: The Imago Dei in Genesis 1* (Grand Rapids, MI: Baker Publishing Group, 2005), 70–74; Marc Z. Brettler, *God is King: Understanding an Israelite Metaphor* (Sheffield: JSOT Press, 1989).

[101] Col. 1:15–20. Gregory describes Christ, the identical *Eikon*, as ἄναξ; it is usually translated as 'king'; see Gilbert, *On God and Man*, 55; Denis M. Meehan, *Three Poems* (Washington, DC: Catholic University of America Press, 1987), 33. Also see Carm. 2.1.13 (PG 37, 1238, 140); 1.1.37 (PG 37, 520, 2); 1.1.5 (PG 37, 429, 65); 2.1.51 (PG 37, 1396, 36).

argues that the description of humankind made as God's *eikon* points to the function of 'God's vice-regent on 'earth'.[102] This resonates with Gregory's interpretation of the human *eikon* in the passage above, and demonstrates further how Gregory applies *eikon* to highlight similarity to God, as he does with respect to Christ.

Whilst royal comparisons may pay tribute to the *eikon*, feminist theologians have critiqued this approach by arguing that it results in a view of the *eikon* of God as solely male.[103] With this in mind, we will examine Gregory's view of the *eikon* in relation to gender, arguing that he applies metaphors such as kingship in order to denote the royal position of the *eikon*, rather than to suggest that the *eikon* is male. From a consideration of his work, it becomes clear that Gregory regards both male and female as imaging God equally. Added to this, Gregory reveals further ideas about the human *eikon* as a unified, dynamic, visible *eikon* through his discussions of female *eikones* and their use of cosmetics.

FEMALE IMAGES AND IDOLS

In the following section I argue that (a) Gregory presents women as *eikones* of God, since Gregory takes care not to represent God according to gender; (b) Gregory argues that women should be treated justly on the basis that they are God's *eikones*; (c) women reveal the *eikon* dynamically in both body and soul and (d) defacing this *eikon*, for example, by means of cosmetics, reduces the *eikon* of God to an idol (εἴδωλον).

In Basil's *Hexaemeron*, which Gregory praises and Gregory Nyssen is reported to have edited, women are mentioned as being created *eikones*.[104] Nonetheless, it is Gregory who receives the most praise

---

[102] Wenham, *Genesis 1–15*, 32.

[103] Rosemary Radford Ruether, 'Misogynism and Virginal Feminism in the Fathers of Church' in Rosemary Radford Ruether (ed.), *Religion and Sexism* (New York: Simon and Schuster, 1974), 150–83, 153; Lone Fatum, 'Image of God and Glory of Man: Women in the Pauline Congregations' in Kari Elisabeth Børresen (ed.), *Image of God and Gender Models in Judaeo-Christian Tradition* (Oslo: Solum Forag, 1991), 56–138, 67.

[104] Or. 43.67 (SC 384, 272–74); Socrates, *HE* 4.26. Scholars have debated the author of Homilies 10 and 11, since they appear in Basil and Gregory Nyssen's works, in PG 30, 9A–61D and PG 44, 274A–298B, respectively. More recently, scholars suggest Basil as the author of Homilies 10 and 11; see Philip Rousseau, *Basil of Caesarea* (Los Angeles, CA: University of California Press, 1994), 318.

for his treatment of women as God's *eikones,* as we shall see shortly.[105] Generally, views in the fourth century are mixed regarding whether or not women are God's *eikones.*[106] Particular interpretations of Paul's first letter to the Corinthians (11:7) mean that early church fathers such as Diodore of Tarsus refuse to allow the possibility of women imaging God:

Therefore the blessed Paul said rightly that the man alone is the image of God and his glory, but the woman is the glory of the man.[107]

Prior to and alongside Paul, the idea that men image God, and women are the glory of men, is evident in two streams of interpretation. Firstly, it appears in pseudepigraphal literature, which interprets the creation narratives designating Adam to be the individual who was created as God's *eikon,* rather than generic humanity. This interpretation occurs by collapsing the two creation narratives in Genesis together, where Adam is created as God's *eikon* (Gen 1) and Eve is made afterwards from Adam's rib (Gen 2).[108] Secondly, Philo presents a male *eikon* by explaining that the spiritual intellect (νοῦς) is superior to the sensory (αἴσθησις) realm, where the former is regarded as a male quality, and the latter as a female quality.[109] This is subject to the following critique: when the *eikon* is depicted as the spiritual intellect (νοῦς), it has been suggested that since νοῦς was a male quality, consequently the *eikon* was also

---

[105] George H. Tavard, *Woman in Christian Tradition* (London: University of Notre Dame Press, 1973), 91; Elisabeth Behr-Sigel, *The Ministry of Women in the Church,* trans. Fr. Stephen Bigham (Pasadena, CA: Oakwood Publications, 1991), 90–91.

[106] The difference between the Cappadocian Fathers' and the Antiochene Fathers' views of women are highlighted by Nonna Verna Harrison, 'Women, Human Identity, and the Image of God: Antiochene Interpretations', *JECS,* 9, no. 2 (2001), 205–49; Nonna Verna Harrison, 'Women and the Image of God according to St. John Chrysostom', in Paul M. Blowers (ed.), *Dominico Eloquio: Essays on Patristic Exegesis in Honor of Robert Louis Wilken* (Grand Rapids: Eerdmans, 2002), 259–79, 262–63. For further work on the subject of women and God's *eikon,* see David G. Hunter, 'The Paradise of Patriarchy: Ambrosiaster on Woman as (Not) God's Image', *JTS,* 43, no. 2 (1992), 447–69.

[107] Diodore of Tarsus, *Fragments on Genesis* 1:26 (PG 33:1564C–1565A); translation, Harrison, 'Antiochene Interpretations', 209.

[108] 4 Ezra 6:54, 7:70; Sibylline Oracles 1:5–37; Jubilees 3:1–35. See Anders Hultgård, 'God and Image of Woman in Early Jewish Religion', in Kari Elisabeth Børresen (ed.), *Image of God and Gender Models in Judaeo-Christian Tradition* (Oslo: Solum Forag, 1991), 35–55, 39–42.

[109] *Opif.* 165; *Spec.*1.200–201; see Richard A. Baer, *Philo's Use of the Categories Male and Female* (Leiden: Brill, 1970), 39ff.

perceived to be male.[110] Since this view does not appear in Gregory's works, he cannot be criticised on this basis. However, as we shall see shortly, Gregory is liable for critique on a different account.

A further idea relating to how women image God emerges in the patristic approach to asceticism, where holy women were said to have become 'manly'.[111] Whilst it is not the purpose of this book to explore Gregory's views on asceticism, I must comment briefly on the concept of the 'manly woman' in his writing.[112] For example, in his oration *In Praise of the Maccabees*, drawing from the second book of the Maccabees, Gregory presents Eleazar's mother as having 'the soul of a man in the body of a woman (ὦ ψυχῆς ἀνδρείας ἐν γυναικείῳ τῷ σώματι)'.[113] Gregory is able to make this move without any sense of confusion, as he and the other fathers were writing within a highly rhetorical context where gender was understood to be fluid to a certain degree.[114] Whilst 'male' and 'female' designated particular qualities, such as courage and intellect versus weakness and ignorance, the fathers believed that human persons could shift and move between them.[115] Ideas such as these have led many feminist theologians to denounce the 'whole patristic and mediaeval tradition' on the basis that all the fathers rejected the possibility that

---

[110] Fatum, 'Image of God and Glory of Man', 67. Also, see *Spec.* 30; *Haer.* 5.32.1; cited by Ruether, 'Misogynism', 153.

[111] Kari Vogt, '"Becoming Male": A Gnostic and Early Christian Metaphor', in Kari Elisabeth Børresen (ed.), *Image of God and Gender Models in Judaeo-Christian Tradition* (Oslo: Solum Forag, 1991), 172–87, 181.

[112] For comments on Gregory's asceticism, see Bradley K. Storin, 'In a Silent Way: Asceticism and Literature in the Rehabilitation of Gregory of Nazianzus', *JECS*, 19, no. 2 (2011), 225–57, 225. The impact of asceticism on the human as the *eikon* of God is generally absent from scholarly writing and would thus benefit from further research. This is evident from the lack of citations in the index of Vincent L. Wimbush and Richard Valantasis, *Asceticism* (Oxford: Oxford University Press, 2002), 623–28.

[113] Or. 15.4 (PG 35, 916B); see 2 Macc. 7:21. This idea is also present in Or. 43.57 (SC 384, 246–48); Carm. 2.1.11 (PG 37, 1029–166). Gregory's work transcends gender; see Vasiliki M. Limberis, *Architects of Piety: The Cappadocian Fathers and the Cult of the Martyrs* (Oxford: Oxford University Press, 2011), 159.

[114] Peter Brown, *The Body and Society: Men, Women, and Sexual Renunciation in Early Christianity* (New York: Columbia University Press, 2008), 10.

[115] Susanna Elm, 'Gregory's Women: Creating a Philosopher's Family' in Jostein Børtnes and Tomas Hägg (eds.), *Gregory of Nazianzus: Images and Reflections* (Copenhagen: Museum Tusculanum, 2006), 171–92, 173; Maud W. Gleason, *Making Men: Sophists and Self-Presentation in Ancient Rome* (Princeton, NJ: Princeton University Press, 1995), passim.

'women were equally theomorphic'.[116] However, it is possible to take a more positive approach to the problem of female 'manliness'. Harrison observes that the language of women 'becoming male' is far from affirming 'culturally entrenched misogyny', but, rather, a way of transcending it.[117] The implications of Harrison's approach are that when Gregory implies that great women are more like men, it is his intention to affirm rather than to denigrate them.

Gregory is consistent in affirming that women image God. His belief in equality originates in his view of God as genderless. Thus, for Gregory, gender is accidental rather than essential to the *eikon* of God.[118] Gregory implies in a number of ways that the *eikon* is not associated with a particular gender. Since Gregory's God has no gender, when God creates an *eikon* of Godself, that *eikon* incorporates both male and female.[119] Furthermore, scholars have argued that the genderless nature of the *eikon* reflects the Septuagint, since a singular human person (ἄνθρωπος) is created as the *eikon* of God in Genesis 1:26–27, after which God 'made them male and female'.[120] The consequences of this are that whilst humans are God's *eikones*, they are gendered as creatures, not as *eikones* of God. This notion is reflected in Gregory's work when he speaks of the *eikon* at creation as 'God's breath'.[121] Further to this, as discussed earlier in this chapter, Gregory describes the human person as a 'new kind of angel'.[122] Since angels are genderless, the genderless nature of the *eikon* is also implied by Gregory's comparison of humans with angels. This leads Gregory to advocate that both men and women should practise virginity,

---

[116] Rosemary Radford Ruether, 'The Liberation of Christology' in Ann Loades (ed.), *Feminist Theology: A Reader* (Louisville: Westminster John Knox, 1990), 138–48, 139; Elizabeth A. Clark, *Women in the Early Church* (Collegeville, Minnesota: Liturgical Press, 1983), 15.

[117] Harrison, 'Male and Female', 447; Nonna Verna Harrison, 'Feminine Man in Late Antique Ascetic Piety', *Union Seminary Quarterly Review*, 48, no. 3–4 (1994), 49–71, 49.

[118] Warren Smith, *Passion and Paradise: Human and Divine Emotion in the Thought of Gregory of Nyssa* (New York: The Crossroad Publishing Company, 2004), 42.

[119] For a survey of the impact of the doctrine of the Trinity on gender in the fourth century, see Virginia Burrus, *Begotten, Not Made: Conceiving Manhood in Late Antiquity* (Redwood, CA: Stanford University Press, 2000).

[120] Phyllis A. Bird, 'Sexual-Differentiation and Divine Image in the Genesis Creation Texts', in Kari Elisabeth Børresen (ed.), *Image of God and Gender Models in Judaeo-Christian Tradition* (Oslo: Solum Forag, 1991), 11–35, 17.

[121] Or. 38.11 (SC 358, 124).   [122] Or. 38.11 (SC 358, 124).

if they desire to live the life of angels.[123] This relates back to God, since the Holy Trinity is virginal in its very nature. In this case, for Gregory, as for the fathers generally, virginity is connected with incorruptibility, for example, the eternal or imperishable nature. For Gregory, taming sexual desire is only one aspect of virginity; more importantly, it is about cleansing and purifying all the senses. Virginity is also practical and concerned with the love of one's neighbour and of God. One result of Gregory's preference for virginity is that gender is not the predominant focus of being created according to God's *eikon*. Rather, Gregory's motivation lies with the life of the *eikon*. For example, in *In Praise of Virginity*, Gregory explains that human persons image God, who lives forever:

> With immortal hands [God] established my form,
> (χείρεσιν ἀθανάτῃσιν ἐμὴν ἐστήσατο μορφήν)
> to it [God] imparted [God's] life. [God] shot spirit into it,
> (τῇ δ' ἄρ' ἑῆς ζωῆς μοιρήσατο ἐν γὰρ ἔηκε
> πνεῦμα)
> which is a portion of the unseen Godhead.
> From soil and breath [God] made a mortal human,
> *Eikon* of the Immortal, for the nature of spiritual intellect is queen to both
> (ἐκ δὲ χοὸς πνοιῆς τε βροτὸς γένετ', ἀθανάτοιο
> εἰκὼν ἡ γὰρ ἄνασσα νόου φύσις ἀμφοτέροισι).[124]

Unlike Nyssen, Gregory does not state that the *eikon* is genderless; nevertheless, it is clear that this is his intention, both from the poem above and throughout his work. Feminist theologians have criticised this, arguing that if we view the *eikon* of God as genderless, then we portray the human person as androgynous.[125] However, Gregory believes that the human

[123] Or. 16.2 (PG 35, 936A–938B); 37.10 (SC 318, 292); 40.18 (SC 358, 234); 43.62 (SC 384, 258–60); Carm. 1.2.1 (PG 37, 523, 11); 1.2.6 (PG 37, 644, 5–9). See Susanna Elm, *'Virgins of God': The Making of Asceticism in Late Antiquity* (Oxford: Clarendon Press, 1994), 156–57; François Bourassa, *Excellence de la virginité: arguments patristiques* (Montréal: Facultés de théologie et de philosophies de la Compagnie de Jésus, 1953), 36–37; Peter Brown, *The Making of Late Antiquity* (Cambridge, MA: Harvard University Press, 1978), 289.

[124] Carm. 1.2.1 (PG 37, 529, 92–97). Gilbert translates 'lordly' here; see *On God and Man*, 92. However, the text reads ἄνασσα, which is a feminine noun meaning 'queen', see *PGL*, 120. It is possible that Gregory is recalling Herodotus' (*Hist.* 3.38) personification when he writes, 'it is, I think, rightly said in Pindar's poem that custom (νόμος) is lord (βασιλεύς) of all'. I am indebted to Nick Wilshere for pointing me towards Herodotus.

[125] Feminist theologians argue that Nyssen employs 'castrational equality', as he excludes both male and female from the *eikon*; Kari Elisabeth Børresen, 'God's Image, Man's Image?' in Kari Elisabeth Børresen (ed.), *Image of God and Gender Models in Judaeo-Christian Tradition* (Oslo: Solum Forag, 1991), 188–207, 198–99.

person images God both individually and collectively; he does not envisage an androgynous human person at creation, rather he understands that human nature represents a single unity which is restored in Christ.

Gregory's view of Christ and how the human person images Christ is pertinent to this discussion, since Gregory writes of women imaging Christ specifically. Gregory is aware of Christ being distinctively male, since he refers to Christ's masculinity in *On Holy Pascha*, where he likens Christ to the male sacrificial lamb.[126] Harrison argues correctly that, for Gregory, Christ's maleness is allegorical rather than literal in this context.[127] Therefore, women are able to image Christ because Christ is God, and as we have established, Gregory does not appropriate gender to God.[128]

Next, we will determine how Gregory includes women when he speaks of human persons imaging Christ. The lines below are from Gregory's poem, *Against Women Wearing Ornaments*, in which Gregory lays out how Christian women should behave. We shall discuss the implications of Gregory's advice shortly; our focus here is that Gregory refers to the Christian woman as an *eikon* of Christ, which reveals that he does not consider Christ's masculinity as something which precludes women from imaging him:[129]

> I have not put my trust in *mythoi*, but if you command me
> Do not become cunning Pandora.
> The race of Pandora are shameless, but you, *eikon* of Christ,
> Must shine with wisdom and understanding (ἀλλὰ σὺ Χριστοῦ
> εἰκὼν σωφροσύνῃ λάμπεο καὶ πραπίσιν).[130]

---

[126] Or. 45.13 (PG 36, 641A).

[127] 'For Gregory, the "maleness" ascribed to Christ in this sense actually refers to his virtue, which is universally human and not his biology'; Nonna Verna Harrison, 'The Maleness of Christ', *SVTQ*, 42, no. 2 (1998), 111–51, 131. Also see Jay Wesley Richards, 'Can a Male Savior Save Women?: Gregory of Nazianzus on the Logos' Assumption of Human Nature', *CSR*, 28, no. 1 (1998), 42–57. Richards offers a critique of the following essay; Rosemary Radford Ruether, 'Can a Male Savior Save Women?' in Rosemary Radford Ruether (ed.), *To Change the World: Christology and Cultural Criticism* (New York: Crossroad, 1981), 45–56.

[128] Or. 31.7 (SC 250, 286–88). Beeley confirms this: 'Christ is born as a single entity', which Gregory describes using both neuter and masculine nouns, thus not 'making either gender into a technical term'; *Trinity and the Knowledge of God*, 130; Harrison, 'The Maleness of Christ', 111.

[129] Contra Elizabeth A. Johnson, 'Redeeming the Name of Christ', in Catherine LaCugna (ed.), *Freeing Theology: The Essentials of Theology in Feminist Perspective* (San Francisco: Harper-San Francisco, 1993), 115–37, 119–20.

[130] Carm. 1.2.29 (PG 37, 893, 125–26); Knecht, *Gegen die Putzsucht der Frauen*, 25. Gregory is referring to Pandora, who is the first woman according to Greek mythology. He argues that women who image Christ should behave differently from Pandora; see Hesiod's *Theogony*.

Gregory goes further than simply recognising that women image Christ. He is so convinced that women are *eikones* of God, in a manner which is not inferior to men, that he employs this argument on behalf of equality for women regarding unfair divorce laws:

There is one maker of man and woman (εἷς ποιητὴς ἀνδρὸς καὶ γυναικός), one sod of clay (εἷς χοῦς) for both, one *eikon* (εἰκὼν μία), one law, one death, one resurrection, in the same way we were born from man and woman.[131]

In this oration, Gregory goes on to show how women are of equal honour to men, to the extent that McGuckin observes, 'the woman is the icon of Christ in this case'.[132] However, whilst Gregory's ethics regarding women's rights in the divorce courts are outstanding, he does not promote freedom and equality in all areas of female life. For example, Gregory's approach to women's attire is extremely conservative. If we leave aside feminist issues, his discussions concerning women and cosmetics warrant consideration, since Gregory's thoughts about women's clothes and cosmetics reveal much about his notion of the *eikon*; namely, that defacing the *eikon*, for example, through the use of cosmetics, reduces the *eikon* of God to an idol (ἔἴδολον).

With great rhetorical flourishes in his orations, Gregory praises his mother Nonna and his sister Gorgonia, for their restraint in not applying cosmetics or wearing expensive jewellery.[133] Gregory honours them in his orations because he considers that Nonna and Gorgonia are protecting themselves as *eikones* by choosing not to apply cosmetics.[134] It is difficult to reconstruct for whose benefit Gregory made these statements, since speaking out against the use of cosmetics was quite general in the Graeco-Roman world.[135] It is possible that Gregory's restrictions are connected

---

[131] Or. 37.6 (SC 318, 284).

[132] John A. McGuckin, *St. Gregory of Nazianzus: An Intellectual Biography* (Crestwood, New York: St. Vladimir's Seminary Press, 2001), 334.

[133] Or. 8.10 (SC 405, 266); 18.8 (PG 35, 993B–996A); Carm. 1.2.2 (PG 37, 585, 85–90); 1.2.29 (PG 37, 885, 15–20); Philip M. Beagon, 'The Cappadocian Fathers, Women and Ecclesiastical Politics', VC, 49, no. 2 (1995), 165–79, 171.

[134] Or. 8.14 (SC 405, 276).

[135] For biblical disapproval of jewellery, see 1 Tim. 2:9; 1 Pet. 3:3. For further information on the use of cosmetics, see Ann M. Stout, 'Jewelry as a Symbol of Status in the Roman Empire' in Judith L. Sebesta and Larissa Bonfante (eds.), *The World of Roman Costume* (Madison: University of Wisconsin, 1994), 77–100, 77; Anette Drew-Bear, *Painted Faces on the Renaissance Stage: The Moral Significance of Face-painting Conventions* (Lewisburg: Bucknell University Press, 1994), 20. For an overview of cosmetics in Ancient Greece, see Michelle M. Lee, *Body, Dress, and Identity in Ancient Greece* (Cambridge: Cambridge University Press, 2015), 67–69. Adornment was also discouraged as it was a means of power for women in the ancient world; Gary

primarily to supporting a non-extravagant and celibate life, since women applying cosmetics were considered to be excessively wealthy and susceptible to committing adultery.[136] So precious is the human *eikon* that she must reserve herself solely for glorifying God. Gregory argues that those who wear cosmetics are in danger of becoming more like idols or actresses on the stage than being *eikones* of God.[137] Moreover, Gregory believes that the use of cosmetics adulterates the *eikon*, as seen below in his poem *Exhortation to Virgins*:[138]

> Let another adulterate the *eikon* of God with coloured complexions,
> A breathing work of art, silent betrayer of things within, . . .[139]
> (ἄλλη χρώμασιν εἰκόνα τὴν θεοῦ νοθευέτω
> πίναξ ἔμψυχος, σιγῶν κατήγορος τῶν ἔνδον)

Consider further Gregory's argument below in *Against Women Wearing Ornaments*.[140] Drawing on the Genesis creation narratives, Gregory imagines God's response to a woman who wears cosmetics as a means of enhancing her beauty. In a section of his poem, employing the rhetorical device of ethopoiia, Gregory assumes God's voice, laying out what God would say to a woman who wears cosmetics:

Who is and whence came the creator? Be gone, one who belongs to another!

> I did not inscribe you, dog! But I moulded an *eikon* of myself.[141]
> How is it that I have an idol in place of a dear form?[142]
> (τίς, πόθεν ὁ πλάστης; ἔρρε μοι, ἀλλοτρίη
> οὔ σ'ἔγραψα, κύων, ἀλλ' ἔπλασα εἰκον' ἐμοῖο
> πῶς εἴδωλον ἔχω εἴδεος ἀντὶ φίλου;)

G. Hoag, 'Decorum and Deeds in 1 Timothy 2:9–10 in light of *Ephesiaca* by Xenophon of Ephesus', *Ex Auditu*, 27 (2011), 134–60, 145.

[136] *Against Wealth*, Carm. 1.2.28 (PG 37, 856–884). Amongst fathers who disproved of women wearing cosmetics were Clement, Tertullian, Saint Cyprian, Ambrose, and Jerome; see Alicia J. Batten, 'Neither Gold nor Braided Hair (1 Timothy 2.9; 1 Peter 3.3): Adornment, Gender and Honour in Antiquity', *NTS*, 55, no. 4 (2009), 484–501, 498.

[137] Or. 8.10 (SC 405, 266); 18.8 (PG 35, 993 B–C); 38.5 (SC 358, 110); Carm. 1.2.2 (PG 37, 538–39, 215–20); 1.2.3 (PG 37, 637, 55–59); 1.2.19 (PG 37, 885, 15–16).

[138] Gregory's authorship of *Exhortation to Virgins* is disputed; see Rudolf Keydell, 'Die Unechtheit der Gregor von Nazianz zugeschriebenen Exhortatio ad Virgines', *BZ*, 43, no. 2 (1950), 334–37. However, Gregory's customary use of the devil in this poem, along with his approach to the life of virgins, is consistent with his thought elsewhere.

[139] Carm. 1.2.3 (PG 37, 637, 57–59).   [140] Carm. 1.2.29 (PG 37, 884–908).

[141] Gen. 1:26 and Gen. 2:6.   [142] Carm. 1.2.29 (PG 37, 887, 46–48).

Gregory's insulting use of 'dog' (κύων) to describe a woman who relies on cosmetics to enhance her beauty may be somewhat shocking for many twenty-first century readers.[143] It highlights that Gregory expects extreme submission regarding how women dress. Interpreters must engage with all Gregory's work, rather than simply his orations, when making claims about his position on ethical concerns. For example, whilst McGuckin and Tavard both praise Gregory for being a leader in female equality, it is possible that they have not taken into account these poems. On the one hand, it is true that Gregory is a great supporter of women, but this claim must be nuanced. When Gregory likens a woman to a dog, he does not intend this to be a statement of praise. We suggest, then, that, in this respect, Gregory did not follow through to a logical conclusion on the question of what it means for a woman to image God.

It is important to recognise that many contemporary readers will not appreciate Gregory's approach to women and cosmetics. That said, the lines above reveal two significant points about Gregory's approach to the *eikon*. Firstly, his play on words around the idea of *eikones* and idols shows that Gregory considers the human *eikon* to be one who bears God's presence uniquely. This recalls the theme explored in Chapter 1, in which Gregory interprets Genesis 1:26–27 in light of contemporary ideas about icons and idols. The addition of cosmetics to a woman's body means that she is no longer an *eikon*, but rather an idol, a term which Gregory generally uses negatively.[144] The same idea appears in Gregory's funeral oration for his sister.[145] Secondly, the defacement of the *eikon* occurs through the body, which is why cosmetics are such an important issue for Gregory. This lends itself to a reading in which the *eikon* functions as the whole human person.

Through an analysis of the creation narratives of the human *eikon* as they occur in Gregory's work, it becomes clear that his vision of the human *eikon* is multifaceted; in which the *eikon* functions both as the

---

[143] It also raises questions of how humans relate to other animals, but to explore this is beyond the scope of the book.

[144] Or. 5.28 (SC 309, 348); 8.10 (SC 405, 266); 39.6 (SC 358, 160); 40.38 (SC 358, 284); Carm. 1.2.1 (PG 37, 532, 136); 1.2.29 (PG 37, 883, 372); 2.1.1 (PG 37, 979, 123). Gregory's use of the phrase εἴδωλον τοῦ καλοῦ in Or. 2.74 (SC 247, 186) leads Anna Williams to suggest that Gregory applies εἴδωλον interchangeably with εἰκών; *The Divine Sense: The Intellect in Patristic Theology* (Cambridge: Cambridge University Press, 2007), 93. However, Gregory does not refer to the human person as an εἴδωλον of God anywhere in his work.

[145] Or. 8.10 (SC 405, 266).

soul and the whole human person, including the body. By examining Gregory's account of angels we have learnt that he does not describe them as *eikones*. In light of this, I argue that not only is Gregory careful to adhere to biblical descriptions, but he also presents visibility as a key aspect of the human *eikon* when he describes her as 'another angel'. This becomes even clearer through the other titles by which Gregory describes the human *eikon*: 'microcosm', 'king', and 'mixed worshipper'. By considering each of these titles closely, it is clear that ethics continues to play an important role in Gregory's understanding of what it means to image God. Most significantly, Gregory speaks of women as *eikones* of Christ specifically, which sets him apart from many church fathers who write on the human *eikon*.

From attending to Gregory's creation narratives, the phrase 'divine, yet vulnerable' encapsulates best Gregory's presentation of the human *eikon*, since this description lends itself to an open interpretation and captures the most significant aspects of Gregory's human *eikon*, rather than representing a reductionist view. Gregory describes the creation of the human *eikon* in such a way that she is vulnerable to the spiritual realm and, more significantly, porous to God; consequently, she is created with the capacity for divinity. This aspect of Gregory's theological anthropology is crucial to my discussion of Gregory's concept of theosis in Chapter 5, in which Charles Taylor's work on the 'porous self' becomes pertinent once more. Human vulnerability also incorporates a negative aspect in light of the devil's hatred of the human *eikon*. The constant wrestling between the devil and the human *eikon* raises many questions regarding both the nature of the fall of Lucifer and his consequent existence. These are questions to which we shall turn in Chaper 4, in which I shall argue that, for Gregory, it is impossible to consider human existence as an *eikon* of God without simultaneously being confronted with questions about the spiritual forces of evil.

4

The Image of God and the Devil

Come into paradise with Jesus in order to understand from what you have fallen.[1]

In Chapter 3, we observed how God mixes the *eikon* with the very dust of the earth in the formation of the human person. This renders the divine *eikon* vulnerable to a certain degree; thus the existence of the human person is divine, through the gift of the *eikon*, yet vulnerable due to being composed of earth. At creation, this dynamic vulnerability of the human *eikon* is positive, since it entails that the human person is porous to God; through the gift of God she possesses the capacity to become divine. Paradoxically, we shall see that this vulnerability, whilst remaining positive, takes on a negative quality through the fall, when the human *eikon* succumbs to the schemes of the devil and his army.[2]

In this chapter, we will continue to establish the prevalence of the devil in Gregory's approach to the existence of the human *eikon*.[3] When Gregory writes about the world (κόσμος), the flesh (σάρξ), and the passions (πάθη) in a combative manner, he envisages the devil at work and, in a sense, the devil is behind the scenes of many acts of evil, as far as Gregory is concerned. However, the pervasiveness of the devil prompts concerns of

---

[1] Or. 45.24 (PG 36, 656C).
[2] For connections between the human *eikon* and warfare, see Carly L. Crouch, 'Made in the Image of God: The Creation of אדם, the Commissioning of the King and the Chaoskampf of YHWH', *JANER*, 16, no. 1 (2016), 1–21.
[3] Sections of this chapter are published as 'Vulnerable, Yet Divine: Retrieving Gregory Nazianzen's Account of the *Imago Dei*' in Oliver Crisp and Fred Sanders (eds.), The *Christian Doctrine of Humanity* (Grand Rapids, MI: Zondervan Academic, 2018), 110–123.

dualism. Recalling Gregory's adherence to the doctrine *creatio ex nihilo,* we will see that he does not err towards dualism. At the same time however, Gregory does not treat the devil as a linguistic constriction, but rather as a 'real' enemy experienced by the human *eikon*. Through a careful analysis of the texts, we will establish that Gregory attributes to the devil a diminishing existence. From here, we will explore Gregory's re-telling of the fall, arguing that he draws upon extra-biblical traditions concerning the 'garments of glory'. By making this move, he depicts the human *eikon* as unable to image God fully after the fall. The argument throughout this chapter concerns the impossibility of considering Gregory's vision of being a human *eikon* in isolation from both the affective experience of the fall and the impact of the devil's envy.

THE DEVIL AND DEMONS

Contrary to Ruether's argument that 'the daemonological aspect, so prominent in non-hellenised Christian asceticism, is largely absent in Gregory', the devil's fall and its consequences occupy a vast space in Gregory's work.[4] Following the Christian tradition, Gregory equates Lucifer to Satan, the devil, and the serpent in the Garden of Eden, as discussed in Chapter 1.[5] Gregory weaves their narratives together into the story of Christ's victory on behalf of humankind:

> ... crushing Satan (Σατάν) quickly under our feet, whether falling like lightning from heaven on account of his former splendour, or fleeing like a serpent due to his later crookedness and his metamorphosis into that which crawls on the ground.[6]

Concerning Lucifer's fall, Gregory follows the tradition occurring in 2 Enoch and Origen, where Satan's downfall is attributed to his longing for the glory of God.[7] Gregory does not attempt to answer the question of how Lucifer came to be proud and hanker after a glory which was not his own, other than to comment that whilst it is hard to move them away from good, angels are able to turn to evil should they choose.[8] For

---

[4] Rosemary Radford Ruether, *Gregory of Nazianzus, Rhetor and Philosopher* (Oxford: Clarendon Press, 1969), 55–128, 149.

[5] Ἑωσφόρος, translated 'Morning Star', Muraoka, *GELS*, 312. Lucifer is the common translation, taken from Latin, meaning 'light-bearer'.

[6] Or. 23.14 (SC 270, 310); Carm. 1.2.1 (PG 27, 531, 120); see Luke 10:18.

[7] Cels. 6.43. For a brief survey on Origen's view on angels and demons, see Carr, *Angels and Principalities*, 168–71.

[8] Or. 38.9 (SC 358, 120).

Lucifer, choosing evil results in elimination from heaven. Once fallen, he does not work alone, but manages to gather up an army of rebel angels, which Gregory refers to as demons.[9] In naming them thus, Gregory follows the Christian tradition where demons are consistently evil.[10] He writes, 'the rebel powers (ἀποστατικαὶ δυνάμεις) subject to him [Lucifer] are craftsmen of evil in the flight from beauty and hosts of evil in us'.[11] Elsewhere in Greek literature, demons are not regarded as being evil necessarily, but are more often intermediary beings. For example, Plato views the demon's role as bridging the chasm between the divine and human.[12]

Gregory draws on two differing traditions which account for the appearance of demons on earth. Firstly, in *On Spiritual Beings*, Gregory states that spiritual beings do not come from bodies, nor do they enter bodies.[13] In this instance, demons stem from Satan's leadership when he draws angels into his rebellion. After this, they become his army and spend their time warring against humanity.[14] Added to this, following early church fathers such as Justin Martyr, Irenaeus, and Clement, Gregory draws from a further tradition regarding the existence of demons on the earth.[15] In a poem where he offers advice to virgins, Gregory observes that whoever mixed the fleshless nature (angels) with flesh (humans) committed a sin.[16] He states that angelic desires produced great giants, which meant that the sins of heavenly beings took up their abode on earth. This tradition originates from Genesis 6:1–4, where the Hebrew phrase 'sons of God' is interpreted as referring to angels. These angels descend to have sexual intercourse with 'daughters of men'.[17] From there,

---

[9] Carm. 1.1.7 (PG 37, 444, 74).

[10] Edward Langton, *Essentials of Demonology: A Study of Jewish and Christian Doctrine, Its Origin and Development* (London: Epworth, 1949), 88; Dale B. Martin, 'When Did Angels Become Demons?', *JBL*, 129, no. 4 (2010), 657–77.

[11] Or. 38.9 (SC 358, 120–22); 45.5 (PG 36, 629B); 22.13 (SC 270, 248); 24.10 (SC 284, 58); 37.7 (SC 318, 284); 39.13 (SC 358, 176); 40.10 (SC 358, 216–18); Carm. 1.1.7 (PG 37, 441–46, 37–97).

[12] *Symp.* 202d–203a.   [13] Carm. 1.1.7 (PG 37, 440, 17–18).

[14] Carm. 2.1.50 (PG 37, 1389, 55–60).

[15] *1 Apol.* 5; *Haer.* 4.16.2; *Dem.* 18; *Strom.* 5.1.10. For a full exploration of Justin's use of this myth, see Annette Yoshiko Reed, 'The Trickery of the Fallen Angels and the Demonic Mimesis of the Divine: Aetiology, Demonology, and Polemics in the Writings of Justin Martyr', *JECS*, 12, no. 2 (2004), 141–71.

[16] Carm. 1.2.2 (PG 37, 617, 490–97).

[17] Loren T. Stuckenbruck, 'The Origins of Evil in Jewish Apocalyptic Tradition: The Interpretation of Genesis 6:1–4 in the Second and Third Centuries BC' in Christoph Auffarth and Loren T. Stuckenbruck (eds.), *The Fall of the Angels* (Leiden: Brill, 2004), 87–118, 88.

1 Enoch 15 interprets Genesis 6:1–4 as the origin of demons on the earth. The 'angels of God' are called 'Watchers', whose offspring with the women on the earth are giants, from whose bodies the evil spirits come forth. The aim of the evil spirits is to corrupt the inhabitants of the earth. Writing on this tradition, VanderKam states that Lactantius (c.a. AD 240–320) is the last writer to employ the Enoch-inspired myth, overlooking the fact that Gregory refers to the tradition in the fourth century.[18] Revealing his preoccupation with evil spirits, Gregory offers a dramatic rendering of the multiple ways in which these sneaky demons intend to entrap the human *eikon*:

From this, the evil beings shot up upon the earth; demons, attendants of the murderous king of evil, phantoms of the night, liars, wantons, teachers of sin, those who mislead others, drunks, lovers of sensuous laughter, stirrers of revelry, diviners, practitioners of ambiguity, argumentative ones, murderous wretches, inhabitants of darkness, hidden ones, shameless beings, sorcerers.[19] They call on approaching; they hate, whilst dragging away. They appear as night and light either without disguise or in ambush. While this is the way of the army, so it is the way of their chief (τοίη μὲν κείνων στρατιή, τοῖος δέ τε ἀρχός).[20]

Note that in the passage above, Gregory refers to the demons as an army. This is due to military service being a popular metaphor for the Christian life in the early church.[21] This stems from Jewish apocalyptic thought, which discussed regularly the warfare between Satan and humankind. In line with this tradition, Gregory frames human existence within a constant wrestle against an army of powerful spiritual enemies.[22]

The idea of warfare between the human *eikon* and Satan is explicit throughout Gregory's work; see, for example, Oration 6, when Gregory speaks on the theme of peace. Gregory delivered this oration after

---

[18] James C. VanderKam, '1 Enoch, Enochic Motifs, and Enoch in Early Christian Literature' in James C. VanderKam and William Adler (eds.), *The Jewish Apocalyptic Heritage in Early Christianity* (Assen, Netherlands; Minneapolis: Van Gorcum; Fortress, 1996), 33–101, 84. 1 Enoch 19:3 and Jubilees 10:1–2 later refer to evil spirits as demons.

[19] φιλομειδέες and χρησμολόγοι are most likely allusions to Aphrodite and Apollo respectively; see Moreschini and Sykes, *Poemata Arcana*, 210–11. Gregory follows a long line of patristic writers who equate heathen gods with demons; see *Cels.* 3.28.

[20] Carm. 1.1.7 (PG 37, 444–45, 73–82).

[21] Gerald Bonner, *The Warfare of Christ* (London; New York: Faith Press; Morehouse-Barlow, 1962), 37.

[22] Or. 2.22 (SC 247, 118); 11.5 (SC 405, 338); 17.9 (PG 35, 796); 19.6 (PG 35, 993); 22.13 (SC 270, 248); 24.15 (SC 284, 74); 38.5 (SC 358, 110); 40.10 (SC 358, 218); 40.14 (SC 358, 226); et al. For consistency with the New Testament, see Norman Hepburn Baynes, 'St. Anthony and the Demons', *JEA*, 40 (1954), 7–10.

reconciling his father, the bishop, with the local monastic community, where there had been a disagreement over the bishop signing a document whose orthodoxy was in question.[23] In this oration, Gregory sets the spiritual battle in context by describing in detail how Satan was an angel who fell from heaven. After this, he moves on to consider how Satan works towards disunity within the Church:

> Hiding himself in the dark quarter of discord, as far as I am concerned, and to those present using for the most part sophistry and cunning against each of us, opening a spot in us through skill, such as would suit himself, so that he might break in with the fullness of his strength, just like a chief with an army, when there is a break in the wall or line of battle.[24]

Gregory continues the theme of warfare throughout the oration and closes by reflecting on Ephesians 6:14, a pericope about spiritual warfare.[25] Like the author of Ephesians, Gregory thinks the battle is not against flesh and blood; rather, it concerns the spiritual powers of darkness. He exhorts his listeners to be 'recognising only one war, against the Evil One and the ranks underneath him'.[26] We will explore this theme in greater depth shortly, demonstrating further how Satan's principal target is the *eikon* and that he works through the world, sinful flesh, and the passions in order to destroy the *eikon*. Firstly, we must consider the question of dualism. Gregory's consistent use of the battle imagery prompts questions regarding what nature of existence he attributes to the fallen angels; namely, does he lean towards dualism by referring so frequently to the battle of the human *eikon* with the devil and demons?

Before we demonstrate that Gregory's approach to the devil and demons is not dualistic, let me clarify my understanding of 'dualism', since scholars have interpreted this in varying ways.[27] Many have discussed the dualism that Christianity inherited from Jewish apocalyptic, which is the concept that the present age is evil due to Satan having dominion over the earth. Frances Young, for example, suggests that whilst a cosmic battle goes on currently, it will end in God's ultimate

---

[23] Calvet-Sebasti (SC 405, 31).   [24] Or. 6.13 (SC 405, 156).

[25] Clint E. Arnold, *Ephesians, Power and Magic: The Concept of Power in Ephesians in Light of its Historical Setting* (Cambridge: Cambridge University Press, 1989), passim; Harold W. Hoehner, *Ephesians: An Exegetical Commentary* (Grand Rapids, Michigan: Baker Academic, 2002), 825.

[26] Or. 6.22 (SC 405, 174).

[27] For five kinds of dualism as cosmic, eschatological, psychological/ethical, anthropological, and literary, see Antoinette Collins, 'Dualism and the (LXX) Book of Genesis', *Phronema*, 14 (1999), 45–52, 46.

triumph, from which she argues for a 'practical dualism' rather than an 'ultimate dualism'.[28] Since, for Gregory, God is the absolute power and always rules, Young is correct in arguing for no 'ultimate dualism', although a 'practical dualism' still implies that Satan may be a match for God. This latter point does not align with Gregory's approach, who, as I shall demonstrate shortly, is adamant that God is supreme at all times. For the sake of being concise, I summarise dualism as 'two absolute powers which are in conflict with one another, eternally preceding reality'.[29] This exemplifies what Gregory does not believe, for he dismisses ideas of dualism where opposing powers of good and evil are equal to one another. In both this and the previous chapter, we have seen that Gregory maintains a strict sense of God as 'One' and adheres to the doctrine *creatio ex nihilo* consistently, both of which illustrate Gregory's antipathy towards dualism. Gregory's aggressive attack on Manichaeism further reveals that he does not consider Satan as an equal and opposite force to God.[30] Added to this, in *On Baptism*, adapting ideas of privation, Gregory states that evil does not exist by itself:

Believe that no aspect of evil has either substance or royalty, or is without beginning, or has a substantial nature by itself, or comes from God (πίστευε μὴ οὐσίαν εἶναί τινα τοῦ κακοῦ μήτε βασιλείαν, ἢ ἄναρχον ἢ παρ' ἑαυτῆς ὑπόστασιν ἢ τοῦ θεοῦ γενομένην); but this is our work and that of the Evil One, which came in afterwards due to our lack of attention, not from the Creator.[31]

Consider also Gregory's approach to Christ's encounters with Satan. As demonstrated in Chapter 2, Christ always rules in Gregory's description of the confrontations between Christ and Satan or his demons, thus demonstrating that God conquers Satan on earth as in heaven. Furthermore, we must take into account Gregory's belief that God created the world intrinsically as 'good'. The demonic powers, along with sin, disrupt

---

[28] Young, *The Making of the Creeds*, 94.

[29] My definition closely follows Philip Edgcumbe Hughes, *The True Image: The Origin and Destiny of Man in Christ* (Grand Rapids: Eerdmans, 1989), 83.

[30] Carm. 1.1.4 (PG 37, 415–23). Gregory also attacks those who say there are many gods, both good and evil; see Carm. 1.1.6 (PG 37, 430, 5–6). For further information about the Manichees, see Iain Gardner and Samuel N.C. Lieu, *Manichaean Texts from the Roman Empire* (Cambridge: Cambridge University Press, 2004), 11; Concetta Giuffré Scibona, 'How Monotheistic is Mani's Dualism?', *Numen*, 48, no. 4 (2001), 444–67; Geo Widengren, *Mani and Manichaeism* (London: Weidenfield and Nicolson, 1961). Manichaeism most likely has its roots in Zoroastrianism; see Susan R. Garrett, *No Ordinary Angel: Celestial Spirits and Christian Claims about Jesus* (New Haven: Yale University Press, 2008), 121.

[31] Or. 40.45 (SC 358, 304); *Princ.* 2.9.2; *Hex. Hom.* 2.4; *Enn.* 1.8.1.

this goodness, but they do not take away its inherent value as created by God. Therefore, dualism does not adequately describe Gregory's approach to the devil, demons, or evil. However, if we are to conclude that Gregory does not err towards dualistic thought, the question remains concerning what kind of existence Gregory attributes to the devil and his minions. This is pertinent particularly when we bear in mind the way in which Gregory emphasises that evil does not exist of its own accord, whilst maintaining a perpetual awareness of the war that Satan and his demons exert against the *eikon*.

When Gregory addresses Satan directly with statements such as 'You have come, O villainous one! I know your plans', he does not appear to be employing Satan as simply a personification of sin or evil.[32] Kalleres and Ludlow have argued this, both stating that Gregory envisaged demons as real spiritual beings.[33] Writing about Gregory's approach to demons in his poetry, Kalleres argues, quite rightly, that Gregory speaks to and describes Satan consistently as though he were a real entity, through whom evil entered the world.[34] In her commentary on the way in which Gregory addresses demons directly, Kalleres concludes that he 'disclosed an intimate knowledge of the devil himself' and that his orations and poems 'illuminate an intense personal demonology'.[35] Certainly, Gregory does not write about spiritual warfare as an impartial observer:

> You have come to me again, Weaver of Wiles (δολοπλόκε),
>   as you are known,
> nourishing yourself within the depth of my heart
> (βένθος ἐμῆς κραδίης ἔνδοθι βοσκόμενος),
> and through much strong shaking of this life,
> desiring to bring the holy *eikon* to bended knee
> (εἰκόνα τὴν ἱερὴν γνὺξ βαλέειν ποθέων).[36]

When we consider Gregory's speech above, which is consistent with discussions elsewhere in his work, we cannot reduce his words to simple rhetoric. Whilst she acknowledges this, Kalleres does not resolve the question concerning how the devil and demons are able to exist, given that

---

[32] Carm. 2.1.54 (PG 37, 1397, 1); Or. 40.10 (SC 358, 216–18); Carms. 2.1.50 – 2.1.60 (PG 37, 1385–1404).

[33] Morwenna Ludlow, 'Demons, Evil and Liminality in Cappadocian Theology', *JECS*, 20, no. 2 (2012), 179–211; Kalleres, 'Demons and Divine Illumination', passim; Robert C. Gregg, *Consolation Philosophy: Greek and Christian Paideia in Basil and the Two Gregories* (Philadelphia: Philadelphia Patristic Foundation, 1975), 151.

[34] Or. 40.10 (SC 358, 218); Kalleres, 'Demons and Divine Illumination', 186.

[35] Ibid., 186.   [36] Carm. 1.2.50 (PG 37, 1385, 1–4).

Gregory does not attribute existence to evil. Ludlow, on the other hand, after establishing that Gregory considers demons to be real, moves on to explore the nature of that reality. Through a close reading of the texts, Ludlow argues that demons are real in the sense that they were created good, along with all that God has created. She states that their wills alone are bad, whilst their ontology remains good. From this point, she argues,

Demons occupy a liminal space: their wills are utterly opposed to God and thus evil, and yet these wills exist in a nature which is part of God's good creation.[37]

Ludlow moves on to argue that demons are not mid-way between good and evil, but that their 'existence paradoxically seems to entail the co-existence of both'.[38] Thus, demons are hybrids in the sense that they are 'neither one thing nor the other'.[39] I support Ludlow's argument concerning the demons' wills. Gregory is consistent in his description of the way in which the devil and demons desire that which is to the detriment of the human *eikon*. There is more to explore, however, with respect to the nature of the existence of demons. Ludlow's argument concerning the liminal space, which demons occupy, demands that demons remain ontologically good. Therefore, they must remain unchanged from their creation, whilst their wills are to incline to evil. However, Gregory suggests that Satan is diminishing ontologically, rather than remaining unchanged, when he writes,

But what persuades me both to suppose and say these things: that they are not immoveable, rather, they are hard to budge, is on account of the 'Morning Star'[40] who was named thus because of his brilliance; both becoming and being named (καὶ γενόμενος καὶ λεγόμενος) 'darkness (σκότος)' on account of his self-elevation.[41]

Through his use of γίγνομαι, Gregory stipulates that Satan was becoming something other than who he was at creation. One meaning of γίγνομαι, according to Lampe, may be 'change the quality of'.[42] Added to this,

---

[37] Ludlow, 'Demons, Evil and Liminality', 189. Ludlow draws her argument largely from Dale B. Martin, *Inventing Superstition* (Cambridge, MA: Harvard University Press, 2004). Elsewhere, liminal is described as a 'blurred borderland that is neither in the material world nor in the spiritual world but in both simultaneously'; Rosemary Guiley, *The Encyclopedia of Demons and Demonology* (New York: Facts On File, Infobase Publishing, 2009), 159–60.

[38] Ludlow, 'Demons, Evil and Liminality', 189.   [39] Ibid., 190.   [40] Is. 14:12–15.

[41] Or. 38.9 (SC 358, 120–22); Carm. 1.1.7 (PG 37, 443, 59–62); Cels. 4.65; Haer. 4.41. For demons as 'diminished' in Evagrius' thought, see Kevin Corrigan, *Evagrius and Gregory: Mind, Soul and Body in the 4th Century* (Surrey: Ashgate Publishing Limited, 2009), 92.

[42] PGL, 315.

Satan is becoming 'darkness', a metaphor which is key to Gregory's overall theology, since darkness is the diminishment and absence of light.[43] Gregory's application of 'Light' as a metaphor for God has long been recognised by those who study our theologian's work.[44] At creation, Lucifer is a light second only to God; as we saw in Chapter 3, angels are named secondary lights because they are closest in proximity to God.[45] In view of this, Lucifer's becoming darkness is significant, since it demonstrates that he is no longer close to God in the heavenly realm, and furthermore, his ability to radiate light is diminishing. Therefore, rather than interpreting demons as occupying a liminal existence, it is possible that Gregory considers their existence to be closer to one which could be described as 'diminishing'. I use the participle intentionally, since, like all creation, demons are dynamic and thus their movement is towards non-being rather than being in a static, diminished state.[46]

Ludlow's argument depends on her stipulation that for the Cappadocians, 'demons were also *good* to the extent that they were superior ontological beings (rational, powerful, etc.)'.[47] She argues this because Gregory states that demons were originally created angels before human *eikones* were created. However, it appears that, from what Gregory writes, a significant shift occurs, in which the devil and demons do not remain superior, in any sense whatsoever, to human *eikones*. In his oration *On Baptism*, Gregory demands that Satan bow down and worship him (and by inference all those who are baptised).[48] His demand for worship suggests that Gregory considers Satan, now fallen from heaven, to be his inferior, either morally or ontologically.

Gregory's demand relates to his beliefs about being and becoming divine, which we will explore further in Chapter 5. We shall see that Gregory is consistent in his approach regarding the superiority of the human *eikon* over the devil and demons because of the victory won by Christ. As we saw in Chapter 2, Gregory writes, 'You have come, indeed,

---

[43] 'il demonio è e produce tenebra', Francesco Trisoglio, 'Il demonio in Gregorio di Nazianzo' in Eugenio Corsini (ed.), *L'autunno del diavolo. 'Diabolos, Dialogos, Daimon' convegno di Torino 17/21 ottobre 1988, volume primo* (Milano: Bompiani, 1990), 249–65, 250.

[44] Alexis Torrance, 'Precedents for Palamas' Essence-Energies Theology in the Cappadocian Fathers', *VC*, 63, no. 1 (2009), 47–70, 62.

[45] Or. 38.9 (SC 358, 120).

[46] Alden A. Mosshammer, 'Non-Being and Evil in Gregory of Nyssa', *VC*, 44 (1990), 136–67, 147.

[47] Ludlow, 'Demons, Evil and Liminality', 192.   [48] Or. 40.10 (SC 358, 218).

you have come O most Evil One, but you have been restrained'.[49]
Regarding the place of this battle between the devil and the *eikon*,
according to Gregory, for the most part it takes place within the *eikon*
herself. This explains why, in one of his poems, Gregory accuses the devil
of 'nourishing yourself within the depth of my heart'.[50] Gregory adopts
the same approach in other poems: 'Flee from my heart O deceitful one,
flee at break-neck speed (φεῦγ' ἀπ' ἐμῆς κραδίης, δολομήχανε, φεῦγε
τάχιστα)'.[51] In her analysis of the Cappadocians, Ludlow suggests that
they envisage demons waging war, both externally and internally. If we
were to focus specifically on Nazianzen, his writing presents warfare as
occurring primarily in the heart.[52] The demons' need to 'nourish' themselves on human hearts suggests that, in order to maintain their existence,
they must find nourishment, rather like parasites. This demonstrates
further their inferiority to the *eikon*, since they need the *eikon* and not
vice versa.

Our final point regarding the diminishing nature of the devil relates,
possibly surprisingly, to Origen's belief about the final restoration (ἀποκατάστασις), which commentators have argued that Gregory follows
implicitly.[53] Contrary to the general view, Gregory does not align himself
explicitly with this; he applies ἀποκατάστασις on as few as six occasions,
and not in such a way so as to suggest universal salvation.[54] Gregory
refers to fire that burns forever (διαιωνίζω); therefore we cannot be certain
of his thoughts regarding ultimate restoration.[55] However, if Gregory is
ambiguous regarding the universal restoration of humankind, he adopts

---

[49] Carm. 2.1.60 (PG 37, 1403, 1). The devil is understood more clearly through his
treatment of the *eikon*; 'I frutti prevalgono sulle radici; il demonio è osservato più nella
sua azione e nei suoi moventi che nella sua natura', Francesco Trisoglio, *San Gregorio di
Nazianzo: Un contemporaneo vissuto sedici secoli fa* (Torino: Effatà Editrice, 2008), 119.

[50] Carm. 1.2.50 (PG 37, 1385, 2).

[51] Carm. 2.1.55 (PG 37, 1399, 7); 2.1.1 (PG 37, 996, 345); Or. 40.35 (SC 358, 278).

[52] Ludlow, 'Demons, Evil and Liminality', 199–200.

[53] Ilaria L.E. Ramelli, *The Christian Doctrine of Apokatastasis: A Critical Assessment from
the New Testament to Eriugena* (Leiden: Brill, 2013), 452; Brian Daley, *The Hope of the
Early Church: A Handbook of Patristic Eschatology* (Cambridge: Cambridge University
Press, 1991), 84; Meehan, *Three Poems*, 42.

[54] For Gregory's use of ἀποκατάστασις, see Or. 30.4 (SC 250, 230) in which Gregory refers
to an argument from the opposition; Or. 30.6 (SC 250, 238), where Gregory's point is
that Christ is God; Or. 31.27 (SC 250, 330) speaks of Christ's own return to heaven;
Or. 40.8 (SC 358, 212) refers to baptism on earth; Or. 41.11 (SC 358, 338) speaks of
Christ's ascension to heaven; and Or. 44.5 (PG 36, 613A) in which Gregory is speaking
about the Church. Lastly, in Or. 2.36 (SC 247, 134) Gregory refers to the final ἀνάστασις,
yet does not imply that he is speaking about those outside the Church.

[55] Or. 40.36 (SC 358, 282).

an explicit approach to his views on the end of the devil. Gregory assures
his readers that God will bring to an end (καταλύω) the devil and kill him
(θανατόω).[56] This leaves us with a condundrum regarding the goodness of
demons, at least with respect to their ontology, since ultimately the devil
must be restored if he is good ontologically. Contrary to this, Gregory
explicitly states that God will ultimately annihilate the devil, which suggests that no goodness will remain at the end. With this in mind, I come
back to my suggestion that Gregory understands the devil's existence to
be one which is 'diminishing'. There is a caveat, however; a diminishing
reality does not mean that the devil is less dangerous to human *eikones*.
Rather it implies the opposite, since his diminishing existence increases
the devil's hatred of the human race, and more specifically, his hatred of
the Church. With an outline of Gregory's view of the devil in place, let us
turn to Gregory's retelling of the 'fall', highlighting the devil's involvement and the impact upon the vulnerable *eikon*.

THE FALL

Gregory does not envisage the human *eikon* falling purely of her own
accord, since he follows Irenaeus in his depiction of the human person in
paradise as a child, who is innocent and easily beguiled.[57] The human
capacity for freedom means that a fall is possible, but not inevitable.[58]
The likelihood of the fall is increased by the human *eikon* sharing paradise with the devil, her deadliest enemy. The devil takes advantage of the
human capacity for freedom and encourages this 'child' to disobey the
only commandment God gave to her:

> If we had remained the very thing which we were and kept the commandment, we
> would have become that which we were not, coming towards the tree of life, after
> the tree of knowledge. And what would we have become? Immortal and consorts
> with God (θεῷ πλησιάσαντες). But since death (θάνατος) came into the world
> through the envy of the Evil One (τῷ φθόνῳ τοῦ πονηροῦ), and filched the human
> person through trickery ...[59]

---

[56] Or. 24.9 (SC 284, 56).

[57] Or. 38.12 (SC 358, 128); 39.7 (SC 358, 160–62); 2.25 (SC 247, 122–24); Carm.1.1.8
(PG 37, 454, 104); *Dem.* 11–12; *Haer.* 4.38.3; see Matthew C. Steenberg, 'Children in
Paradise: Adam and Eve as "Infants" in Irenaeus of Lyons', *JECS*, 12, no. 1 (2004), 1–22;
Althaus, *Die Heilslehre des heiligen*, 66–67.

[58] Or. 14.25 (PG 35, 889C–982B); 38.12 (SC 358, 126); 37.13 (SC 318, 298).

[59] Or. 44.4 (PG 36, 612A–B).

For Gregory, the *eikon* is wounded through the process of the fall, rather than eradicated completely.[60] In the West, it is customary to think that humans are in need of a judge who will dispense pardon to them after the fall, whereas Gregory, following the Eastern tradition, envisages the *eikon* as being in need of a healer and a helper: 'Since these things required a greater aid, an even greater aid befell'.[61]

The consequences of the fall upon the *eikon* are multitudinous. Any notion that the fall leaves the *eikon* unaffected is dispelled by Gregory's language concerning Christ's purpose in dying on the cross: 'to triumph over the serpent . . . and heal Adam and restore the fallen *eikon* (τὴν εἰκόνα πεσοῦσαν)'.[62] Whilst at creation, human *eikones* are angelic rulers through their status as God's *eikones*; for the most part, after the fall they lapse into an existence of perpetual struggle. In paradise, the devil is the principal enemy of Adam and Eve; outside paradise, they experience the additional strain of being clothed with 'garments of skin (χιτῶνες δερματίνους)'.[63] Gregory understands these to represent a duller, more earthly flesh than previously. The result of this is severe, since now human *eikones* struggle to apprehend God,[64] rather than functioning as those who are 'initiated into that which is spiritual'.[65] This negative shift may be described as growing 'spiritual cataracts'. Drawing from Romans, Gregory describes fallen human persons hyperbolically as murderers, adulterers, idolaters, and worst of all in Gregory's mind, they experience mortality.[66]

It should be evident from this discussion thus far that living as a radiant *eikon* of God is even more challenging after the fall than it was in paradise. Before we examine this challenging existence in more depth, let us clarify Gregory's view of how the fall occurs. Gregory assumes his own responsibility for the sin in the world, as he ascertains that he himself has eaten the fruit from the forbidden tree in paradise, a notion which is central to the Eastern tradition.[67] In identifying with this initial

---

[60] Or. 38.14 (SC 358, 136); 1.4 (SC 247, 76–78); 7.23 (SC 405, 240); 16.8 (PG 35, 944D–45A); 38.14 (SC 358, 128); 40.7 (SC 358, 210). See Edmund J. Rybarczyk, *Beyond Salvation: Eastern Orthodoxy and Classical Pentecostalism on Becoming Like Christ* (Carlisle: Paternoster Press, 2004), 58.

[61] Or. 38.12 (SC 358, 132). Gregory portrays healing as primary and pardon as secondary; see Or. 22.13, (SC 270, 246–48).

[62] Or. 24.4 (SC 284, 46); Carm. 1.1.9 (PG 37, 460, 53–59).

[63] Or. 38.12 (SC 358, 130).   [64] Or. 38.13 (SC 358, 132).

[65] Or. 38.11 (SC 358, 126).   [66] Or. 38.13 (SC 358, 132); see Rom. 1:26–32.

[67] Or. 19.14 (PG 35, 1060C–D); 22.13 (SC 270, 248); 37.7 (SC 318, 284); 38.12 (SC 358, 128); Carm. 1.1.4 (PG 37, 420, 54); 1.1.9 (PG 37, 463, 82–86); 1.1.10 (PG 37, 466,

consumption, Gregory sits in the tradition of the Eastern fathers whereby he displays an awareness of historical events, but tends 'more to collapse history and read past events as present'.[68] This highlights further how he interprets the creation narratives in Genesis, and the way in which he is able to read himself, and indeed every human person, into the account traditionally referred to as the 'fall of humanity'.[69]

In the biblical narrative, Eve, Adam, and the serpent take lead roles in the drama of the fall. Likewise, Gregory's discussions of the fall move between these three characters; he himself identifies with Adam.[70] In Chapter 3, we discussed that Gregory can be generous in his approach to women, at least with regards to their identity as *eikones* of God, if not with respect to those who apply cosmetics! He portrays Eve in a variety of ways, from relative compassion through to degrees of contempt, since she is described both as someone who 'suffered as one who was more tender',[71] and also as 'an enemy' and 'antithetic' to Adam.[72] Added to this, Gregory attributes no small degree of blame to the 'malice of the devil', since it was the Evil One who tricked Adam and Eve into eating from the tree of knowledge.[73] This in turn led to their banishment from paradise.[74] In light of what we have discussed thus far, concerning the consistency in Gregory's writing of the devil's envy of human *eikones*, it is no surprise that Gregory portrays the devil as wanting to see them banished from paradise and destroyed.[75] However, Gregory does not refer to the devil in order to deny human responsibility for sin, and does not imply that human persons might utter the excuse, 'the devil made me do it'.[76] Rather, he follows a biblical narrative, whereby the serpent is

---

16–21). See Moreschini (SC 358, 51); Berthold Altaner, 'Augustinus und Gregor von Nazianz, Gregor von Nyssa' in Berthold Altaner (ed.), *Kleine patristische Schriften* (Berlin: Akademie Verlag, 1967), 277–85, passim.

[68] Louth, 'The Fathers on Genesis', 574.

[69] Richard J. Clifford, 'The Hebrew Scriptures and the Theology of Creation', *Theological Studies*, 46, no. 3 (1985), 507–23.

[70] Or. 22.13 (SC 270, 248).   [71] Or. 38.12 (SC 358, 128).

[72] Or. 18.8 (PG 35, 8993B).

[73] Or. 38.12 (SC 358, 128); 36.5 (SC 318, 250–52); 39.7 (SC 358, 162); 44.7 (PG 36, 613D–616A); Carm. 1.1.9 (PG 37, 457, 9).

[74] Or. 39.13 (SC 358, 176–78).

[75] Or. 6.10 (SC 405, 146); 36.5 (SC 318, 250); 40.10 (SC 358, 216–18); 44.4 (PG 36, 619B); Carm. 1.1.7 (PG 37, 443, 65); 1.1.10 (PG 37, 466, 16–20); 1.2.1 (PG 37, 531, 120); *Haer.* 1.10.1; Daniel R. Schultz, 'The Origin of Sin in Irenaeus and Jewish Pseudepigraphical Literature', *VC*, 32, no. 3 (1978), 161–90.

[76] Don Cupitt, 'Four Arguments against the Devil', *Theology*, 64, no. 496 (1961), 413–15, 413; Or. 16.15–17 (PG 35, 953C–957C); 22.13 (SC 270, 348).

responsible for the temptations, but at the same time maintains that human persons should resist those temptations.

Let us examine the experience of the fall itself and its effects upon the *eikon,* considering first Gregory's retelling of the biblical narrative.[77] In Genesis, Adam and Eve's banishment from the Garden of Eden proceeds as follows: firstly, Adam and Eve eat the fruit from the tree of knowledge (Gen 3:6), after which they discover they are naked and experience shame (Gen 3:7–10); then the Lord makes garments of skins for them (Gen 3:21) and banishes them from the garden (Gen 3:23–24). Observe in Gregory's allegorical reading the series of events below in relation to the account in Genesis:

> ... immediately, on account of the evil, all at once (ὁμοῦ) he was expelled from the tree of life and from paradise (Gen 3:23–24) and from God and he was clothed in garments of skin (χιτῶνες δερματίνους, Gen 3:20), probably the more earthly, duller flesh (παχύτης), both mortal (θνητός) and obstinate (ἀντίτυπος). And this first thing he knew was his own shame, and he hid from God (Gen 3:7–8).[78]

After Adam and Eve have eaten from the tree of knowledge, Gregory describes a number of actions occurring simultaneously: Adam is expelled from paradise, expelled from God's presence, and clothed in earthly, dull flesh, after which he experiences shame for the first time. Note that in Genesis, Adam is ashamed because he is naked,[79] whereas, for Gregory, being naked (ἁπλότης) is a good thing because it implies simplicity.[80] Gregory suggests that the first human is ashamed because he is covered in earthly, dull flesh (παχύτης).[81] Before we explore the implications of this, Gregory's use of παχύτης demands attention, since this interpretation of the nature of the 'garments of skin' is key to his reading of the biblical narrative.

---

[77] Gregory follows a particular tradition of interpretation; see Heerak Christian Kim, *The Jerusalem Tradition in the Late Second Temple Period: Diachronic and Synchronic Developments Surrounding Psalms of Solomon 11* (Maryland, U.S.A.: University Press of America, 2007), 40–42; Derek Krueger, *Liturgical Subjects: Christian Ritual, Biblical Narrative, and the Formation of the Self in Byzantium* (Philadelphia, PA: University of Pennsylvania Press, 2014), 147–49.

[78] Or. 38.12 (SC 358, 130).   [79] Gen. 3:10, γυμνός.   [80] Or. 38.12 (SC 358, 128).

[81] Gary A. Anderson, 'The Garments of Skin in Apocryphal Narrative and Biblical Commentary' in James L. Kugel (ed.), *Studies in Ancient Midrash* (Cambridge, Mass.: Harvard University Press, 2001), 101–43, 130. The same order appears in *In Praise of Virginity*, Carm. 1.2.1 (PG 37, 531, 119–22), but is different in *On the Soul*, Carm. 1.1.8 (PG 37, 455, 112–18), where the coats of skin are worn before departure from the garden. Since Gregory does not mention shame in *On the Soul*, the change in sequence does not imply a change in the object of shame being earthly flesh rather than nakedness.

Lampe translates παχύτης as 'grossness' or 'materiality',[82] which may be supplemented by Liddell, Scott, and Jones, who highlight the notion of 'dullness'.[83] The concepts of materiality and dullness lead us towards understanding Gregory's intentions, but do not fully convey the sense in which Gregory appeals to παχύτης. Gregory's purpose becomes clearer when we consider παχύς, since it generally describes that which is 'earthly' and 'of this world'.[84] This is imperative to Gregory's narrative, since it draws out the striking contrast between the depiction of the human *eikon* as 'another angel' at creation and the description of her after eating from the tree of knowledge.[85] In short, she is created angelic and divine, with the potential of living forever, but quickly becomes mortal. Concerning Gregory's use of παχύτης, Daley and Harrison note that translation is problematic, both settling on 'coarse'.[86] This translation is only loosely accurate and does not fully convey Gregory's intentions. It is important to take into account not only his particular use of παχύτης, but also his previous descriptions of the human *eikon* as naked (implying purity and simplicity) and angelic. Furthermore, Gregory himself explains that παχύτης causes the human person's 'mortality'.[87] Like Irenaeus, Gregory interprets death as a gift for the couple who have been banished from paradise. Death is a gift because it puts an end to sin.[88] Nevertheless, the addition of the garments of skin, and consequent loss of glory, 'is nothing but a shorthand way of referring to a cataclysmic shift in the ontological status of human persons',[89] where the destiny of humanity has been interrupted by the jealousy of the devil, who compromised the theosis and divine life of the *eikon*.[90]

Whilst our analysis of Gregory's appeal to παχύτης has demonstrated the enormous impact of this thicker, duller, and more earthly flesh upon the *eikon*, it does not explain fully Gregory's interpretation of the banishment scene in Genesis. Gregory's interpretation becomes clearer when we explore the tradition which developed around the Genesis narrative, namely, the 'garments of glory'.

---

[82] *PGL*, 1054.   [83] LSJ, 1351.   [84] *PGL*, 1054.

[85] Or. 38.11 (SC 358, 126); 45.7 (PG 36, 635C); Carm. 1.2.15 (PG 37, 777, 156).

[86] Daley, *Gregory of Nazianzus* (London: Taylor & Francis, 2006), 123; Nonna Verna Harrison, *Gregory Nazianzen: Festal Orations*, PPS (Crestwood, New York: St. Vladimir's Seminary Press, 2008), 50.

[87] Or. 38.12 (SC 358, 130).   [88] *Haer.* 3.23.7; Or. 38.12, SC 358, 130.

[89] Anderson, 'Garments of Skin', 143.

[90] Rousse, 'Les anges et leur ministère', 147. See Or. 36.5 (SC 316, 250–52); Carm. 1.2.14 (PG 37, 755–65).

'GARMENTS OF GLORY'

The tradition 'garments of glory', also known as 'robes of glory', appears in sources as varied as Rabbinic, Gnostic, Islamic, Manichaean, and particularly the Syriac Christian tradition.[91] It appeals to Adam's identity as a king and ruler,[92] being read in conjunction with Psalm 8:6 (8:5), where humanity is crowned or clothed with 'glory and honour', as discussed in Chapter 4.[93] The tradition has a complex reception, taking numerous twists and turns that are beyond the scope of this study.[94] For the sake of my argument here, I shall focus on the strand which concerns the interpretation of the following Scripture passages: Genesis 2:25 (Adam and Eve are naked and without shame), Genesis 3:7 (Adam and Eve perceived their sin and felt shame), and Genesis 3:21 (the Lord gave them garments of skin). Due to its particular exegesis of these verses, the 'garments of glory' tradition drew the conclusion that Adam and Eve lost a glorious covering before being given the garments of skin.[95] The key point here is that Adam and Eve experience shame because of their loss of glory and the addition of their garments of skin, and not because they become aware of their nakedness, which is how the Genesis pericope is often read.

The 'garments of glory' tradition is evident in early church fathers such as Didymus the Blind,[96] John Chrysostom,[97] and Ephrem the Syrian,

---

[91] For example, Saint Ephrem, *Hymns on Paradise*, trans. Sebastian P. Brock (Crestwood, New York: St. Vladimir's Seminary Press, 1990). For further explanation, see Ross Shepherd Kraemer, *When Aseneth Met Joseph: A Late Antique Tale of the Biblical Patriarch and His Egyptian Wife, Reconsidered* (Oxford: Oxford University Press, 1998), 266–67; Hannah Hunt, '"Clothed in the Body": The Garment of Flesh and the Garment of Glory in Syrian Religious Anthropology' in Markus Vincent (ed.), *Studia Patristica 64* (Leuven: Peeters Press, 2013), 167–76.

[92] Crispin H.T. Fletcher-Louis, *All the Glory of Adam: Liturgical Anthropology in the Dead Sea Scrolls* (Leiden: Brill, 2002), passim; Stephen N. Lambden, 'From Figleaves to Fingernails: Some Notes on the Garments of Adam and Eve in the Hebrew Bible and Select Early Postbiblical Jewish Writings' in Paul Morris and Deborah Sawyer (eds.), *A Walk in the Garden: Biblical, Iconographical and Literary Images of Eden* (Sheffield: JSOT Press, 1992), 74–90.

[93] James L. Kugel, *Traditions of the Bible: A Guide to the Bible as It Was at the Start of the Common Era* (New York: Harvard University Press, 2009), 113; Sebastian P. Brock, 'Jewish Traditions in Syriac Sources', *JJS*, 30, no. 2 (1979), 212–32, 221–23.

[94] Andrei A. Orlov, *From Apocalypticism to Merkabah Mysticism: Studies in the Slavonic Pseudepigrapha* (Leiden: Brill, 2007), 329–32.

[95] Peterson describes the effects of the garments of skin upon the human person as a metaphysical change; Erik Peterson, 'Theologie des Kleides', *BM*, 16 (1934), 347–56.

[96] *In Gen.* See Peter D. Steiger, 'The Image of God in the Commentary *On Genesis* of Didymus the Blind' in Frances M. Young, Mark J. Edwards, and Paul Parvis (eds.), *Studia Patristica*, 42 (Leuven: Peeters Publishers, 2006), 243–48.

[97] *Hom. On Gen.* 16.

yet it is not explicit in Gregory's work, leaving scholars to disagree over whether he knew of the convention.[98] Sykes argues that Gregory appeals to the tradition without offering any evidence to confirm his argument. Anderson's appeal that Gregory draws from this tradition considers Gregory's sequence of events during the fall in just one oration.[99] Building on Anderson's argument, we shall explore Gregory's use of the tradition by considering the account of the fall in his poetry also. The ambiguity lies in the fact that Gregory does not refer to the garments of glory during his recounting of the fall. Nevertheless, we shall see that Gregory's ideas were informed by this tradition, and that he wove it subtly into his writing in two key ways. Firstly, recall that Gregory retold the Genesis narrative in such a way that Adam and Eve were ashamed of their earthly, dull flesh, and not ashamed of their nakedness. This approach is identical to the 'garments of glory' tradition, in which Adam is not ashamed of his nakedness, but rather his coat of skin. Secondly, as we have already discussed, Gregory describes the human person as 'another angel' at creation on a number of occasions; whilst human persons were different from the angels in heaven, nevertheless, like angels, Gregory speaks of human persons metaphorically as lights, which is comparable with human *eikones* shining gloriously.[100] This notion is explicit in his poetry:

> The mortal human is your glory anew (σὸν βροτὸς αὖ κλέος ἐστιν),
>   whom you placed here as an angel, composing songs of
>   praise of your splendour, O Light.[101]

When Gregory describes the mortal human as God's glory, he recalls the 'garments of glory' tradition, in which Adam was created as the glory of God. Hints of this tradition running through Gregory's work serve to remind us once more how highly Gregory regarded the human person at creation, precisely because she is made as God's *eikon*. Furthermore, Gregory appeals implicitly to the tradition to highlight how the glory is dulled through the fall through the donning of the garments of skin. Gregory adapts the tradition to incorporate his view of the vulnerability of humanity. The 'garments of glory' tradition is suggestive of an almost invincible quality regarding the first human persons, whereas Gregory presents them as both glorious, yet vulnerable, as they listen to the devil's lies guilelessly.

---

[98] For a negative argument, read Bouteneff, *Beginnings*, 174.

[99] Moreschini and Sykes, *Poemata Arcana*, 248; Anderson, 'Garments of Skin', 129–30.

[100] Or. 40.5 (SC 358, 206); Carm. 1.1.4 (PG 37, 418, 33).

[101] Carm. 2.1.38 (PG 37, 1327, 25–26); 2.1.45 (PG 37, 1366, 186); Or. 39.7 (SC 358, 162).

For Gregory, there is a qualitative change in humanity's flesh, owing to the fall. Before the fall the human *eikon* is open to the divine will; after the fall she struggles to apprehend God. Even whilst wearing the 'robe of glory', the *eikon* apparently remains vulnerable to evil through the temptations of the devil, but even more so when shrouded in thick, dull flesh. This results in a shift in the ontology of human persons, whereby through eating from the tree of knowledge, they move from being 'spiritually alive'[102] to being 'mortal'.[103] Hence, Gregory's ontology and epistemology are one and the same. The donning of earthly, dull, and mortal flesh entails an epistemological breakdown for the *eikon*, or, as Kalleres puts it, the fall 'resulted in the loss of this delicate balance of noetic and sensory which had enabled man to know God'.[104] Through the gift of the *eikon* at creation, the human person is able to 'see and experience the radiance of God',[105] whereas the earthly, dull flesh affects the *eikon* in such a manner that she no longer automatically relates to God.[106] This relates to the use of παχύνω in the Septuagint, where it is applied as a metaphor to denote that which is 'mentally dull'.[107] If we read παχύτης with this in mind, the effects of the fall become clearer still: unlike the angels and her former self, the *eikon* is now mentally dull regarding her ability to relate to and apprehend God. No longer is she wearing 'garments of glory', but instead thick, dull earthly flesh which prevents her from apprehending God:

'Heaven is high, but the earth is deep'. And who of those who have been cast down by sin shall ascend? Who, still being enshrouded by the gloom below and the dullness of the flesh (τῆς σαρκὸς τὴν παχύτητα) will meditate on the whole spiritual intellect purely with the whole spiritual intellect, and gaze upon that which is stable and invisible, whilst mingled with that which never stands still?[108]

Whilst being clothed with earthly, mortal, dull flesh and experiencing an epistemological breakdown may seem consequence enough, the *eikon* has yet further challenges to face, namely a continued battle with the devil, the world, the flesh, and the passions, to which we shall turn next.

---

[102] Or. 38.11 (SC 358, 124).
[103] Or. 7.19 (SC 405, 228); 24.3 (SC 284, 44); 38.12 (SC 358, 128).
[104] Kalleres, 'Demons and Divine Illumination', 169.   [105] Or. 38.11 (SC 358, 126).
[106] Or. 28.2 (SC 250, 102–04).   [107] Is. 6:10; Muraoka, *GELS*, 541.
[108] Or. 2.74 (SC 247, 186); 28.4 (SC 150, 108).

THE WORLD, THE FLESH, AND THE DEVIL

From fornication and all other deadly sin; and from all the deceits of the world, the flesh and the devil, *Good Lord, deliver us.*

The prayer above, found in the Litany of the 1662 *Book of Common Prayer*, gathers together the essence of Gregory's frequent prayers regarding the threats to the *eikon*; for the devil, sinful flesh, and the world form serious obstacles to the *eikon* achieving her full divinity. Next, we explore further the pervasiveness of the devil in Gregory's thought about the existence of the *eikon* by considering the continual battle between the devil and the *eikon*, which focuses attention on the vulnerability and divinity of the *eikon*.

In Chapter 1, we saw that Gregory uses myriad epithets for the devil, the author of the maltreatment experienced by the *eikon*. In no less than thirteen consecutive poems, Gregory describes the devil's assault upon the *eikon* using vivid language.[109] Six of the thirteen poems are entitled *Against the Evil One*, which offers an indication of Gregory's preoccupation with the work of the devil. In these poems, Gregory presents the constant temptation to sin as the means through which the devil attempts to destroy the *eikon*:

> And if the destroyer of the *eikon* trips me up (εἰ δὲ σκελίζει μ' ὁ
> φθορεὺς τῆς εἰκόνος),
> Who might become my guardian, save you, Lord?[110]

In the lines above, the *eikon* is vulnerable and in need of help and protection from the temptations of the devil. Whilst the *eikon* is vulnerable to a certain degree, she is not expected to be passive in her response to the devil, since Gregory appeals to human responsibility and highlights that humans have a degree of freedom to choose not to sin:

> But if you, tongue, do not accept the mire (τὸν βόρβορον)
> But if at least you, hand, do not accept what is worse,
> Thus may the *eikon* in us remain imperishable (οὕτως ἂν
> εἰκὼν ἡμῖν ἄφθαρτος μένῃ).[111]

On the basis of the above lines, it is clear that Gregory envisages human persons as being responsible for resisting sin. The devil may seek to

---

[109] Carms. 2.1.54–2.1.67 (PG 37, 1397, 11–1407, 8). For translations of the first eight poems as prayers, see Kalleres, 'Demons and Divine Illumination', 161–68.
[110] Carm. 2.1.65 (PG 37, 1407, 6–7).
[111] Carm. 2.1.61 (PG 37, 1405, 6–8). See Wis. 12:1.

influence human persons, but he cannot force them into sinning; rather, there is a battle to be fought and won. Sometimes humans win their battle with the devil through making good choices, as seen below when Gregory states his determination to preserve the gift of the *eikon*, in spite of the devil's desire to destroy him:

> Strike the skin but the soul is unwounded,
> I shall render the divine *eikon*, the portion, to Christ,
> O Human-killer
> (. . .εἰκόνα θείην παρστήσω Χριστῷ, τὴν λάχον, ἀνδροφόνε).[112]

However, in spite of Gregory's best efforts, the *eikon* is not invincible and is subject to harm, just like the body, as the human *eikon* is a unity. The poem entitled *Lament* demonstrates that the *eikon* is extremely vulnerable to the extent that she can be destroyed:

> The *eikon* is being destroyed (εἰκὼν κενοῦται): what word will offer help?
> The *eikon* is being destroyed (εἰκὼν κενοῦται): gift of excellent God.
> The *eikon* is violated (ὑβρίζετ' εἰκὼν) . . .[113]

Above, Gregory uses κενόω, which, as we saw in Chapter 2, is well-known to contemporary theologians because there has been much discussion concerning the way in which the author of Philippians (2:6) applies it to Christ. However, Gregory does not appear to have Christ's kenosis in mind at this point.[114] A significant difference between Christ and his *eikon* is evident here: Christ chose his kenosis, and through it effected the unity of divinity and humanity, whereas Gregory's poem suggests that the human *eikon* is being destroyed against her will. I have chosen to translate κενόω as 'destroy' rather than 'empty' because four lines previously in the poem, Gregory writes that the devil longs to kill human persons today as much as he wanted to kill them in paradise. Therefore, it follows that κενόω relates to the life of the *eikon*, since it is precisely her life that the devil longs to destroy.[115] Gregory uses κενόω to show that on succumbing to temptation, the human person's divine life begins to be destroyed, in the same way that the first *eikones* became mortal after

---

[112] Carm. 2.1.50 (PG 37, 1389, 61–62).

[113] *Lament*, Carm. 2.1.61 (PG 37, 1404, 1–3); 1.2.28 (PG 37, 881, 340–45); 2.1.70 (PG 37, 1418, 1–5).

[114] Cousar, *Philippians and Philemon*, 50–59; Nicholas T. Wright, 'ἁρπαγμός and the meaning of Philippians 2:5–11', *JTS*, 37, no. 2 (1986), 321–52.

[115] PGL, 743, 1.A.4. Lampe highlights that Gregory employs κενόω in *On the Son* to denote destruction. Note that Paul also uses κενόω to mean nullify/destroy in 1 Cor. 1:17.

eating from the tree of knowledge. The devil's interest in the life of the *eikon* supports my overall argument concerning the dynamic existence of the *eikon*. Through the schemes of the devil, Gregory reveals that the *eikon* does not remain statically imperishable; rather, she is subject to movement and change.

Unfortunately for the *eikon*, the devil is not the only challenge to her life, as noted at the beginning of this chapter. The world and the flesh present further challenges, and, as I shall argue, relate closely to the devil. As discussed in Chapter 3, when Gregory reflects on God's creation of the world, he describes it in positive terms, observing the order and harmony in which the world was created. We also saw that at creation, the human person was described as a microcosm and that this was decidedly positive. Conversely, here we focus on the occasions when Gregory refers to the fallen world negatively, standing in a long line of church fathers who use the concept of 'the world (κόσμος)' as a means of making a direct contrast to that which is good.[116] In doing this, they follow Paul, when he makes such comments as, 'Do not be conformed to this world' (Rom 12:2).[117]

Gregory's approval of withdrawal from the world is apparent throughout his orations and poetry. For example, in his oration *On Athanasius, Bishop of Alexandria*, Gregory praises Athanasius concerning his time in Egypt, during which he devoted himself to asceticism.[118] Gregory portrays Athanasius as finding a middle way of walking through rigorous asceticism and being in community, showing that Gregory himself was not inclined towards a totally solitary existence. In walking the 'via media', Gregory 'defies Max Weber's categories of "world-rejecting" and "inner-worldly asceticism".'[119] On reading the texts, it becomes clear that when Gregory renounces the world, he is rejecting the sin in the world, rather than the world itself; in other words, he is applying the term 'world' as a metaphor for sin:

---

[116] PGL, 771, section C7c demonstrates the concept of 'the world' as a metaphor for sin; also see Elizabeth A. Clark, *Reading Renunciation: Asceticism and Scripture in Early Christianity* (Princeton, NJ: Princeton University Press, 1999), 41; James E. Goehring, *Ascetics, Society, and the Desert: Studies in Early Egyptian Monasticism* (Harrisburg, PA: Trinity Press International, 1999), 76.

[117] Or. 21 (SC 270, 110–92).   [118] Especially Or. 21.19 (SC 270, 148).

[119] Andrea Sterk, *Renouncing the World Yet Leading the Church: The Monk-Bishop in Late Antiquity* (Cambridge, Massachussets: Harvard University Press, 2004), 7. See Max Weber, *Sociology of Religion* (Boston: Beacon Press, 1963), 166–83.

I have long desired to be dead to the world and to be alive to the life which is hidden in Christ (ἐβουλήθην ἐν καιρῷ μὲν παντὶ νεκρωθῆναι τῷ βίῳ καὶ ζῆσαι τὴν ἐν Χριστῷ κεκρυμμένην ζωὴν) ... [120]

Here, Gregory is reminiscent of Paul, who writes about being dead to sin, but alive to Christ.[121] If we read Gregory in light of Paul, Gregory's use of κόσμος as a euphemism for sin is logical, because Paul often uses the term negatively since it became the place where sin is present.[122] For Gregory, this negative experience of the world relates to the devil; this is evident because Gregory calls him 'the world-ruler'.[123] See the passage below, where Gregory posits the devil as the world-ruler who should not be obeyed:

Honour the unity, stand in awe of the archetype, live with God, not the world-ruler (κοσμοκράτωρ) ... He was a murderer from the beginning. He overpowered the first human person through disobedience, and he brought in the life of labour, and he laid down law to punish and be punished, on account of sin.[124]

In the passage above, Gregory states clearly that the world-ruler is in opposition to God. Yet earlier in the same oration Gregory commends the audience to submit themselves to their earthly rulers and does not indicate that this might compromise their submission to God.[125] There-fore, the world-ruler to which Gregory refers in the passage above must be the devil, since Gregory's description of the world-ruler as a 'murderer from the beginning' is a direct citation from John 8:44, where Jesus is

---

[120] Or. 19.1 (PG 35, 1044A); Paul Gallay, *La vie de Saint Grégoire de Nazianze* (Lyon: Emmanuel Vitte, 1943), 128.

[121] Rom 6:11, 'οὕτως καὶ ὑμεῖς λογίζεσθε ἑαυτοὺς [εἶναι] νεκροὺς μὲν τῇ ἁμαρτίᾳ ζῶντας δὲ τῷ Θεῷ ἐν Χριστῷ Ἰησοῦ'. See Joseph A. Fitzmyer, *Romans: A New Translation with Introduction and Commentary*, the Anchor Yale Bible (New Haven: Doubleday, 1993), 438.

[122] 1 Cor. 2:12; Rom. 5:12; Rom. 12:2; 1 Cor. 6:2; 1 Cor. 2:8; James takes the same approach, see Ja. 1:27; 4:4; Hermann Sasse, 'κόσμος' in Gerhard Kittel (eds.), Θ-Κ TDNT, vol. 3 (Grand Rapids: Eerdmans, 1971), 867–98, 892.

[123] For Gregory using 'world-ruler' as an epithet for the devil, see Or. 1.4 (SC 247, 77); 8.12 (SC 405, 272); 11.4 (SC 405, 338); 14.21 (PG 35, 884C); 17.9 (PG 35, 976C); 19.6 (PG 35, 1049C). For identification of the 'world-ruler' with the devil in John 12:31, 14:30, see George R. Beasley-Murray, *John*, WBC (Mexico: Thomas Nelson Publishers, 2000), 263; Jutta Leonhardt-Balzer, 'The Ruler of the World, Antichrists and Pseudo-Prophets: Johannine Variations on an Apocalyptic Motif' in Catrin H. Williams and Christopher Rowland (eds.), *John's Gospel and Imitations of Apocalyptic* (London: T&T Clark, 2013), 180–99, 189. For the history of κοσμοκράτωρ, see Wilhelm Michaelis, 'κοσμοκράτωρ', ibid., ed. Geoffrey William Bromiley (1966), 913–14. He relates this term to the devil in Eph 6:12. For 'world-ruler' as a description of Caesar, see Or. 20.4 (SC 270, 64); 39.9 (SC 358, 166).

[124] Or. 17.9 (PG 35, 976B–D).   [125] Or. 17.6 (PG 35, 972D–973A).

talking to the Jews unambiguously about the devil.[126] Whilst Gregory refers to the concept of the devil as the world-ruler infrequently, he applies the concept to the effect that those living on earth wrestle with a spiritual enemy who attempts to rule the world to their detriment. In light of this, when Gregory composes poetry with titles such as *On Dying to the World*, we should be aware that behind this is the warning that the devil resides in the world.[127] This confirms why he urges repeatedly,

Let us flee worldly desires, let us flee the world which leads us astray and the world-ruler, let us be cleansed by the Creator, let us honour the *eikon*, let us stand in awe of the call, let us change this life (τιμήσωμεν τὴν εἰκόνα, αἰδεσθῶμεν τὴν κλῆσιν, μεταθώμεθα τὴν ζωήν).[128]

Above, Gregory displays his high view of the divine *eikon*; indeed, it is precisely because human persons are made according to the *eikon* of God that they should flee from 'the world'. Note though that Gregory is speaking of the world negatively here because he is also speaking of the devil. Observe the same pattern below with respect to the flesh.

In Chapter 3, we saw that the way in which Gregory presents the creation of the human person is as a unity. This is due to his particular approach to the mixture (μῖξις) of the *eikon* and dust, where God's divine *eikon* transforms dust or flesh, precisely because these are vulnerable (or porous) to God.[129] We discussed also that Gregory's high esteem for the *eikon* means that he envisages the body as being made spiritual by the *eikon*.[130] On occasion, Gregory continues to speak of flesh positively, even after the fall, implying that through its unity with the *eikon*, it too can be lifted up to heaven: '… yet let the *eikon* be cleansed from impurity, and let the yoked flesh (τὴν ὁμόζυγον σάρκα) be raised up high'.[131] In the same way, there are times when Gregory is positive that the *eikon* retains her predominance over dust/clay after the fall:

Let not my soul journey over the earth, weighed down with dust like a leaden
    weight sucked into the depths;
but let dust give way to the winged Spirit and *eikon* (πνεύματι δὲ πτερόεντι καὶ
    εἰκόνι χοῦν ὑποεῖξαι),
as evil melts down like wax in fire.[132]

---

[126] Contra Martha Pollard Vinson, *St. Gregory of Nazianzus: Select Orations* (WA, DC: Catholic University of America Press, 2003), 91.

[127] Carm. 1.2.48 (PG 37, 1384, 1–3).   [128] Or. 19.6 (PG 35, 1049B–C).

[129] Contra Brown, *Body and Society*, 34; Ellverson, *The Dual Nature of Man*, passim.

[130] Carm. 1.2.18 (PG 37, 787, 13–15).   [131] Or. 16.15 (PG 35, 953).

[132] Carm. 2.1.45 (PG 37, 1361–62); 2.1.45 (PG 37, 1357–58); Or. 14.7 (PG 35, 865C), et al.

Gregory's presentation of flesh is confused by the fact that he sometimes speaks in negative terms about the *eikon* wrestling fervently against the clay in order to reassume her predominance. Below, he presents a different picture from the one we saw above where the *eikon* transformed the dust into that which is spiritual:[133]

> But you, fleeing the work of clay (ὕλης), in harmony with that which is above,
> As spiritual intellect is in harmony with spiritual intellect in the divine harmony
> And warring against the flesh you bring aid to the *eikon* (καὶ σαρκὶ πολεμοῦσα
> βοηθεῖς τῇ εἰκόνι).[134]

Lines such as those above lead some commentators to conclude that Gregory's anthropology is dualistic, which does not take the whole picture of Gregory's anthropology into account.[135] There are occasions when Gregory is positive about the unity of *eikon* and flesh, as we saw earlier; if one neglects to take these into account, one may assume incorrectly that Gregory is referring to the actual human body when he speaks about 'flesh' or 'clay'. However, when Gregory refers to flesh (σάρξ) alongside the *eikon* (εἰκὼν θεοῦ) in terms of wrestling or combat, he applies the terms metaphorically to denote the human struggle with sinful nature, and he appears to have in mind notions of the devil in the background.[136] Lampe concurs that often in the writings of the early church fathers, flesh (σάρξ) is used to mean 'not co-terminous with the body, but human nature viewed in active opposition alike to God and to the spiritual effects of grace'.[137] This particular presentation of flesh echoes Paul when he writes, 'For I know that nothing good dwells within me, that is, in my flesh (σάρξ)'.[138] Indeed, Gregory follows Paul so closely that what has

---

[133] Or. 32.27 (SC 318, 142); 32.30 (SC 318, 148).

[134] Carm. 1.2.3 (PG 37, 634, 13–15).

[135] Gregory Telepneff, 'Theopascite Language in the Soteriology of Saint Gregory the Theologian', *GOTR*, 32, no. 4 (1987), 403–16, 415; Hofer, *Christ in the Life of Gregory of Nazianzus*, 50–51; Ellverson, *The Dual Nature of Man*, 62–66.

[136] Or. 26.10 (SC 284, 250); Carm. 1.1.10 (PG 37, 469, 58); 1.2.3 (PG 37, 634, 15); 2.1.28 (PG 37, 1287, 1–2); 2.1.46 (PG 37, 1378, 1–14).

[137] *PGL*, 1224.

[138] Rom. 7:18; also see Rom. 6:19; 2 Cor. 10:2; Col. 2:18; Gal. 5:16 and *Cels.* 2.25.8. On this, read Dale B. Martin, *The Corinthian Body* (New Haven: Yale University Press, 1999), 173. For more on the variety of σάρξ in Paul, see Eduard Schweizer, 'σάρξ' in Gerhard Kittel and Gerhard Freidrich (eds.), *Σ TDNT*, vol. 7 (Grand Rapids: Eerdmans, 1971), 98–151, 125–30; Bruce L. Martin, *Christ and the Law in Paul* (Eugene, OR: Wipf & Stock, 2001), 105; Bede Benjamin Bidlack, *In Good Company: The Body and Divinization in Pierre Teilhard de Chardin, SJ and Daoist Xiao Yingsou* (Leiden: Brill, 2015), 8.

been written concerning Paul's use of σάρξ could also be said of Gregory: 'all parts of the body constitute a totality known as flesh, which is dominated to such a degree that wherever flesh is, all forms of sin are present'.[139] The way in which the devil relates to the concept of sinful flesh appears in the poem *Against the Flesh*, where Gregory draws together flesh and Belial, another name for the devil:

Deadly flesh, black sea of ill-minded Belial (σάρξ ὀλοὴ βελίαο κακόφρονος οἶδμα κελαινόν),
Deadly flesh (σάρξ ὀλοή), root of branching sufferings,
Deadly flesh, a companion of the cosmos which flows below (σάρξ ὀλοὴ κόσμοιο κάτω ῥείοντος ἑταίρη),
Deadly flesh, adversary of the heavenly life (σάρξ ὀλοὴ ζωῆς ἀντίμαλ' οὐρανίης),
Flesh, hated and desired, sweet battle, mistrustful good,
Always tasting of the human-slaying tree (ἀνδροφρονοιο φυτοῦ πάντοτε γευόμενη),
Slimy filth, muddy fetters, heavy leaden weight,
Unconquerable beast born from wrangling matter (ὕλης ἔκγονε μαρναμένης),
Evil boiling, both tombstone and fetter of your mistress
Of the heavenly *eikon*, which we have assigned to us from God (εἰκόνος οὐρανίης τὴν λάχομεν θεόθεν),
Will you not stop your shameless evil?[140]

This section of the poem serves to highlight how Gregory does not envisage the devil and the flesh as distinct from one another; rather, he sees them as interwoven, with the work of sinful flesh being instigated by the devil.[141] Setting his vivid portrayal of the enemy of the *eikon* in the context of the biblical narrative, Gregory draws from Genesis 3:6, where the human *eikon* made the mistake of tasting fruit from the forbidden tree. Recall that Gregory interprets the serpent in paradise as the same persona as the devil. Thus, the allusion to the forbidden tree recalls the devil, who was responsible for tempting the first human *eikones*. Whilst Gregory does not provide a systematic treatment of how sinful flesh and the demonic powers are enmeshed, he presents an idea that sinful flesh and the devil are constantly related; the devil tempts human *eikones* through their flesh, which leans in the direction of sin after the fall because it is covered with 'garments of skin', as we saw earlier. This becomes

[139] Danker and Bauer, *Greek-English Lexicon*, 915.
[140] Carm. 2.1.46 (PG 37, 1378, 1–11). Also see Or. 2.91 (SC 247, 206–08); 11.4 (SC 405, 336–38); 24.15 (SC 284, 74); 33.12 (SC 318, 218); Carm. 1.1.9 (PG 37, 456, 125–30).
[141] David Brakke, 'The Making of Monastic Demonology: Three Ascetic Teachers on Withdrawal and Resistance', *Church History*, 70, no. 1 (2001), 19–48, 22.

clearer still in a poem where Gregory is concerned with the 'sufferings of his soul'.[142] He explains that through his spiritual intellect he is drawn toward good, but through flesh and blood he is drawn towards Belial. Through the lines below we see an aspect of how the devil and flesh work together, for the fallen flesh means that there is now a propensity to sin, which is exploited by the devil:

> The other consists of both flesh and blood, and it is willing
> To receive Belial, being drawn to nether darkness (ζόφος) ...[143]

Gregory envisages a fallen world in which the flesh and the devil work together, since flesh is weak and easily manipulated by the devil, who attempts to draw the faithful into darkness. Gregory applies ζόφος to denote darkness, which is commonly used in Greek poetry to describe the underworld, and later in Jude and 2 Peter to denote the place where God puts the angels whom God wants to punish.[144] Through this, the diminishing existence of the devil becomes clear once again, since Gregory positions him as belonging 'below' rather than experiencing the fullness of existence, which comes from being close to God. Furthermore, observe the complex existence of the *eikon*. As demonstrated at the beginning of this section, Gregory speaks positively about the human person even after the fall on some occasions, portraying that on the one hand the divinity of the *eikon* after the fall is intact enough that the sinful flesh gives way, but at the same time the *eikon* is vulnerable to the temptation of the devil through the flesh. Rather than presenting his readers with a definitive conclusion about a static *eikon*, Gregory presents us with the complexities of human existence, the negative aspects of which Gregory explains by the presence of a spiritual enemy.

Unfortunately for the *eikon*, the devil does not only attempt to destroy her through the flesh, since he works also through the passions to offer a further challenge to the *eikon*; a challenge which requires no slight resistance.[145] See below that when Gregory writes about Christ saving the cosmos, Christ finds his *eikon* 'confounded with passions':

---

[142] Carm. 2.1.45 (PG 37, 1353–78).   [143] Carm. 2.1.45 (PG 37, 1359, 75–76).
[144] 2 Pt. 2:4, 17; Homer *Il.* 21:56.
[145] Contra J. Patout Burns, 'The Economy of Salvation: Two Patristic Traditions' in Everett Ferguson (ed.), *Doctrines of Human Nature, Sin, and Salvation in the Early Church* (New York: Garland, 1993), 224–46, 228.

He lit a lamp, his own flesh, and he swept the house, cleansing the world from sin, he sought the coin, the royal *eikon* confounded with passions (τὴν βασιλικὴν εἰκόνα συγκεχωσμένην τοῖς πάθεσι); he called together the friendly powers to himself, on finding the coin.[146]

The vulnerability of the *eikon* becomes evident further through the passions since, as we observe above, Christ came to earth precisely to seek out 'the royal *eikon* confounded with passions'.[147] The passions are relevant to this study in two ways, since Gregory relates them both to the work of the devil and the *eikon*. Much of the debate relating to passions in the work of the early church fathers concerns whether the passions are neutral or intrinsically prone to sin, following Platonic[148] or Stoic[149] thought respectively.[150] Since the complexity of the passions and their classical heritage has been much discussed elsewhere, I shall refer only to the aspects of the passions relevant to my study on Gregory's approach to the devil and the *eikon*.[151] Much like his approach to the world and the flesh, Gregory does not define the passions systematically, although Gregory does inform his reader that he conceives the passions internally and that they require restraint; he also pronounces judgment upon those who yield to the passions.[152] Gregory argues further that sinful flesh works together with the passions, since the 'fleshy person' is the 'lover of passions'.[153]

---

[146] Or. 38.14 (SC 358, 136). Cf. Matt. 18:12–14; *Haer.* 3.19.3.

[147] Also, see Or. 2.18 (SC 247, 114); 2.26 (SC 247, 124); 2.91 (SC 247, 206–08).

[148] Plato varies on pathos; a positive stance can be seen in *Phaed.* 246ab, 253c–254b.

[149] John Rist, *Stoic Philosophy* (Cambridge: Cambridge University Press, 1969), 31–36.

[150] It is debated whether Paul follows Stoic thought, as he mentions passions on three occasions and on each occasion he is negative; 1 Thess. 4:5; Rom 1:26; Col 3:5.

[151] It is beyond the scope of this study to survey Gregory's entire use of πάθη, although I note that in addition to passions, Gregory also refers to the passion of Christ, Or. 3.7 (SC 247, 250); 4.7 (SC 309, 98); 5.9 (SC 309, 308); 32.23 (SC 318, 134); Carm. 1.2.33 (PG 37, 941, 176); suffering, Or. 18.22 (SC 405, 296); 20.8 (SC 270, 74); Carm. 2.1.19 (PG 37, 1271–79, 1–104); and bad theology, Or. 27.6 (SC 250, 84). God has no passions, Or. 25.17 (SC 284, 198); Carm. 1.1.10 (PG 37, 470, 64); angels have no passions, Carm. 1.2.1 (PG 37, 525, 35–40). For an overview of passions from Plato to Stoicism and beyond, see Christopher C.H. Cook, *The Philokalia and the Inner Life: On Passions and Prayer* (Eugene, OR: Wipf & Stock, 2012), 47–57; Kallistos Ware, 'The Meaning of "Pathos" in Abba Isaias and Theodoret of Cyrus' in Elizabeth A. Livingstone (ed.), *Studia Patristica*, 20 (Leuven: Peeters Press, 1989), 315–22, 315; Teresa M. Shaw, *The Burden of the Flesh: Fasting and Sexuality in Early Christianity* (Minneapolis: Fortress Press, 1998), 44–48.

[152] Or. 2.30 (SC 247, 128); 2.34 (SC 247, 132); 25.4 (SC 284, 164). For Gregory's judgment, see Or. 2.43 (SC 247, 146).

[153] Carm. 1.2.34 (PG 37, 963, 243). This betrays the Stoic influence; see Richard Sorabji, *Emotion and Peace of Mind* (Oxford: Oxford University Press, 2000), 394.

For a definition of the passions, we may look to Evagrius, Gregory's early protégé, who writes about the nature of the passions as 'a pleasure hostile to humanity, born of free will, and compelling the mind to make improper use of the creatures of God'.[154] The only occasion upon which Gregory is positive about the passions concerns consolation; when people require consolation, those responding must not be passionless (ἀπαθής).[155] Passions themselves may not be inherently evil, although they may be used by demons who desire to take up residence in a human person. This is evident in Gregory's poem *Against Anger*, where he writes, 'I am full of raging anger, living with a demon (θυμῷ χολοῦμαι τῷ συνοίκῳ δαίμονι)'.[156] Finally, Gregory makes clear that the passions, like evil spiritual beings, must be fought:

> Let us wrestle against the rulers, against the authorities, against the hidden perse-cutors and tyrants, against the world rulers of this darkness, against the spiritual beings of evil in the heavenly realms, and amongst the heavenly beings, against the internal war, within us and in the passions (πρὸς τὸν ἔνδον καὶ ἐν ἡμῖν αὐτοῖς τὸν ἐν τοῖς πάθεσι πόλεμον), against those insurrections rising up on a daily basis.[157]

In the passage above, a war occurs in the passions since the devil attempts to destroy the *eikon* by making use of the weakness already present through the passions. As we discussed earlier in this chapter, Gregory envisages the war against the devil as occurring within the human person. This points towards a parasitic demonic activity that requires the human *eikon* as a means of continuing its existence, which in turn supports my argument earlier on in this chapter that the devil and demons live a diminishing existence.

RESISTING THE DEVIL

Throughout the latter half of this chapter, I have argued that Gregory presents the devil working through the world, the flesh, and the passions. Attending to these in depth has highlighted the extent to which Gregory incorporates spiritual beings, their fall, and subsequent war on the human *eikon* into his overall theology. Being aware that this narrative of warfare is rather bleak, Gregory offers a defence of why God allows the devil to

---

[154] Translation in Cook, *The Philokalia and the Inner Life*, 55. For the Greek text, see SC 438. Gregory Nyssen was also an active influence upon Evagrius; see Ilaria L.E. Ramelli, 'Evagrius and Gregory: Nazianzen or Nyssen? Cappadocian (and Origenian) Influence on Evagrius', *GRBS*, 53 (2013), 117–37, 130.

[155] Or. 7.1 (SC 405, 180–82).   [156] Carm. 1.2.25 (PG 37, 813, 1).

[157] Or. 11.4 (SC 405, 338); 2.91 (SC 247, 206). Also see Eph. 6:12; *Princ. Praef.* 5.111.

continue thus, and why Christ did not annihilate him completely. The reasons offered by Gregory are three-fold: firstly, Christ wanted the devil and his minions to fight one another as a means of their punishment; secondly, those who struggle against the demons for virtue would win eternal glory; and thirdly, the devil might deal out punishments 'afterwards' to those who have followed him on earth.[158] Gregory's second point emphasises the free will of the human *eikon*, since she may choose whether or not to succumb to the temptations of the devil and his underlings, no longer being a slave to sin. However, Gregory does not account for the occasions upon which he himself attributes sickness, for example, to demonic activity; his justification for the continued existence of the devil does not explain certain physical illnesses which could hardly be resisted or be said to be within the human person's control.[159] Gregory is possibly aware of the inadequacy of his defence to a certain extent, which is why he laments the continued presence of the devil, in spite of having defended Christ's decision to allow the devil to continue to exist:

Would that evil (ἡ κακία) be destroyed utterly, both the first seed of evil, and the Evil One who sowed the weeds in us while we were sleeping.[160]

In light of Gregory's lament above in which he wishes that the devil would be destroyed completely, I am inclined to suggest that his defence of why the devil remains is not wholly sufficient. He might have argued further that the devil remains because he serves as a perpetual reminder of the catastrophic outcome when created beings, angelic or human, choose to worship themselves instead of God.

Gregory situates his writing about the devil within the realm of his own experience which, for Gregory, demonstrates that the devil and his minions remain vigorous in their attempt to destroy the *eikon*. As a response to this, he offers multiple ways in which to combat the devil. The initial means of victory over the devil is through Christ. As we explored in Chapter 2, Christ, the identical *Eikon,* conquered the devil both through the pattern of his life and in defeating death. Through this, the human *eikon* is able to enter into Christ's protection by being incorporated into Christ's death and resurrection by the Holy Spirit at baptism, which we will discuss in Chapter 5.[161] Gregory writes frequently regarding further means of protection and resistance available to the human *eikon*, recommending vigilance:

---

[158] Carm. 1.1.7 (PG 37, 445, 80–95).   [159] Carm. 2.1.89 (PG 37, 1442–45).
[160] Or. 19.14 (PG 35, 1060C).   [161] Or. 40.10 (SC 358, 216–18).

Keep yourself inaccessible, both in word and deed and life and thought and movement. The Evil One interferes with you from every side, he scopes you out everywhere, where he may strike, where he may wound. Do not let him find any corner laid open and ready for his blow. The purer he sees you, the more he is eager to stain you (ὅσῳ καθαρωτέραν ὁρᾷ, τοσούτῳ μᾶλλον σπιλῶσαι φιλονεικεῖ), for the stains on a brilliant garment are all the more visible.[162]

Whilst the *eikon* must be on her guard, vigilance is meaningless without faith in the Trinity and cooperation with God.[163] The nature of cooperation with God that Gregory advocates is the Christian life of asceticism.[164] Brakke has highlighted that asceticism as a means of victory over the devil is an area of research which is considerably lacking, since demonological theory has been deemed subjective in recent times. Thus, discussions on asceticism have turned towards topics which relate more closely to ideas of the body and the constructions of ascetic practices and institutions, such as monasteries.[165] This overlooks the primary world-view of the early church fathers; and more specifically, if we were to omit a discussion of the devil and demons when considering Gregory's theology and theological anthropology, his whole theological worldview regarding humankind would begin to unravel.

For Gregory, like church fathers before him, asceticism is concerned with resisting the devil, being built intrinsically into Christian life, since it forms the way of the 'new eschatological life granted in baptism within the confines of the present life'.[166] In order to live ascetically, Gregory recommends fasting, tears, silence, care of the poor, resisting wealth, virginity, prayer, and making the sign of the cross, which together form the means of remaining alert to God and to the devil's schemes.[167] Furthermore, Gregory suggests that human *eikones* must attempt to

---

[162] Or. 37.12 (SC 318, 296).

[163] Or. 2.21 (SC 247, 116–18); 6.22 (SC 405, 174–76); 11.4 (SC 405, 336–38).

[164] Or. 16.15–16 (PG 35, 953C–956D); 24.15 (SC 284, 74); 36.6 (SC 318, 254–56); see John Chryssavgis, *In the Heart of the Desert: The Spirituality of the Desert Fathers and Mothers* (IN: World Wisdom Inc., 2008), 37–40.

[165] Brakke, 'Making of Monastic Demonology', 19–20.

[166] John Behr, *Asceticism and Anthropology in Irenaeus and Clement* (Oxford: Oxford University Press, 2000), 17.

[167] Resisting wealth, Carm. 1.2.28 (PG 37, 863–81); 2.1.45 (PG 37, 1362); against women wearing ornaments, Carm. 1.2.29 (PG 37, 884–908); fasting, Or. 21.10 (SC 270, 130); care of the poor, Or. 14 (PG 35, 858A–909C); virginity, Carm. 1.2.1 (PG 37, 521–78); 1.2.2 (PG 37, 578–632); 1.2.3 (PG 37, 632–32); tears, Carm. 2.1.34 (PG 37, 1319); silence, Carm. 2.1.34 (PG 37, 1307–22); 2.1.35 (PG 37, 1322–25); prayer, Carm. 2.1.55 (PG 37, 1399–1400); 2.1.65 (PG 37, 1047); sign of the cross, Carm. 2.1.56 (PG 37, 1401, 11).

know and understand their identity in Christ, which means that they are becoming divine.[168] Overall, a significant amount of effort is required to resist the devil and stand against his army. The obvious place to begin is at baptism, since, as we shall see in Chapter 5, Gregory equates this with a seal of protection by the Holy Spirit.

This chapter has demonstrated that the human *eikon* incites envy from the devil because she is 'a living being ... being made god by her inclination towards God'.[169] This occasions a life of struggle and temptation as the devil seeks to destroy the *eikon*. I aimed to establish that any consideration of the *eikon* must take place alongside a discussion of the devil, although in making this move we must question the nature of the devil's existence. Responding to this, I argued that the devil and demons are not evil ontologically, since originally they were part of God's good creation. Catastrophically, they fell away from the near presence of God, and their subsequent role of continuing to do harm means that they are diminishing according to their existence, being compelled to work through the world, the flesh, and the passions as they endeavour to defeat the *eikon*.

Against the backdrop of the extra-biblical narrative, we have observed that the addition of the garments of skin add a further layer of vulnerability to the *eikon*, since they are accompanied by a propensity to sin. Through the garments, an ontological and epistemological change occurs in the existence of the *eikon*. She shifts from being angelic, spiritually alive and able to apprehend God, to being mortal, dull, and struggling to know God. Let us turn to the healing, restoration, and theosis of the *eikon*, through which we discuss further how Gregory presents the 'divine, yet vulnerable' *eikon*.

---

[168] Or. 1.4 (SC 247, 76–6); Carm. 2.1.54 (PG 37, 1399, 3–4).
[169] Or. 38.11 (SC 358, 126).

5

Theosis and the Divine Image

We have explored Gregory's vision of the human *eikon*, in which the *eikon* relates not only to the soul but also to the whole, dynamic human person. This argument has been formed in light of the unity of Christ, the identical *Eikon*, and against the backdrop of Genesis 1:26–27, which draws together beliefs about icons and idols. Gregory's account incorporates the struggles of being human, which, as a matter of priority, attempts to describe human experience rather than focusing solely upon the question, 'What is the *eikon*?' Drawing his inspiration from biblical and extra-biblical narratives, Gregory locates the human *eikon* in a cosmological battle with the forces of evil, which is only won through participation in Christ and the protection offered by the Holy Spirit.

This chapter continues to read the texts in light of biblical and extra-biblical narratives by turning to the healing and restoration of the human *eikon*. We will explore what Gregory may mean when he describes the *eikon* as 'divine', or as 'becoming a god'. We ask, 'how do we interpret the following claim?':

Who will renew the creature, and set forth the *eikon*, and fashion creatures for the world above, and even greater than that, to say we will be god and make others gods (τὸ μεῖζον εἰπεῖν θεὸν ἐσόμενον καὶ θεοποιήσοντα)?[1]

Whilst Gregory varies his description of the progressive divinity of the *eikon*, contemporary scholars usually refer to this as 'theosis'; a

---

[1] Or. 2.73 (SC 247, 186).

convention which I will follow here.[2] In order to respond to the question of how to interpret theosis, we will draw together the diverse aspects of Gregory's vision of the human *eikon* explored throughout this book. Hitherto, I have argued that Gregory's approach to the divine *eikon* encompasses beliefs relating to ontology, function, ethics, relationship, and experience. We have seen that the human *eikon* both participates in and functions like the identical *Eikon*, Christ. Here, we move on to argue that Gregory's depiction of theosis is best interpreted literally. To support this claim, we will examine together (a) Gregory's theological anthropology, in which God creates the human person to be specifically vulnerable (or porous) to the spiritual realm, (b) Gregory's doctrine of the Holy Spirit, in which the Spirit is consubstantial with the Father and the Son, (c) his view of baptism as a sacrament through which genuine transformation occurs, and (d) the interaction between the human *eikon* and the devil before and after baptism. I begin by locating my argument within contemporary discussions which pertain to Gregory's understanding of theosis. We shall see that there is little agreement amongst commentators on how we should interpret the vision of theosis found in the texts.

SPEAKING OF THEOSIS

By the fourth century, while Gregory was writing, the idea of a human becoming a god was well established in the church, although it was not defined explicitly until the late fifth/early sixth century, by Dionysios the Areopagite.[3] He defined theosis as 'attaining of likeness to God and union with Him so far as this is possible'.[4] It was not until the fourteenth century that Gregory Palamas defined an approach to theosis which distinguishes

---

[2] All of Gregory's theosis vocabulary is listed in Vladimir Kharlamov, 'Rhetorical Application of Theosis in Greek Patristic Thought' in Michael J. Christensen and Jeffrey A. Wittung (eds.), *Partakers of the Divine Nature: The History and Development of Deification in the Christian Traditions* (Grand Rapids, MI: Baker Academic, 2007), 115–31, 123–27. I shall not repeat his work here.

[3] Dionysios wrote circa AD 500, adopting the name of Paul's convert in Athens (Acts 17:34). An unknown Syrian, he is also known as Pseudo-Dionysios.

[4] *On Ecclesiastical Hierarchy 1*, PG 3, 376A; trans. Russell, *Doctrine of Deification*, 248. Russell draws attention to the Platonic echoes in Dionysius' words.

between God's energies and God's essence. This then became the accepted approach to theosis in Orthodox theology, albeit interpreted with different emphases, and received diversely by contemporary Eastern and Western theologians.[5] Note that Gregory Palamas writes at a much later time period than Nazianzen, in a different historical context, responding to different theological problems.

Theosis contributes significantly to Western notions of soteriology and theological anthropology. Whereas the Christian West has tended to explore salvation in juridical categories, the Christian East's focus on theosis leans more towards the restoration of the created identity of the human person and her subsequent potential. Rooted in the belief that the human person is made in the image and likeness of God, her potential is realised through theosis. Gregory himself was aware that the notion of 'becoming a god', or 'becoming divine', was a challenging or even shocking concept to grasp, since he offered the proviso 'dare I say' on more than one occasion when he spoke of theosis; but as Florovsky writes, 'it is the only adequate phrase to express what is meant'.[6]

As we shall discuss shortly, commentators question precisely what Gregory means when he writes, 'I shall make the divine *eikon* present to Christ (εἰκόνα θείην παραστήσω Χριστῷ)'.[7] Also, questions arise relating to passages such as the one below:

Know from where you have your being, from where you draw breath, your ability to think and greatest of all, your capacity to know God, to hope for the kingdom of heaven, the same value as angels, the perception of glory, which now is in mirrors and riddles, but then will be more perfect and more pure, for the potential to become a son of God, an heir together with Christ, even, dare I say, become god yourself (τολμήσας εἴπω καὶ θεὸν αὐτόν)?[8]

---

[5] The notion of energies and essence as key to Palamas' doctrine of theosis has been challenged by Doru Costache, 'Experiencing the Divine Life: Levels of Participation in St Gregory Palamas' on the Divine and Deifying Participation', *Phronema*, 26, no. 1 (2011), 9–25, and Anna N. Williams, 'Light from Byzantium: The Significance of Palamas' Doctrine of Theosis', *Pro Ecclesia* 3, no. 4 (1994), 483–96.

[6] Or. 14.23 (PG 35, 887A); 36.11 (SC 318, 264); 38.7 (SC 358, 116); Georges Florovsky, 'Lamb of God', *SJT*, 4, no. 1 (1951), 13–28, 19.

[7] Carm. 2.1.50 (PG 37, 1389, 61–62); 1.2.18 (PG 37, 787, 14).

[8] Or. 14.23 (PG 35, 888A).

The response to Gregory's portrayal of the divinity of the *eikon* ranges as widely as suggesting that it is metaphorical,[9] rhetorical,[10] real,[11] or ontological.[12] At the same time, while commenting on theosis, scholars often leave these categories undefined. When no categories are applied, comments about theosis become even more vague, such as, 'an extraordinary kind of being in a state of blessedness'.[13] However, when we consider below the number of different strands which Gregory weaves into his vision of theosis, it is not surprising that confusion abounds. Gregory includes in his discussions on theosis: ideas about God,[14] the Holy Spirit,[15] knowledge of God,[16] confession of correct doctrine,[17] pastoral responsibility,[18] baptism,[19] mystery,[20] immortality,[21] Christian

[9] Kharlamov, 'Rhetorical Application of Theosis', 115–31, 126; Norman Russell, *The Doctrine of Deification in the Greek Patristic Tradition* (Oxford: Oxford University Press, 2004), 213–25; Jules Gross, *The Divinization of the Christian according to the Greek Fathers*, trans. Paul Onica (Anaheim, California: A&C Press, 2002), 197; Norris, *Faith Gives Fullness*, 50; Paul M. Collins, 'Between Creation and Salvation: Theosis and Theurgy' in Vladimir Kharlamov (ed.), *Theosis: Deification in Christian Theology*, vol. 2 (Cambridge: James Clarke & Co., 2012), 192–204, 67; Winslow, *Dynamics of Salvation*, 179–200.

[10] Vladimir Kharlamov, 'Basil of Caesarea and the Cappadocians on the Distinction between Essence and Energies in God and its Relevance to the Deification Theme', in Vladimir Kharlamov (ed.), *Theosis: Deification in Christian Theology*, vol. 2 (Cambridge: James Clarke & Co., 2012), 100–45, 120; Norris, *Faith Gives Fullness*, 51.

[11] Susanna Elm, *Sons of Hellenism, Fathers of the Church: Emperor Julian, Gregory of Nazianzus, and the Vision of Rome* (Berkeley: University of California Press, 2012), 180; Beeley, *Trinity and the Knowledge of God*, 119.

[12] John A. McGuckin, 'The Strategic Adaptation of Deification in the Cappadocians' in Michael J. Christensen and Jeffery A. Wittung (eds.), *Partakers of the Divine Nature: The History and Development of Deification in the Christian Traditions* (Madison: Fairleigh Dickinson University Press, 2007), 95–114, 95.

[13] Torstein Theodor Tollefsen, 'Theosis according to Gregory' in Jostein Børtnes and Tomas Hägg (eds.), *Gregory of Nazianzus: Images and Reflections* (Copenhagen: Museum Tusculanum, 2006), 257–70, 259.

[14] Carm. 1.1.10 (PG 37, 469, 56–61); Or. 23.12 (SC 270, 304).

[15] Ors. 31, 40, 41, passim.

[16] Or. 14.23 (PG 35, 887A); 28.17 (SC 250, 134–36); 38.5 (SC 358, 110–12).

[17] Or. 23.12 (SC 270, 304); 31.4 (SC 250, 282); 34.12 (SC 318, 218).

[18] Or. 2.22 (SC 247, 118–20); 2.73 (SC 247, 186).

[19] Carm. 1.1.9 (PG 37, 464, 90–94); Or. 40 (SC 358), passim. See Hilarion Alfeyev, 'The Deification of Man in Eastern Patristic Tradition (with special reference to Gregory Nazianzen, Symeon the New Theologian and Gregory Palamas)', *Colloquium*, 36, no. 2 (2004), 109–22, 116.

[20] Or. 38.11 (SC 358, 124–26). Theosis is perceived as a mystery that takes place within the human person 'through God's supernatural power, and as such is essentially unutterable'; Georgios I. Mantzaridis, *The Deification of Man* (Crestwood, NY: St. Vladimir's Seminary Press, 1984), 127.

[21] Or. 38.13 (SC 358, 134); Carm. 1.1.8 (PG 37, 452, 75).

life,[22] participation,[23] Christ's sufferings,[24] doing good,[25] and spiritual warfare.[26] Theosis is both present and eschatological, since becoming divine is a process which is only realised at the 'Final Day'.[27] Furthermore, Gregory incorporates soteriology, following early theologians such as Irenaeus and Athanasius, who understood the divinity of human persons in terms of a divine exchange:[28]

Let us become like Christ, since Christ became like us. Let us become gods for his sake, since he became human for our sakes (γενώμεθα θεοὶ δι 'αὐτόν, ἐπειδὴ κἀκεῖνος δι 'ἡμᾶς ἄνθρωπος).[29]

In an attempt to find a way of speaking about theosis, various classifications have been offered. One of the most recent was made by Russell who, extending the work of Gross, categorised the ways in which the early church fathers used theosis language as nominal, analogical and metaphorical.[30] The metaphorical method comprises of two sub-categories: the ethical and the realistic approaches. The ethical approach involves attainment of likeness to God through ascetical endeavour; to be in the likeness of God means to possess divine attributes acquired through the imitation of Christ. In the realistic approach, theosis is participation in the divine that 'in some sense' transforms the human person.[31] It appears that for Russell, the ethical approach involves behaving like God, whereas the realistic approach entails becoming like God, where theosis effects a transformation in the person being deified, albeit this

---

[22] Carm. 1.1.2 (PG 37, 622, 555–64).

[23] Or. 7.23 (SC 405, 240); Frederick W. Norris, 'Deification: Consensual and Cogent', *SJT*, 49, no. 4 (1996), 411–28, 413.

[24] Carm. 2.1.34 (PG 37, 1313, 83).   [25] Or. 17.9 (PG 35, 976B–D).

[26] Or. 2.22–25 (SC 247, 118–24); 11.5 (SC 405, 338–40); 17.9 (PG 35, 976B–D); 40.10 (SC 358, 216–18).

[27] Or. 4.121 (SC 309, 286–88); 14.20 (PG 37, 881D–884B); 20:1 (SC 270, 56–58); 43.48 (SC 384, 226–28); Moreschini, *Filosofia e letteratura*, 34–36; Kenneth Paul Wesche, 'The Doctrine of Deification: A Call to Worship', *Theology Today*, 65, no. 2 (2008), 169–79, 176.

[28] *Haer.* 5, Praef.; *De Incarn.* 54.

[29] Or. 1.5 (SC 247, 78); 29.19 (SC 250, 218); 30.14 (SC 250, 256); 32.14 (SC 318, 114); Carm. 1.1.11 (PG 37, 471, 9–10); 1.2.14 (PG 37, 762, 92); 2.1.1 (PG 37, 971, 15–20); 2.1.34 (PG 37, 1313, 83–84).

[30] For information on the additional categories of theosis as educational, ethical, mystical, and ritual, see Collins, 'Theosis and Theurgy', 192.

[31] Russell, *Doctrine of Deification*, 3.

remains a metaphor.[32] The nature of the transformation that takes place and how it occurs is unclear according to Russell's analysis. Russell engages with Donald Winslow's seminal work on theosis in Gregory's writing; Winslow defines theosis as a metaphor consisting of spatial, visual, epistemological, ethical, corporate, and social aspects.[33] Reducing Winslow's six-dimensional metaphor, Russell describes the application of theosis in Gregory's work as having 'five different senses'. These are: intermingling with God through the incarnation of the Son (Or. 1.5), baptismal (Or. 7.22), ethical (Or. 30.4), eschatological (Or. 7.21), and analogous (Or. 42.17).[34] Russell states that Gregory is only interested in theosis as imitation, overlooking the occasions when Gregory states that he participated in the *Eikon* (μετέλαβον τῆς εἰκόνος, καὶ οὐκ ἐφύλαξα).[35]

It is possible that commentators, such as Russell, locate the divinity of the *eikon* as metaphorical because they focus on the only occasion on which Gregory states that the creature is not God:

> Let us say then, on the one hand, that a creature is 'of God', (κτίσα δέ, θεοῦ μὲν λέγεσθω) for even this is a great thing to be said about us, but 'God', not at all (θεὸς δὲ μηδαμῶς). Only then will I accept graciously that a creature is God, whenever even I become literally God. It is like this: If it is God, it is not a creature, for the creature is classed with us who are not the gods. But if it is a creature it is not God, for it began in time.[36]

As a result of Gregory's caution demonstrated above, some commentators adopt a sceptical approach arguing that Gregory does not mean what he writes.[37] The debate about theosis in Gregory's work sometimes functions in a manner akin to those arguments in biblical studies, which occur when scholars make their argument through proof-texting. Gregory's corpus is so vast that if we locate our argument in light of only one passage, it is quite easy to argue for approaches which are either metaphorical,

---

[32] For an alternative classification, see Ivan P. Popov, 'The Idea of Deification in the Early Eastern Church' in Vladimir Kharlamov (ed.), *Theosis: Deification in Christian Theology*, vol. 2 (Cambridge: James Clarke & Co., 2012), 42–82. He classifies Clement of Alexandria, Origen, the Cappadocians, Ps. Dionysius, and Maximus the Confessor as 'idealist', which he claims is rooted in Neo-Platonist participation; ibid., 43–45.

[33] Winslow, *Dynamics of Salvation*, 193–98.   [34] Russell, *Doctrine of Deification*, 223.

[35] Or. 38.13 (SC 358, 134); Russell, *Doctrine of Deification*, 214.

[36] Or. 42.17 (SC 384, 86). Note that Gregory's usual connotation of Creator/creature difference negates any belief that creatures exist eternally.

[37] Or. 42.17 (SC 384, 86). For example, Kharlamov, 'Rhetorical Application of Theosis', 115–31, 126; Norman Russell, *The Doctrine of Deification in the Greek Patristic Tradition* (Oxford: Oxford University Press, 2004), 213–25.

rhetorical, real, or ontological. Responding to the sceptics, Elm argues that Gregory's theosis is 'real' and not a 'metaphor'.[38] She builds her argument on the grounds that Gregory's approach to theosis is worked out principally in two orations: *In Defence of His Flight to Pontus* and *Against Julian*.[39] Elm is correct in her assessment, although it is clear neither what she means by 'real', nor how her approach demonstrates that theosis is not a metaphor. I hope to build on her claim through the course of this chapter, at the same time arguing for a broad understanding of Gregory's theosis. In light of our discussion thus far, I propose that Gregory considers the divinity of the *eikon* relationally, functionally, ethically, experientially and ontologically; moreover, relating to every aspect of her life.

Philosophical Influences

Before we move on, we must pause to consider the philosophical context of Gregory's beliefs. In the same way that commentators debate what Gregory might mean by theosis, they also contend from where he drew his primary influences. Theosis sounds very like apotheosis, the process through which the Roman emperor or people of distinction were made divine.[40] Note however that Christian theosis does not occur in Gregory's writing with a prefix. By using a neologism, Gregory expresses 'becoming god' as a distinctively Christian belief. That said, debates abound regarding whether Gregory drew primarily from Platonic or Stoic sources in order to construct his account.

---

[38] Susanna Elm, 'Priest and Prophet: Gregory of Nazianzus's Concept of Christian Leadership as Theosis' in Beate Dignas, Robert Parker, and Guy G. Stroumsa (eds.), *Priests and Prophets among Pagans, Jews and Christians* (Leuven: Peeters, 2013), 162–84, 177–78.

[39] Or. 2 (SC 247, 84–240), popularly entitled *On Priesthood*; Or. 4 (SC 309, 86–292).

[40] For a review of the process, see Aleš Chalupa, 'How Did Roman Emperors Become Gods? Various Concepts of Imperial Apotheosis*', *Anodos: Studies of the Ancient World*, 6, no. 7 (2007), 201–07. If we read as far back as Homer, often θεός is linked to acts of speaking; Walter Burkert, 'From Epiphany to Cult Statue: Early Greek Theos' in Alan B. Lloyd (ed.), *What is a God?: Studies in the Nature of Greek Divinity* (London: Duckworth 1997), 15–34. Nock suggests that the semantic field for θεός is so wide that it can be used to denote anything which is 'the incalculable non-human element in phenomena'; Arthur D. Nock, 'A Diis Electa' in Zeph Stewart (ed.), *Essays on Religion and the Ancient World* (Oxford: Clarendon Press, 1972), 232–76, 260.

Many commentators argue that Gregory follows a Platonic under-standing of theosis.[41] Andrew Louth explains that the Platonic concept of 'becoming like God as far as possible' (φυγὴ δὲ ὁμοίωσις θεῷ κατὰ τὸ δυνατόν) was so familiar to the fathers that Genesis 1:26 would have been heard in light of this, as we discussed briefly in Chapter 1.[42] Consequently, he argues that ὁμοίωσις in Genesis 1:26 would have been interpreted by the fathers as a process of assimilation, like that found in Plato's *Theaetetus*.[43] When speaking of our theologian, however, we must bear in mind, as Maslov and Elm have both observed, that Gregory does not actually appeal directly to Plato's phrase.[44] Maslov has suggested a further philo-sophical metaphor of Stoic origin as a precursor for Gregory's theosis: '*oikeiosis pros theon* or "familiarity" with the divine, both pre-given and subject to self-conscious cultivation'.[45] Maslov observes that whilst the phrase does not occur together with theosis, 'Gregory combines each with the notion of ascent to God (*anabasis*)'.[46]

Whilst I agree that Gregory's theosis is connected to journeying towards God, I believe that there is more to be said. It is interesting that with the exception of theologians such as Molac and Tollefsen, discus-sions about Gregory's primary inspiration for theosis do not account for biblical inspiration.[47] We have seen that Gregory plays on beliefs about images and idols, which is evident through his interpretation of the creation narratives in Genesis. He conflates Genesis 1 and 2 to establish that the human *eikon* was made from the dust of the earth and God's breath. Furthermore, we saw in Chapter 1 that the ancient cultures considered a close affiliation between the image of a god and the god itself. With this in mind, it is not difficult to understand how Gregory envisaged the human *eikon* as a god. Added to this, elsewhere in the Old

---

[41] Gross, *Divinization of the Christian*, 266; Hubert Merki, ὁμοίωσις θεῷ. *Von der platonischen Angleichung an Gott zur Gottähnlichkeit bei Gregor von Nyssa* (Freiburg, Swizerland: Paulusverlag, 1952), 105.

[42] *Theaet.* 176a; Louth, 'The Fathers on Genesis', 573; Sedley, 'The Ideal of Godlikeness', 309.

[43] Contra Boris Maslov, 'The Limits of Platonism: Gregory of Nazianzus and the Invention of Theosis', *GRBS*, 52 (2012), 440–468. The Greek development of theosis through Neo-Platonic philosophers such as Plotinus differed radically from the earliest Christian notions of theosis; David Litwa, *Becoming Divine: An Introduction to Deification in Western Culture* (Eugene, Oregon: Wipf & Stock, 2013), 102–17.

[44] Maslov, 'Limits of Platonism', 447; Elm, *Sons of Hellenism*, 178.   [45] Ibid., 178.

[46] Maslov, 'Limits of Platonism', 450.

[47] Other verses connected with theosis are marginally explored by Tollefsen, 'Theosis according to Gregory', 258–59. See also Philippe Molac, *Douleur et transfiguration*, 104.

Testament, the explicit mention of human persons as gods occurs in Exodus 7:1 and Psalm 81:6 (82:6), to which Jesus appeals in John 10:35, all of which Gregory draws from when discussing theosis.[48]

Observe below Gregory's reflection on the narrative of the human person as made in the *eikon* of God. Beginning with Psalm 8, and continuing with an abundance of Pauline ideas, Gregory clearly understands theosis to be the telos of the *eikon* which is apparent in Scripture:

> What is the human person that you are mindful of her?[49] What is this new mystery about me? I am small and great, lowly and lofty, mortal and immortal,[50] earthly and heavenly. I share these things with the world below, those things with God; these things with the flesh, those things with the Spirit. It is necessary for me to be buried with Christ,[51] to rise with Christ,[52] to inherit together with Christ,[53] to become a son of God,[54] indeed to be called god myself (θεὸν αὐτὸν κληθῆναι) ...[55] This is the great mystery for us, that God wills this for us, having been made man on our account and become poor, that God might raise our flesh, and restore the *eikon* and fashion the human person anew (ἀνασῴσηται τὴν εἰκόνα καὶ ἀναπλάσῃ τὸν ἄνθρωπον), that we might all become one in Christ, who was made perfectly in each one of us, as much as he is in himself. [56]

In the passage above, we may see that becoming a god must be understood in light of Christ and the salvation history, as narrated in the Bible. Theosis revolves around the created purpose of the *eikon*, who, after being damaged, is restored through Christ. This is not a theme drawn from either Plato or Stoicism, and whilst Gregory is influenced undoubtedly by the philosophical worldview of the fourth century, it is difficult to dispute that Gregory drew his inspiration and understanding from biblical narratives.

Thus far in this chapter we have located Gregory's view of theosis within the context of contemporary discussions. These relate primarily to the following: (a) questions of linguistics, i.e. is Gregory speaking metaphorically or literally?; and (b) debates about Gregory's primary source of influence, i.e. was he drawing from Plato or the Stoics? In order to answer b), I have sought to establish some of the ways in which Gregory draws on

---

[48] Or. 40.6 (SC 358, 206) and Ep. 101.44 (SC 208, 54) respectively. See Carl Mosser, 'The Earliest Patristic Interpretations of Psalm 82, Jewish Antecedents, and the Origin of Christian Deification', *JTS*, 56, no. 1 (2005), 30–74, 58. Scholars have scoured Jewish sources to investigate how Jn. 10:35 relates to Ps. 81:6 (82:6); James S. Ackerman, 'The Rabbinic Interpretation of Psalm 82 and the Gospel of John', *HTR*, 59, no. 2 (1966), 186–91.

[49] Ps. 8:4–6.   [50] 1 Cor. 15:53.   [51] Rom. 6:4; Col. 2:12.   [52] Col. 2:13; 3:1.

[53] Rom. 8:17.   [54] Jn. 1:12; 11:52; Rom. 8:14–16.   [55] Ps. 81:6.

[56] Or. 7.23 (SC 405, 238–40).

biblical images and the whole salvation narrative in his construction of theosis. We will continue to explore these later in the chapter. Now we return to the question of how to interpret Gregory's view of theosis. By attending closely to Gregory's theological anthropology, high pneumatology, and discussions of baptism, I will argue that Gregory's theosis is best understood literally. Moreover, we shall see how he incorporates ontology, relationality, functionality, ethics, and experience into his overall view of theosis. Let us begin by examining Gregory's approach to the Spirit, to whom he attributes the action of deifying the *eikon*.

THE HOLY SPIRIT AND THEOSIS

Soul, why do you delay? Sing praise of the Spirit . . .
Let us stand in awe of the mighty Spirit, who is the same as God,
    through whom I know God,
through whom God is present, and who forms me into a god in
    this world (καὶ ὅς θεὸν ἐνθάδε τεύχει).[57]

Two inseparable reasons for the Spirit's indispensability to the healing and theosis of the *eikon* are: (a) Gregory's doctrine of God and (b) the Spirit's activity both in the Church and the lives of individual Christians; or, in other words, the Spirit's identity in the transcendent and immanent Trinity.[58]

We begin with a brief overview of Gregory's argument for the Spirit's deity. As discussed in Chapter 2, Gregory upholds the Nicene Christian tradition of professing faith in one God:

---

[57] Carm. 1.1.3 (PG 37, 402, 1–4).

[58] Full-length studies on Gregory's approach to the Holy Spirit include Thomas A. Noble, 'The Deity of the Holy Spirit according to Gregory of Nazianzus' (Ph.D. Diss., Edinburgh, 1989); Daniel G. Opperwall, 'The Holy Spirit in the Life and Writings of Gregory of Nazianzus' (Ph.D. Diss., Open Access Dissertations and Theses: McMaster, 2012). Both studies claim to be the first ever study on Gregory's approach to the Holy Spirit, but Noble's study is the forerunner. Shorter overviews exist; see Philip Kariatlis, '"What then? Is the Spirit God? Certainly!" St Gregory's Teaching on the Holy Spirit as the Basis of the World's Salvation', *Phronema*, 26, no. 2 (2011), 81–102; Christopher A. Beeley, 'The Holy Spirit in the Cappadocians: Past and Present', *Modern Theology*, 26, no. 1 (2010), 90–119; Christopher A. Beeley, 'The Holy Spirit in Gregory Nazianzen: The Pneumatology of Oration 31' in Andrew Brian McGowan, Brian Edward Daley, and Timothy J. Gaden (eds.), *God in Early Christian Thought: Essays in Memory of Lloyd G. Patterson* (Leiden, Netherlands: Brill, 2009), 151–62. For Origin's influence upon Gregory's pneumatology, see Noble, 'Deity of the Holy Spirit', 25–30.

We have one God because there is one Godhead. Though there are three in which to believe, they derive from One and have reference to it. While one is not more, one is not less, than God. One is not before and another after. They are not split in will or divided in power (οὐδὲ βουλήσει τέμνεται, οὐδὲ δυνάμει μερίζεται). Nor does there exist that which is in things divisible. In short, the Godhead exists undivided in beings divided.[59]

Gregory's belief that God is One means that he fights vociferously for the deity of the Spirit in an attempt to persuade the other bishops to acknowledge this doctrine. In an oration dedicated to the Holy Spirit, Gregory combats his opponents' criticism that he was introducing a strange and unscriptural God.[60] He argues his case for the Spirit by citing Scripture. For example, when discussing the Holy Spirit's unique identity that differentiates the Spirit from the Father and the Son within the Godhead, Gregory cites the occasions in the Bible where the Spirit proceeds in the Spirit's own right, rather than only at the bidding of the Father and the Son.[61] Since the Spirit is God, Gregory is adamant that the Spirit is a distinct identity (ὑπόστασις) and attempts to convince his opponents by listing the behaviour of the Holy Spirit in Scripture, with expressions such as 'He speaks, he decrees, he is grieved, he is vexed ...'[62]

As far as Gregory is concerned, anything less than the Spirit's equality within the Godhead would result in a plethora of gods. Gregory argues that since God is One, the Holy Spirit is consubstantial with the Father and the Son:

What then? Is the Spirit God? Absolutely! Is he consubstantial (ὁμοούσιον)? Yes, if [the Spirit] is God.[63]

Gregory's language is thus explicit regarding the Spirit's consubstantiality, which contrasts with Basil, who, whilst arguing for the divinity

---

[59] Or. 31.14 (SC 250, 302), translation adapted from Lionel Wickham and Frederick Williams, *St. Gregory of Nazianzus: On God and Christ: The Five Theological Orations and Two Letters of Cledonius*, PPS (Crestwood, New York: St. Vladimir's Seminary Press, 2002), 127–28.

[60] Or. 31.3 (SC 250, 278). For a discussion on the uses of Adam and Eve with the argument of the Holy Spirit, see Alexander Golitzin, 'Adam, Eve and Seth: Pneumatological Reflections on an Unusual Image in Gregory of Nazianzus's Fifth Theological Oration', *ATR*, 83, no. 3 (2001), 537–46.

[61] Or. 31.26 (SC 250, 326–28); 25.15 (SC 284, 194). For further comment, see Arthur H. Armstrong, *The Cambridge History of Later Greek and Early Medieval Philosophy* (Cambridge: Cambridge University Press, 1967), 445.

[62] Or 31.6 (SC 250, 286); 31.29 (SC 250, 332–36).

[63] Or. 31.10 (SC 250, 292). This was a 'radical claim to make'; Behr, *The Nicene Faith*, vol. 2, 363.

of the Holy Spirit, refuses to support explicitly the statement that the Spirit is consubstantial with the Father and the Son, due to his belief that the Church must not depart from biblical language concerning doctrine.[64] Gregory's conviction that the bishops must declare their belief in the consubstantiality of the Holy Spirit results in his resignation when he does not achieve his aim. In a poem entitled *On His Own Life*, Gregory provides a dramatic account of this event, in which he depicts himself making a sacrificial resignation to preserve unity in the Church:

> Now I become Jonas the prophet. I am giving myself as a victim for the safety of the ship, even though it will be a case of the innocent encountering the waves.[65]

Gregory's emphasis on the distinctiveness in personhood speaks to Western Christians in the twenty-first century as we continue to explore the nature of the Trinity. A consequence of our focus on relationality in the West is that the Holy Spirit can either be reduced to a mere bond of love between the Father and the Son or worse, overlooked almost entirely.[66] Gregory, however, is keen to demonstrate that the Spirit is equally God, rather than merely a bond of union between the Father and the Son. Before moving on to explore the impact of Gregory's pneumatology upon our interpretation of the divinity of the human *eikon*, we establish further the significance of the Spirit to the life of the Church.

The Spirit calls those who are pastors and bishops,[67] guides the leaders of the Church,[68] unifies the Church,[69] reveals correct doctrine,[70] purifies through fire,[71] renews,[72] inspires preaching,[73] and, for Gregory particularly, the Spirit is one who plays him as though he were a musical instrument.[74] The work of the Holy Spirit does not end there, since it is through the Spirit that the 'Father is known and ... the Son is glorified and known'.[75] Gregory applies knowledge (γνῶσις) to describe the Spirit's revelation of the Father and the Son; thus he does not express knowledge

---

[64] See Ep. 102.1 (SC 208, 70–72) for Gregory's comments on the travesty of the Holy Spirit not being recognised in the Creed in the way Gregory thought to be correct.

[65] Carm. 2.1.11 (PG 37, 1839–50); trans. Meehan, *Three Poems*, 128.

[66] Kallistos Ware, 'The Trinity: Heart of Our Life' in James S. Cutsinger (ed.), *Reclaiming the Great Tradition* (Downers Grove, IL: Intervarsity Press, 1997), 125–46, 133.

[67] Or. 33.13 (SC 318, 184).   [68] Or. 12.2 (SC 405, 350).

[69] Or. 34.6 (SC 318, 206–08).   [70] Or. 29.1 (SC 250, 176).

[71] Or. 41.12 (SC 358, 340).   [72] Or. 7.15 (SC 405, 218); 8.20 (SC 405, 290).

[73] Or. 12.1 (SC 405, 348).   [74] Or. 12.1 (SC 405, 348).   [75] Or. 41.9 (SC 358, 336).

in terms of the intellect of a human person, but rather in terms of revelation of a relationship with God.[76]

John Egan has argued, quite rightly, that Gregory's understanding of the knowledge of God is also linked to his perception of light and illumination, since those who know God through the Holy Spirit are illumined.[77] Further to Egan's valuable contribution, note that Gregory also connects both knowledge and illumination to the concept of life in the Spirit. This becomes clear through Gregory's use of Psalm 12 (13), which he applies as a means of stating that those who do not know God are in danger of death:

If you are blind and without illumination, 'illumine your eyes, so that you may never sleep in death'.[78]

Above, Gregory links the knowledge of God and illumination to life, since those who guard against death remain spiritually alive. Accordingly, a further significant role of the Spirit is to give life to the believer through the knowledge of God.

Thus far, we have observed the lengths to which Gregory goes to argue that the Holy Spirit is consubstantially God, and how Gregory presents the Spirit as one who gives life, providing significant gifts to the Church. With this in mind, we now turn to consider how Gregory links the Holy Spirit intrinsically to the theosis of the human *eikon*. Theosis must not be expressed on a Christological basis alone; rather, it should be developed in conjunction with a robust pneumatology.[79]

In discussing the Spirit's identity, Gregory moves between the transcendent Trinity, the Spirit's economy within creation,[80] the Church, and the life of Christian individuals; this leads to his claim that the Spirit must be God, since it is the Spirit who deifies believers. Gregory's confession of belief 'in the Almighty Father, and in the Only Begotten word, and in the Holy Spirit

---

[76] For example, Matt. 1:25 uses γιγνώσκω to explain that Mary and Joseph did not have sexual intercourse until after Jesus was born. Whilst Gregory clearly does not present this type of relationship through his use of γιγνώσκω, he would have been aware of its wide semantic field.

[77] John P. Egan, *The Knowledge and Vision of God according to Gregory Nazianzen: A Study of the Images of Mirror and Light* (Paris: Institut catholique de Paris, 1971), passim. His argument is supported by Beeley, *Trinity and the Knowledge of God*, 104.

[78] Or. 40.34 (SC 358, 276); Ps. 12.3 (13:3).

[79] The significance of the Holy Spirit is often overlooked; Myrrha Lot-Borodine, *La Déification de l'homme, selon la doctrine des Pères grecs* (Paris: Les Éditions du Cerf, 1970), 12.

[80] Or. 41.11 (SC 358, 338).

who is also God',[81] is crucial to theosis; for it means that it is God who deifies believers. See below how Gregory asserts this in various orations:

If I was still worshipping a creature, or I was baptised into a creature, I would not be being made god nor would I have transformed my first birth (οὐκ ἂν ἐθεούμην οὐδὲ τὴν πρώτην μετεποιούμην γέννησιν).[82]

Therefore the Holy Spirit is always participated in, but does not participate; perfecting but is not perfected, filling but is not filled; sanctifying but is not sanctified, deifying but is not deified (θεοῦν, οὐ θεούμενον).[83]

If [the Spirit] is ranked with me, how does [the Spirit] make me god, or how does [the Spirit] attach me to deity (πῶς ἐμὲ ποιεῖ θεόν, ἢ πῶς συνάπτει θεότητι)?[84]

Through the Spirit's presence the language of theosis is set within the doctrine of God.[85] It is God who saves and deifies; theosis is a gift and not something which human persons are able to manufacture for themselves:

I, too, myself am an *eikon* of God, from the glory above, although I have been placed below (εἰκών εἰμι καὶ αὐτὸς Θεοῦ, τῆς ἄνω δόξης, εἰ καὶ κάτω τέθειμαι). I am not persuaded that I am saved by one who is of equal honour. If the Holy Spirit is not God, let [the Spirit] be made God first and then let [the Spirit] deify me who is of equal honour to [the Spirit].[86]

As I have already argued, the deifying of the *eikon* by the Spirit attracts the envy of the devil. Before moving on to demonstrate how the Spirit acts as a shield for the *eikon* when the devil attacks her, I must make one further point regarding Gregory's doctrine of the Spirit, which relates to the distinction between God and the newly-formed god. Theologians such as Zizioulas and Torrance have argued that the pre-Palamite distinction between God's energies and essence is evident in Gregory Nazianzen's work, and that, consequently, Gregory presents a picture in which the human *eikon* participates in God's energies but not in God's essence.[87] Torrance builds his argument on the premise that in speaking about the doctrine of God, both Palamas and Nazianzen apply the metaphor of

---

[81] Or. 12.6 (SC 405, 360); 3.6 (SC 247, 248–50); 21.37 (SC 270, 190–92); 33.16 (SC 318, 192).

[82] Or. 40.42 (SC 358, 296).   [83] Or. 41.9 (SC 358, 334).

[84] Or 31.4 (SC 250, 280–82).

[85] Louis Bouyer, *The Spirituality of the New Testament and the Fathers*, trans. Mary P. Ryan (London: Burns and Oates, 1963), 348–50.

[86] Or. 34.12 (SC 318, 218).

[87] Zizioulas, *Being as Communion*, 91; Or. 12.1 (SC 405, 348); Torrance, 'Palamas' Essence-Energies Theology', 61.

light.[88] However, since many other authors, including biblical writers, apply light as a metaphor for God, this does not build a strong case for a Palamite distinction of God's energies and essence in the work of Nazianzen.[89] Torrance bases his argument upon the metaphor of light, as Gregory does not apply frequently the language of activity (ἐνέργεια) in relation to God, and even when Gregory speaks of the ἐνέργεια of God, it is as a concession to his opponents.[90]

Rather than focusing upon God's activity, Gregory speaks of God's power (δύναμις) on numerous occasions.[91] Gregory makes it explicit that God's power precedes activity, thus any 'activity presupposes power', a sequence which Gregory Nyssen also applies.[92] In his discussions of God's power, Nazianzen varies between descriptions of the power of God, the power of Christ,[93] and the power of the Spirit.[94] Through his application of power, Gregory does not imply that being or nature lie behind power, either in his discussions of the Son or the Spirit:

Each of the Trinity is in entire unity as much with [Godself] as with the partnership, by identity of being and power (ἀλλὰ τὸ ἓν ἕκαστον αὐτῶν ἔχει πρὸς τὸ συγκείμενον οὐχ ἧττον ἢ πρὸς ἑαυτό, τῷ ταὐτῷ τῆς οὐσίας καὶ τῆς δυνάμεως).[95]

... to persuade all humankind as best as I am able, to worship the Father, and the Son and the Holy Spirit, one divinity and power (τὴν θεότητά τε καὶ δύναμιν), for to God belongs all glory, honour, authority, for age upon age. Amen.[96]

---

[88] Torrance, 'Palamas' Essence-Energies Theology', 61–63.

[89] For example, φῶς is given 'theological rank' in John and 1 John; see Hans Conzelmann, 'φῶς' in Gerhard Kittel and Gerhard Freidrich (eds.), *Φ-Ω TDNT*, vol. 9 (Grand Rapids: Eerdmans, 1974), 310–58, 343.

[90] According to a TLG (Thesaurus Linguae Graecae) search (10/06/2016, 11.16 AM), ἐνέργεια appears on only 27 occasions in texts regarded to be authentic to Gregory. See, for example, Or. 29.16 (SC 250, 210). Here Gregory discusses the challenge from his opponents that Father must designate either substance (οὐσία) or activity (ἐνέργεια). Gregory argues that Father designates relation (σχέσις), moving on to say that if Father must designate activity, then activity must also apply to begottenness.

[91] According to a TLG search (10/06/2016, 11.20 AM), δύναμις appears on 282 occasions in texts regarded to be authentic to Gregory.

[92] Or. 29.7 (SC 250, 190). See Michel R. Barnes, *The Power of God: Dunamis in Gregory of Nyssa's Trinitarian Theology* (Washington, DC: Catholic University of America Press, 2001), 293.

[93] Or. 2.98 (SC 247, 216); 29.17 (SC 250, 212); 30.20 (SC 250, 268); 38.18 (SC 358, 146).

[94] Or. 30.1 (SC 250, 226); 31.26 (SC 250, 326); 32.21 (SC 318, 128); 41.11 (SC 358, 338); 41.14 (SC 358, 344); 42.22 (SC 384, 100).

[95] Or. 31.16 (SC 250, 306); translation, Wickham and Williams, 2002, 129.

[96] Or. 31.33 (SC 250, 342). Also see Or. 1.7 (SC 247, 80–82); 22.12 (SC 270, 242–44); 31.28 (SC 250, 330); 40.41 (SC 358, 292); 41.7 (SC 358, 330); 43.67 (SC 384, 272–74).

And we know the Father and the Son and the Holy Spirit as God ... but we know the name is one and the same; likewise we know one and the same nature and being and power of Godhead (οὕτω καὶ θεότητος φύσιν καὶ οὐσίαν καὶ δύναμιν).[97]

In the examples above and throughout his corpus, Gregory does not distinguish between God's being and God's power in the manner that Torrance suggests when he speaks about energies and essence.[98] Rather, Gregory's distinctions lie between the relations of the Father, the Son, and the Spirit.[99] Nor does Gregory imply that the human *eikon* is subsumed into God's being through her theosis; she retains her identity as God's *eikon* whilst she is becoming a god, as we shall see shortly.[100] This identity causes her problems with the devil, to which we turn next.

The Holy Spirit and the Devil

The *eikon* has an enemy who is attempting to destroy her; namely, the devil. Relating to the prevalence of the devil and demonic powers in Gregory's work, the final role of the Spirit that we will discuss here involves the Spirit's function as a shield in the battle between the devil and the *eikon*.[101]

The Spirit's involvement in the theosis of the *eikon* means that the *eikon* moves towards being enlightened, thus gaining life and increasing in her likeness to God. This evokes the envy of the devil, who steps in and attempts to lead the *eikon* into sin.[102] The devil does not want the *eikon* to fulfil her destiny in becoming a god, which means that any enlightenment and enlivening causes him great vexation. However, the *eikon* is not left without help and protection when the enemy is waging war on her:

Don't be afraid of the battle. Protect yourself with water, protect yourself with the Spirit (προβαλοῦ τὸ πνεῦμα), in whom every single burning missile of the Enemy (τοῦ πονηροῦ) is put out.[103]

---

[97] Ep. 101.68 (SC 208, 66).

[98] In support of the argument that the Cappadocians do not purport a distinction within God between God's energies and God's essence, see Jean-Philippe Houdret, 'Palamas et le Cappadocians', *Istina*, 19 (1974), 260–71.

[99] σχέσις, Or. 29.16 (SC 250, 210).

[100] Contra Børtnes, who argues that Gregory uses a double process of metaphor and metonymy, resulting in a move towards 'a transcendent point where there is no longer any difference between eikon and archetype'; see 'Rhetoric and Mental Images', 53.

[101] Or. 2.82 (SC 247, 196–98).

[102] Or. 38.9 (SC 358, 120–22); 40.34 (SC 358, 276–78).   [103] Or. 40.10 (SC 358, 216).

Above, Gregory reveals his ideas about how the Holy Spirit functions in the war between the *eikon* and the devil. The Spirit protects the *eikon*; thus the narrative of this war is not consistently gloomy, but rather Gregory offers hope and reassurance that the *eikon* is not left to battle alone. However, the devil's attacks do not stop with each individual *eikon*, but also he attempts to destroy the Church. Observe this below through the way in which Gregory considers both God and the devil being involved in the discussion concerning the Trinity. He goes so far as to suggest that those who do not profess that the Spirit is God are listening to demonic spirits:

> If, on the one hand, my friends, you do not confess the Holy Spirit to be uncreated (ἄκτιστον), nor to be eternal (ἄχρονον), this is clearly the action of an enemy spirit.[104]

The devil, commanding the army of enemy spirits, is as active in the battle over true doctrine as he is in other areas of believers' lives. It should not surprise us that Gregory is concerned about the devil's interference in the doctrine of the Holy Spirit. Since Gregory states explicitly that the Holy Spirit deifies the *eikon* and that the devil is envious of the theosis of the *eikon*, it is logical that the devil should attempt to interfere with the doctrine that provides a rigorous account of theosis.

The Spirit: In Summary

We have seen that Gregory goes to great lengths not only to argue on behalf of the deity of the Spirit, but also to put forward numerous arguments concerning the Spirit's involvement in the life of the Church. These range from revealing a deeper knowledge of God, bringing life, protecting those who believe in God from the attacks of the devil, through to deifying the human *eikon*. It is incomprehensible that Gregory would have envisaged the Spirit, as experienced in the Christian life, to have no real impact or effect upon the *eikon*. In light of this, I propose that Gregory's immense effort to argue the consubstantial deity of the Holy Spirit means that he views the Spirit's role in the theosis and protection of the *eikon* as more than a figure of speech.[105] It is possible to incorporate Gregory's account

---

[104] Or. 41.7 (SC 358, 328).
[105] For other discussions of the role of the Holy Spirit in Gregory's doctrine of theosis, see Beeley, *Trinity and the Knowledge of God*, 263; Russell, *Doctrine of Deification*, 222; Winslow, *Dynamics of Salvation*, 371.

of the divinity of the Holy Spirit into how we interpret Gregory's discussion of theosis. This connects directly to my argument that Gregory's theological anthropology specifically demands that the human person is vulnerable to God. Gregory's worship of the Spirit suggests that he has a firm understanding of the God who genuinely deifies the 'porous' (vulnerable) self of the believer in a manner that can be said to be ontological or, as Elm puts it, 'real'. Relating Gregory's theological anthropology directly to theosis, I suggest that the *eikon* is vulnerable to the Holy Spirit to such a degree that the Spirit transforms the *eikon* into a god, as God intended at creation; thus the Spirit fulfils that which Christ made possible through his incarnation, death, and resurrection, and, furthermore, what the *eikon* could not achieve for herself. Gregory envisages this transformation occurring in numerous ways, primarily through baptism.

BAPTISM AND THE IMAGE OF GOD

Let us become clean by our Creator, let us honour the *eikon*, let us venerate the call, let us pursue life (μεταθώμεθα τὴν ζωήν). Why do we make ourselves low having been born in the high place?[106]

Gregory generally depicts baptism as the occasion during which the *eikon* is restored to her former potential of becoming divine through the Holy Spirit. Gregory's high view of the sacrament leads Winslow to comment that no early church father esteems baptism more than Gregory.[107] Having concluded that the Spirit's restoration and theosis of the *eikon* is not a figure of speech for Gregory, we build on this argument by considering Gregory's discussions of baptism, the sacrament through which the Holy Spirit is bestowed.[108] Baptism begins the theosis of the

---

[106] Or. 19.6 (PG 35, 1049B–C).

[107] Donald F. Winslow, 'Orthodox Baptism – A Problem for Gregory of Nazianzus' in Elizabeth A. Livinsgstone (ed.), *Studia Patristica*, 14 (Berlin: Akademie-Verlag, 1976), 371–74, 371.

[108] Gregory's baptism has attracted a certain amount of attention from scholars, who have approached it from a number of angles. For baptism and the Holy Spirit, see Noble, 'Deity of the Holy Spirit', 61–74. For philosophical approaches to baptism, see Elm, 'Inscriptions and Conversions', 1–35; Elm, 'O Paradoxical Fusion!', 296–316. For baptismal practice, see Everett Ferguson, *Baptism in the Early Church: History, Theology, and Liturgy in the First Five Centuries* (Grand Rapids: Eerdmans, 2009), 592–602; Ferguson, 'Gregory's Baptismal Theology and the Alexandrian Tradition' in Christopher A. Beeley (ed.), *Re-Reading Gregory of Nazianzus* (Washington, DC: The Catholic University of America Press, 2012), 67–84. For baptism and Christ, see Althaus, *Die Heilslehre des heiligen*, 153–80.

eikon; this differs from Onica, who argues that the sacraments are only linked extrinsically to patristic theosis and that the doctrine can survive theologically without it.[109] Gregory understands baptism to effect a real change in the *eikon*, precisely because of the presence of the Holy Spirit.[110] This broadens our understanding of the divinity of the *eikon*, although we shall see that the negative aspect of her vulnerability remains through the work of the devil and the persistence of the threat of sin.

Practice of Baptism

We cannot assume knowledge of the exact baptism rite which Gregory used, since no record of the liturgy that Gregory proclaimed in services has survived.[111] Bradshaw argues that liturgical practices in the fourth century were less standardised than has been thought previously; therefore, in order to represent Gregory's approach to baptism as faithfully as possible, we will explore the practice revealed in his oration *On Baptism*.[112] Gregory provides some information about the practice of the rite, which consists of 'words and deeds'.[113]

Gregory informs us that, whereas baptism occurred most commonly at Epiphany, Easter, and Pentecost, it could also take place at Theophany in Constantinople.[114] He did not think that very young children were guilty of sin, although for anyone wanting to belong to Christ a seal was

---

[109]   Or. 40.6 (SC 358, 206–08); Paul Onica, in the introduction to Gross, *Divinization of the Christian*, xii.

[110]   Gregory writes that he is aware of five kinds of baptism: Israel's baptism in the cloud and the Sea, the baptism of repentance, the baptism of water and the Spirit, and baptisms of martyrdom and penance; see Or. 39.17 (SC 358, 186–88).

[111]   Bryan D. Spinks, *Early and Medieval Rituals and Theologies of Baptism: From the New Testament to the Council of Trent* (Aldershot: Ashgate, 2006), 47. I am indebted to Ferguson's outline of Gregory's practice; see *Baptism in the Early Church*, 592–602.

[112]   Paul F. Bradshaw, *The Search for the Origins of Christian Worship: Sources and Methods for the Study of Early Liturgy* (London: SPCK, 2002), x. For a succinct collection of the available initiation rites in the fourth century, see Thomas M. Finn, *Early Christian Baptism and the Catechumenate: West and East Syria* (Collegeville, MN: Liturgical Press, 1992).

[113]   Or. 40.45 (SC 358, 304–06). Gregory also refers to baptism in other orations, particularly Ors. 8, 18 and 39. Gregory was fearful that he himself had not been baptised when he experienced a fierce storm whilst at sea; see Carm. 2.2.1 (PG 37, 994, 322–26).

[114]   Or. 40.24 (SC 358, 250). Moreschini (SC 358, 16–22) has convincingly dated Oration 40 to AD 381. For an argument supporting the dating in AD 380, see Jan M. Szymusiak, 'Pour une chronologie des discours de S. Grégoire de Nazianze', *VC*, 20 (1966), 183–89, 184–85. See also Maxwell E. Johnson, *The Rites of Christian Initiation: Their Evolution and Interpretation* (MN: Liturgical Press, 2007), 136.

necessary; consequently, our theologian actively encourages the baptism of infants over the age of three. He achieves this through applying an analogy from Exodus 12:23–32, where the doorposts were anointed in order to keep safe the first-born.[115] Before the catechumens came to baptism, they underwent rigorous preparation, followed by the confession of sin and exorcisms.[116] Whilst Winkler is not writing about Gregory in her summary of baptismal preparation, her words describe his thoughts accurately when she writes, 'The preparation as a whole is viewed as a drama-like battle with Satan'.[117] Only after the exorcisms does Gregory invite the catechumens over the threshold.[118] It is clear that Gregory understands the sacrament of baptism to represent the door into the Church:

While you are a catechumen, you are in the porch of piety. It is necessary for you to come inside, to stride across the courtyard, to observe the holy things, to peep into the holy of holies, to come to be with the Trinity (μετὰ τῆς τριάδος γενέσθαι).[119]

In order to 'come to be with the Trinity', the public confession of Trinitarian faith is vital at baptism:

... the confession (ὁμολογία) of the Father, and the Son and the Holy Spirit. I entrust this to you today; in this I will baptise you together, and I will raise you up together. I give you this companion and patronage throughout all of life, the one divine nature and power found singly in three and bringing the three together as distinct, not inconsistent in essences (οὐσίαις) or natures (φύσεσιν).[120]

Gregory states firmly that people should not delay baptism. However, his statements concerning baptism are compromised somewhat in Gorgonia's funeral oration, when he was obliged to say that she was purified in spite of being baptised late in life.[121] Gregory's father was also baptised later in life, concerning which Gregory offers a dramatic rendition of events.[122]

---

[115] Or. 40.28–29 (SC 358, 262–64).   [116] Or. 40.31 (SC 358, 268).

[117] Or. 40.27 (SC 358, 258). Gabriele Winkler, 'The Original Meaning of the Prebaptismal Anointing and its Implications', in Maxwell E. Johnson (ed.), *Living Water, Sealing Spirit* (Collegeville, MN: The Liturgical Press, 1995), 58–81, 75. Also see Edward Yarnold, *The Awe-Inspiring Rites of Initiation: The Origins of the R.C.I.A.*, 2nd ed. (Edinburgh: T&T Clark, 1994), 9–11.

[118] Or. 40.16 (SC 358, 230).

[119] Or. 40.16 (SC 358, 230–32). See Hilarion Alfeyev, 'Membership of the Body of Christ: Sacraments of Initiation', *GOTR*, 43, no. 1–4 (1998), 565–72, 567.

[120] Or. 40.41 (SC 358, 292); 40.43 (SC 358, 298).   [121] Or. 8.20 (SC 405, 290).

[122] Or. 18.13 (PG 35, 999C–1001B). For a discussion of Gregory's linking of the charisms to baptism, see Killan McDonnell and George T. Montague, *Christian Initiation and Baptism in the Holy Spirit: Evidence from the First Eight Centuries* (MN: Liturgical Press, 1991), 226–28.

Elm has shown that the reason behind Gregory's urging folk to be baptised was because baptism was considered by some as such a profound act of purification that subsequent sin became an unpardonable impossibility.[123]

Gregory extols the virtues of baptism at great length in his oration, *On Baptism*, in which he describes baptism as a gift (δῶρον),[124] grace (χάρισμα),[125] unction (χρῖσμα),[126] garment of incorruption (ἀφθαρσίας ἔνδυμα),[127] seal (σφραγίς),[128] and bath (λουτρόν).[129] Gregory's depiction of baptism as a bath relates to the purification of the *eikon* that takes place through the sacrament.[130] In an allegorical reading of Luke 17:14, Gregory compares the cleansing of the *eikon* that occurs at baptism to the occasion upon which Jesus heals the lepers:

> If you were covered head to toe with leprosy (that formless evil), after you had been scraped clean from the evil matter and received the healed *eikon* (ἀπεξέσθης δὲ τῆς κακῆς ὕλης καὶ τὴν εἰκόνα σώαν ἀπέλαβες), show the purification to me as your priest.[131]

Gregory also refers to baptism as illumination (τὸ φώτισμα).[132] Whilst discussing the Holy Spirit, we discussed that Gregory understands illumination as pertaining to life. The appearance of illumination in conjunction with baptism also denotes life, as seen in Gregory's description below:

---

[123] Elm, 'Inscriptions and Conversions', 3.   [124] Or. 40.4 (SC 358, 202).

[125] Or. 40.4 (SC 358, 202).   [126] Or. 40.4 (SC 358, 204).

[127] Or. 40.25 (SC 358, 256).

[128] Or. 40.4 (SC 358, 204). σφραγίς recalls the typology which saw the prophylactic seal of the Spirit in baptism as an antitype of the blood of the Passover lamb that was sprinkled upon the doorposts of the Israelites; Geoffrey W.H. Lampe, *The Seal of the Spirit: A Study in the Doctrine of Baptism and Confirmation in the New Testament and the Fathers*, 2nd ed. (London: SPCK, 1967), 116.

[129] Or. 40.4 (SC 358, 204).

[130] A version of this section is published as 'Divine, Yet Vulnerable: The Paradoxical Existence of Gregory Nazianzen's *Imago Dei*', *Studia Patristica.*, vol. XCV, The Fourth-Century – Cappadocian Writers – Including Papers Presented at the Eighteenth International Conference on Patristic Studies, Oxford, 10–15 August 2015, Marcus Vincent (ed.) (Leuven: Peters Press, 2017), 281–290.

[131] Or. 40.34 (SC 358, 276–78).

[132] Or. 40.4 (SC 358, 202). Illumination occurs in almost every section of Oration 40, also see Or. 39.1 (SC 358, 150); 39.14 (SC 358, 180). It is a usual name for baptism; Joseph Ysebaert, *Greek Baptismal Terminology: Its Origins and Early Development* (Nijmegen: Dekker and Van de Vegt, 1962), 158–78.

The Illumination is the brightness of souls, the transposition of life, a question of the conscience toward God.[133] The illumination is an aid in our weakness. The illumination is the renunciation of flesh, following of the Spirit, fellowship of the Word, amendment of the creature, a flood over sin, participation in light, an end of darkness. The illumination is a vehicle toward God,[134] a fellow traveller with Christ, support of faith, perfection of spiritual intellect, a key to the kingdom of heaven, exchange of life, abolition of slavery, release from chains, a remodelling of our very composition (συνθέσεως μεταποίησις).[135]

Above, baptism is the beginning of the process of entering into life, since Gregory envisages the sacrament as both present and eschatological. Elm has written extensively on Gregory's use of Platonic cosmology in relation to baptism, observing that his particular use of inscription language describes a moment of cosmological change alongside a lifelong process of conversion, concluding that whilst restoration begins at baptism, it instigates a process, rather than being a 'one-off' event.[136] Elm does not connect the lengthy process to spiritual warfare, since her argument is not concerned with this. In light of her thesis, it is worth noting the implications for the *eikon*, who remains vulnerable to the threats and disruptions of the devil. This occurs to an even greater degree when baptism is a process, rather than an event, since the continuation of theosis means the continuation of envy from the devil.

Sacrament and Symbol

It should be evident from the discussion so far that Gregory expects baptism to have a tremendous effect upon the Christian, as long as it is carried out correctly and faith in the Trinity is confessed. The fact that baptism is a sacrament plays a significant role in Gregory's expectation of the ontological transformation of the *eikon*. Observe below Gregory's explanation of the cleansing which occurs through baptism:

Since we are doubly made, I mean of soul and body, and our nature is, on the one hand, visible, and on the other, invisible, so is the cleansing double; through water, I say, and the Spirit. Whilst being received bodily the one is seen and the other

---

[133] For further examples of baptism representing life, see Or. 33.17 (SC 318, 196).

[134] Concerning ὄχημα πρὸς θεόν, 'its content is essentially to denote baptism as the action of the Holy Spirit raising the soul from earthly life to heavenly life'; Jean Daniélou, *Primitive Christian Symbols* (Baltimore: Helicon Press, 1963), 88.

[135] Or. 40.3 (SC 358, 200–02).

[136] For example, χαρακτήρ, σφραγίς, τύπος, and γράμμα. See Elm, 'Inscriptions and Conversions', 4.

encounters it apart from the body and is invisible. While the one is symbolic, the other is true (ἀληθής) and cleansing the depths.[137]

Gregory's description above further confirms my argument concerning the necessity of human vulnerability, or porosity, to God. Gregory argues that the way in which water cleanses the body at baptism symbolises a 'real' cleansing of the whole human person. This is only possible because the human person is created to be vulnerable to God and thus able to receive cleansing in the whole of her person.

Gregory explains that baptism is at once both symbolic and true because it consists of both water and the Spirit. For this reason, we may consider baptism as a symbolic occasion through which a real encounter with the Spirit occurs. Martos explains the juxtaposition of symbol and reality by discussing Gregory's understanding of the 'seal'. The early fathers understood the biblical metaphor as a metaphysical reality. They thought that the seal must be real because the Scriptures speak of the realities of faith. However, it could not be a physical reality, since the Spirit makes no physical mark on the body of a person. Therefore, it was an invisible or metaphysical reality which was impressed on the image of the person who received it.[138] This relates to Charles Taylor's notion of the premodern, 'porous' self that was discussed in Chapter 3. Not only does Gregory go to great lengths to argue for the deity of the Spirit, the same Spirit is also present in the sacrament through which Gregory expects a transformation of the *eikon*. This explains why Gregory refers to the power (δύναμις) of baptism on a number of occasions.[139] In making this move, he reminds the reader of the Spirit's power through which the human *eikon* is transformed during baptism.

Gregory implies that he views the Holy Spirit working through the Eucharist in the same way, although he does not offer an oration dedicated to the subject of the Eucharist, nor does he offer details about the rite itself.[140] On the few occasions where he mentions the Eucharist, Gregory varies his descriptions of it as a mystery (μυστήριον), a sacrifice

---

[137] Or. 40.8 (SC 358, 212). Gregory is insistent throughout Ors. 39 and 40 that baptism must be in both the Spirit and in water because human persons are both body and soul and Christ is both divine and human.

[138] Joseph Martos, *Doors to the Sacred: A Historical Introduction to Sacraments in the Christian Church* (London: SCM Press, 1981), 49; Evgeny Lampert, *The Divine Realm: Towards a Theology of the Sacraments* (London: Faber and Faber, 1944), 110–11.

[139] Or. 40.7 (SC 358, 210); 40.21 (SC 358, 242); 40.23 (SC 358, 246); 40.26 (SC 358, 258).

[140] Sterk, *Renouncing the World*, 138.

(θυσίας), and spiritual bread (πνευματικὸς ἄρτος).[141] Nevertheless, this modest amount that Gregory writes is significant as he refers directly to the healing and theosis of the *eikon* as a result of the consummation of the consecrated bread and wine. In an oration in which he discusses the ideal philosopher's life, he writes,

Come, stand with me at my side, close to the holy things and this mystical table as I celebrate theosis through these (δεῦρό μοι στῆθι τῶν ἱερῶν πλησίον καὶ τῆς μυστικῆς ταύτης τραπέζης κἀμοῦ τοῦ διὰ τούτων μυσταγωγοῦντος τὴν θέωσιν).[142]

Through his comment above, Gregory suggests that participation in the Eucharist continues the theosis experienced through the Holy Spirit at baptism. Furthermore, physical healing illustrates the work of the Holy Spirit at the Eucharist. Gregory describes in detail how his father, mother, and sister all experience healing from varying physical ailments through eating and drinking the consecrated bread and wine.[143] In the case of his father's healing at the Eucharist, Gregory refers specifically to the power (δύναμις) of the Holy Spirit, as he does when speaking about baptism.[144] It appears that Gregory envisages the Holy Spirit's role in the Eucharist intrinsic to the efficacy of the sacrament, in the same way that he envisages the Holy Spirit working through baptism.

However, transformation through the power of the Holy Spirit, whether at baptism or the Eucharist, attracts unwanted attention from the devil. Even after the seal of baptism and participating in the Eucharist, the human *eikon* remains vulnerable; this vulnerability is both positive, as the human person is participating in God through the Spirit, and also negative, since she is vulnerable to the schemes of the devil.

BAPTISM AND THE DEVIL

The devil is ever present before, during, and after baptism. This is because Gregory envisages baptism as the sacrament through which the *eikon* receives the healing that Christ has actuated; for this reason, Gregory describes it as 'a restoration of the *eikon* wounded by evil'.[145] Baptism

---

[141] Or. 2.4 (SC 247, 90–92); 2.95 (SC 247, 212–14); 4.52 (SC 309, 156); 18.29 (PG 35, 1020C–1021B); Ep. 171, Gallay *Lettres*, 2, 60–61; Or. 14.1(PG 35, 860A).

[142] Or. 25.2(SC 284, 160).

[143] Father, Or. 18.28–29 (PG 35, 1017C–1021B); Mother, Or. 18.30 (PG 35, 1021B–1024B); Gorgonia, Or. 8.18 (SC 405, 284–86).

[144] Or. 18.29 (PG 35, 1020C–1021B). [145] Or. 40.7 (SC 358, 210).

increases the divinity of the *eikon,* acting as a safeguard and a sign of authority against the demonic realm.[146] However, the illumination, puri-fication, and theosis brought about by baptism causes the devil to envy the *eikon* as at creation. Setting his oration *On Baptism* in the context of a battle, Gregory writes, 'Therefore let us be baptised so that we might be victorious'.[147] The divinity and vulnerability of the *eikon* become extremely apparent through the behaviour of the devil at baptism.

The theme of spiritual warfare is even more prevalent at baptism than at any other time in the Christian life, since the devil does not want the *eikon* to begin, or to continue, the process of becoming a god.[148] Gregory explicitly states that those who delay baptism are allowing the Evil One to cheat them.[149] He attributes this to the devil's deceptive nature:

He is actually darkness, but he feigns light (ὄντως σκότος ἐστί, καὶ φῶς ὑποκρίνεται). When he no longer has the strength for open warfare, he plots in secret and becomes an 'honest' adviser, although he is really evil.[150]

Gregory exhorts his audience to know the adversary's plot and defend themselves. He assures them that they do not fight unarmed; as we observed earlier, the Holy Spirit acts as a shield for the *eikon*. After a long tirade directed at the devil's schemes, Gregory concludes by observ-ing that the devil even attacks those who are young: 'he attaches himself to all ages, to every form of life, let him be rejected on all fronts'.[151] Here we see that life itself is under threat, since the devil is interested in all human *eikones*. The battle with the devil does not end in baptism, despite the effectiveness of the sacrament, since the devil appears immediately afterwards:

After baptism, if the pursuer and tempter of light (ὁ τοῦ φωτὸς διώκτης καὶ πειρασμής) makes an assault upon you - and he will make an assault upon you, mark my words, for he even made an assault upon the Logos, my God ... you have a means of conquering.[152]

Following Christ's temptation in the Gospels, Gregory offers examples of how those baptised will be tempted by Satan.[153] The logic of this is that in the Gospel accounts, Christ's temptations occur immediately after his baptism; thus Gregory demonstrates that those baptised should model their lives on Christ's life. This is where we see that the divinity of the

---

[146] Or. 40.4 (SC 358, 204).   [147] Or. 40.11 (SC 358, 218).
[148] Or. 40.10 (SC 358, 216); 40.16 (SC 358, 230).   [149] Or. 40.14 (SC 358, 226).
[150] Or. 40.16 (SC 358, 230).   [151] Or. 40.16 (SC 358, 232); 40.17 (SC 258, 232–34).
[152] Or. 40.10 (SC 358, 216).   [153] Matt. 4:1–11; Luke 4:1–13.

eikon is not only ontological, but also functional, since Gregory argues that the *eikon* should function in a divine manner throughout her life on earth. Said another way, Gregory believes that the newly baptised should offer the same response to the devil as modelled by Christ. Firstly, Gregory observes that the devil attempted to persuade Christ to turn stones into bread when Christ was hungry.[154] Gregory informs those who are baptised that if the devil tries the same trick on them, they should

resist him with the saving word, which is the bread sent from heaven and giving graciously life to the world (τὸν λόγον ἀντίθες τὸν σωτικόν, ὅς ἐστιν ἐξ οὐρανοῦ πεμπόμενος ἄρτος καὶ τῷ κόσμῳ τὸ ζῆν χαριζόμενος).[155]

After this, in Matthew's Gospel, the devil tries to tempt Christ into throwing himself off the temple in order to prove his divinity (Matt. 4:5–7; Luke 4: 9–12); likewise, Gregory writes, 'If he should plot against you through empty glory ... do not be brought down through exaltation'.[156]

After warning those who are baptised that the devil is well-acquainted with Scripture and therefore particularly wily and evil, Gregory concludes his discussion of spiritual warfare by drawing from the example given in Matthew 4:8–10 and Luke 4:5–6, where the devil shows Jesus all the kingdoms of the world and offers to give them to Jesus if he agrees to worship the devil. During this final piece of advice, Gregory addresses the question of how those who are baptised should respond when Satan tries to tempt them to bow down and worship him (the devil). In Matthew 4:10, Jesus responds, 'Away with you, Satan! For it is written, "Worship the Lord your God, and serve only him"'. Whilst Gregory offers a slightly different answer than that which appears in the Gospels, he does recommend a response that involves the newly baptised believers addressing the devil directly. Although Gregory addresses the devil in several prayers and poems, it is the only occasion in his public orations where Gregory suggests speaking to the devil in this way:

If he should overcome you with insatiate desire, tracing out all the kingdoms, in one moment of time and view as though they belonged to him, demanding worship, look down on him as one who is poor. Say, confident in the seal, 'I, myself, am also an *eikon* of God, I have not yet been thrown down through pride from the glory above, like you. I am clothed in Christ; I have been remodelled Christ by baptism, you ought to worship me!' He will depart, I know well,

---

[154] Or. 40.10 (SC 358, 216); Matt. 4:2–4, Luke 4:2–4.   [155] Or. 40.10 (SC 358, 216).
[156] Or. 40.10 (SC 358, 216).

yielding and being shamed by these words, as he was by Christ the first light, thus will he depart from those who are enlightened by that same Christ.[157]

In a single, fluid move, Gregory provides three reasons why the devil should worship the newly baptised. Firstly, she is an *eikon* of God; secondly, she is clothed in Christ; and thirdly, she is remodelled Christ. These three explanations appear to correspond with the three stages of creation, baptism, and subsequent theosis, as revealed in Scripture. Observe these thus: as discussed in Chapter 3, in his oration *On the Theophany*, Gregory follows Genesis 1:26 by depicting the human person at creation as God's *eikon*.[158] This forms the first reason why Gregory expects worship from Satan, since Gregory argues that God's *eikon* is worthy of worship. Gregory's second reason for expecting worship from Satan is 'being clothed in Christ', a metaphor which relates to baptism in Paul's letter to the Galatians: 'As many of you as were baptised into Christ have clothed yourselves with Christ' (Gal 3:27). Gregory follows Paul in his appropriation of baptism as a sacrament which clothes the believer in Christ; this brings a renewed identity for the newly baptised as one who is a restored child of God. Gregory's third and final reason for Satan worshipping the newly baptised is because they have been 'remodelled Christ'. Gregory uses μεταπεποιόω to describe this action, which we could also translate as 'change the quality of'.[159] The overall notion is one of a change in the human person, who after baptism is worthy of worship.

Whilst Gregory's demand for worship has been described as a 'self-professed divinity', he is speaking to all those who have been baptised, explaining that anyone who has been 'sealed' is worthy of receiving worship from the devil.[160] In demanding worship, Gregory does not envisage himself or other believers committing idolatry, since he is strongly opposed to 'that first and last of all evils, idolatry and the transfer of worship from the Creator to the creatures'.[161] Therefore, the fact that he is commanding the devil to bow down and worship those who are

---

[157] Or. 40.10 (SC 358, 218). Ἐὰν ἐξ ἀπληστίας καταπαλαίῃ σε, πάσας ὑποδεικνύων τὰς βασιλείας, ὡς αὐτῷ διαφερούσας, ἐν μιᾷ καιροῦ ῥοπῇ τε καὶ ὄψεως, ἀπαιτῶν τὴν προσκύνησιν, ὡς πένητος καταφρόνησον. Εἰπέ, τῇ σφραγῖδι θαρρήσας· Εἰκὼν εἰμι καὶ αὐτὸς Θεοῦ· τῆς ἄνω δόξης οὔπω δι' ἔπαρσιν, ὥσπερ σύ, καταβέβλημαι· Χριστὸν ἐνδέδυμαι, Χριστὸν μεταπεποίημαι τῷ βαπτίσματι· σύ με προσκύνησον. Ἀπελεύσεται, σαφῶς οἶδα, τούτοις ἡττημένος καὶ ᾐσχυμμένος, ὥσπερ ἀπὸ Χριστοῦ τοῦ πρώτου φωτὸς οὕτω τῶν ἀπ' ἐκείνου πεφωτισμένων.

[158] Or. 38:11 (SC 358, 124).   [159] PGL, 860.

[160] Kalleres, 'Demons and Divine Illumination', 163.   [161] Or. 38.12 (SC 358, 128–30).

baptised prompts further enquiry. On the one hand, one might respond to Gregory's demand by suggesting it is simply a rhetorical response. However, if we follow this argument through to its logical conclusion, we might reduce all of Gregory's work to having little real meaning. Added to this, when Gregory responds to the devil in this way, yet again, Gregory is treating the human *eikon* quite literally as a visible image, to which the devil must bow down. As we saw in Chapter 1, Gregory also depicts Basil like this, and in Chapter 3, we saw that Gregory treats women as physical, divine *eikones*. How is it that Gregory, who despises idolatry, would advocate that a human *eikon* should receive worship, even though she has been remodelled Christ? What does he reveal through this expectation? Gregory's application of προσκυνέω is central to our answer.

προσκυνέω

Gregory's appropriation of προσκυνέω, which I have translated as 'worship', is of great significance, since it can be interpreted in varying ways.[162] For example, Fulford has opted to translate προσκυνέω as 'reverence',[163] whereas Harrison has also used 'worship'.[164] Lampe offers a number of translations including 'make obeisance to an emperor, venerate, revere, worship deified men, adore, worship of pagan images'.[165] Liddell, Scott, and Jones offer a similar variation: 'Make obeisance to the gods or their images, fall down and worship, throw a kiss to a god, do reverence to, respect'.[166] Expanding our search to the New Testament reveals that προσκυνέω refers to the reverence or worship paid to human persons; meaning that they were considered to belong 'to a superhuman realm'.[167] Whilst the range of interpretation is broad, it points towards an act of reverence being paid to a person or deity who is considered to be 'divine'.

In the eighth and ninth centuries, during the Byzantine iconoclast controversy, a distinction was made between προσκυνέω and λατρεύω; the former encompassed the worship of images and icons, whereas the latter

---

[162] A version of this section is published as 'Gregory Nazianzen on the Devil and the Image of God: 'Worship me!'' in Marcus Vincent and Allan Brent (eds.), *Studia Patristica*, (Leuven: Peeters Press, 2016), 181–190.

[163] Fulford, *Divine Eloquence*, 96.   [164] Harrison, *Festal Orations*, 106.

[165] *PGL*, 1174–76. Aristotle includes it in his list of ways to honour men who are famous for doing good; *Rhetoric*, 1361a. For comments on Gregory's use of προσκυνέω in Oration 4, see Alois Kurmann, *Gregor von Nazianz: Oratio 4 gegen Julian. Ein Kommentar* (Basel: Friedrich Reinhardt, 1988), 270–73.

[166] LSJ, 1518.   [167] Danker and Bauer, *Greek-English Lexicon*, 82–83.

was used for the worship of God alone.[168] However, this division occurred many centuries after Gregory was writing; therefore it would be anachronistic to assume he had this particular distinction in mind. Since our primary concern is how Gregory himself has applied προσκυνέω, let us turn to the texts in which Gregory describes the action of προσκυνέω. He uses the verb on over ninety occasions and in a variety of ways, from attacking the worship of idols,[169] to defending the deity of the Holy Spirit.[170] Added to this, as we saw in Chapter 3, Gregory applies προσκυνέω to describe the human person as a 'mixed worshipper', which means that God mixes breath with dust in order to form a unified, dynamic living person. One key purpose of this newly created human *eikon* is to worship God.[171]

Let us note that Gregory proclaims, 'I worship the Father, I worship the Son, I worship the Holy Spirit (προσκυνῶ πατέρα, προσκυνῶ τὸν υἱόν, προσκυνῶ τὸ πνεῦμα τὸ ἅγιον)'.[172] Since Gregory uses προσκυνέω to express his adoration of the Trinity and also in defence of the deity of the Spirit, we may assume that he understands it to be an appropriate action to denote human reverence of God. By following the convention in the Gospels, and by choosing to use this particular verb to depict how the devil should be responding to the *eikon*, Gregory implies that he considers the *eikon* worthy of being worshipped in a manner akin to the way in which God is worshipped. Said another way, Gregory considers the *eikon* to be 'divine' after baptism. In light of this, we return to the question posed at the end of the previous section: 'How is it that Gregory, who despises idolatry, would advocate that a human *eikon* should receive worship, even though she has been remodelled Christ?'

There are two responses to this: The first is that Gregory intended the devil to bow to the presence of Christ in the believer, and did not imagine that his reader would think he was suggesting that those baptised were now worthy of worship on their own account.[173] However, in his response to the devil, Gregory does not simply say, 'I am an *eikon* of

---

[168] *PGL*, 1032. Gregory often applies λατρεία to the service or adoration of God by angels, Or. 17.12 (PG 35, 980C), and people; Or. 26.5 (SC 284, 236); 11.6 (SC 405, 342); 23.1 (SC 270, 280); 37.18 (SC 318, 304). On two occasions, Gregory uses the verb λατρεύω apologetically in order to argue that one cannot serve that which is created rather than God; Or. 5.28 (SC 309, 350); 37.17 (SC 318, 306).

[169] Or. 4.81 (SC 309, 206).   [170] Or. 40.42 (SC 358, 296).

[171] Or. 38.11 (SC 358, 126).   [172] Or. 37.24 (SC 318, 318); 20.5 (SC 270, 66).

[173] I am grateful to Ben Fulford for this suggestion at the Society of the Study of Theology conference in Nottingham, in April 2015, where I presented a paper concerning this question.

God'; rather he says, 'I, myself, am *also* an *eikon* of God (my italics, εἰκών εἰμι καὶ αὐτὸς Θεοῦ)'. The use of καὶ αὐτὸς implies that there is another *eikon* of God, which exists in addition to human *eikones*. In the context of the oration, this other *eikon* can only refer to the devil or Christ. I reject the former, on the basis that Gregory does not actually refer to angels, fallen or otherwise, as *eikones* of God anywhere in his orations or poetry, as I discussed in Chapter 3. Hence, when Gregory says, 'I, myself, am *also* an *eikon* of God', it is most likely that he would intend his reader to understand him as saying, 'Christ is the *Eikon* of God and I am also an *eikon* of God'. Therefore, it is possible that Gregory intends the devil not only to worship the presence of Christ within the restored, baptised *eikones*, but also to worship them on their own account, precisely because they are *eikones* of God, like Christ.

After baptism, the *eikon* is worthy of worship because of the incarnation, death and resurrection of Christ and the work of the Holy Spirit through baptism. However, we are still left wondering: How does Gregory reconcile the devil's worship of the *eikon* with his strict under-standing of a monotheistic faith? It is possible that Gregory was incorpor-ating a pseudepigraphal tradition, in which it was legitimate to worship the *eikon*, namely, *Life of Adam and Eve*.[174]

WORSHIPPING THE IMAGE OF GOD

As we saw in Chapter 1, Gregory was in no doubt about the books of Scripture, which he thought should be in the canon.[175] At the same time, Gregory appealed to numerous extra-biblical sources to inform his poetry and orations. We will explore here the possibility that Gregory incorporated a theme from the pseudepigraphal tradition, *Life of Adam and Eve*, in which Satan refuses to worship the human *eikon*. Whilst in pseudepigraphal literature there are a number of works where a human figure is worshipped, only one of those, to my knowledge, connects the worship of the *eikon* to the fall of the devil, as Gregory has done in our

---

[174] As far as I am aware, the shared themes between *On Baptism* and *Life of Adam and Eve* have been observed by just one other scholar: Nathan A. Lunsford presented a paper arguing that Gregory drew on *Life of Adam and Eve* at the Annual General Meeting of the North American Patristics Society in 2013. Quite astonishingly, we came to similar conclusions from across the globe, unaware of each other's work.

[175] Carm. 1.1.12 (PG 37, 471–74).

passage under consideration, namely, *Life of Adam and Eve.*[176] It is the earliest extant 'witness of a tradition in which Adam at his creation is worshipped by angels'.[177] Defying conclusive agreement regarding dating, scholars argue as widely as from the third century BC through to the seventh century AD.[178] It survives in a number of versions, all of which are concerned with the lives of Adam and Eve after they have been banished from the Garden of Eden until their deaths. It is the Latin version, *Life of Adam and Eve (Vitae Adae et Evae)*, well known as *Vita*, that is most relevant to my argument.[179] Sanders has argued that some early Jewish, and subsequently early Christian, communities must have thought highly of these pseudepigraphal texts as to share them so widely.[180] From the dating of various manuscripts of the *Vita* tradition, we know that the 'document enjoyed wide circulation amongst Christians'.[181] Added to this, Cameron writes that with regards to the spread of discourse it is necessary to

draw on a range of material far wider than what would eventually become the New Testament canon, if we are to do justice and if we do not wish to give a false impression of unity.[182]

---

[176] Other sources in which a human figure is worshipped include *Similitudes of Enoch*, Ethiopian *Enoch* 48:5, 62:6–9, 46:5; Alexander the Great's encounter with Jewish high priest in Josephus (*Ant.* 11:331–335); Simon ben Onias in *Sirach* 44:1–50:11, where a Jewish high priest is worshipped. I am thankful to Crispin Fletcher-Louis for pointing me to these references.

[177] Crispin H.T. Fletcher-Louis, 'The Worship of Divine Humanity as God's Image' in Carey C. Newman, James R. Davila, and Gladys S. Lewis (eds.), *The Jewish Roots of Christological Monotheism* (Leiden: Brill, 1999), 112–28, 114.

[178] Gary A. Anderson, Michael E. Stone, and Johannes Tromp, *Literature on Adam and Eve: Collected Essays* (Leiden: Brill, 2000); Michael E. Stone, *A History of the Literature of Adam and Eve* (Atlanta: Scholars Press, 1992).

[179] For a synoptic presentation of English, Armenian, Georgian, Greek, Latin, and Slavonic texts, see Gary A. Anderson and Michael E. Stone, *A Synopsis of the Books of Adam and Eve*, 2nd rev. ed. (Atlanta, Ga.: Scholars Press, 1999). For the most recent critical edition, see Jean-Pierre Pettorelli et al., *Vita latina Adae et Evae*, vol. 19, CCSA (Turnhout, Belgium: Brepols, 2013). The Greek version is entitled the *Apocalypse of Moses* (abbreviated here as *Ap.Mos.*).

[180] James Sanders, 'Why the Pseudepigrapha?' in James H. Charlesworth and Craig A. Evans (eds.), *The Pseudepigrapha and Early Biblical Interpretation* (Sheffield: JSOT Press, 1993), 13–19.

[181] Michael D. Johnson, 'Life of Adam and Eve' in James H. Charlesworth (ed.), *The Old Testament Pseudepigrapha* (Garden City, New York: Doubleday, 1985), 249–95, 252.

[182] Averil Cameron, *Christianity and the Rhetoric of Empire: The Development of Christian Discourse* (Berkeley: University of California Press, 1991), 41.

However, since it is not clear exactly how the tradition was received, I shall attempt a 'heuristic comparison', which compares themes rather than analysing identical language.[183] In the discussion that follows, I do not claim that Gregory was reading *Vita* or indeed that he was reading the Greek version from which the relevant fragment is missing, rather that the tradition relayed is one with which Gregory was familiar.

When Gregory says to the devil 'you should worship me', he draws attention to the fact that unlike the devil, he has not fallen from heaven, saying, 'I have not yet been thrown down through pride from the glory above, like you'.[184] In *Vita* 12–14, the devil's refusal to worship the *imago* of God is a key component in the devil's banishment from heaven. God creates Adam as God's *imago*, after which the archangel Michael calls the other angels to come and worship the *imago* of God: 'And having gone out Michael called all the angels saying, "Worship the *imago* of the Lord God, just as the Lord God has instructed"'.[185] The devil not only refuses, but assuming a rather arrogant position replies, 'he ought to worship me'.[186] Michael does not give up, but rather intensifies his command, saying, 'Worship the *imago* of God. If you do not worship him, the Lord God will become angry with you'.[187] The devil's response is to continue to refuse to worship Adam as God's *imago*, the consequence of which is that he is cast out of heaven.[188] As Levison writes, 'Adam's being the image becomes the source of enmity between Satan and himself'.[189] In light of this, I propose that Gregory is aware of the tradition where there is a conversation between Michael and the devil, when Gregory declares to the devil, '*You* ought to worship *me*', as though he is indignant that the devil has previously refused to worship the human *eikon* of God. In both *On Baptism* and *Vita*, the opponent of the devil and the devil himself are seen to be speaking in the first person. In

---

[183] For this method, see Ann Conway-Jones, *Gregory of Nyssa's Tabernacle Imagery in its jewish and Christian Contexts* (Oxford: Oxford University Press, 2014).

[184] Or. 40.10 (SC 358, 218). Since the *Vita* text is in Latin rather than Greek, I shall use the Latin *imago* rather than *eikon* when citing *Vita*.

[185] *Vita* 14.

[186] *Vita* 14, 'ille me debet adorare', see Pettorelli et al., *Vita latina Adae et Evae*, 459.

[187] 'adora imaginem dei. si autem non adorare ris, irascetur tibi dominus deus' ibid. The passage in *Vita* simply 'illustrates the plausibility that the notion of Adam having been worshipped (and the legitimacy principle it implies) had emerged in pre-Christian Judaism'; David Steenberg, 'The Worship of Adam and Christ as the Image of God', *JSNT*, 39 (1990), 95–109, 98. For Adam's created glory, see Robin Scroggs, *The Last Adam: A Study in Pauline Anthropology* (Philadelphia: Fortress Press, 1966), 95–109.

[188] *Vita* 16.   [189] Levison, *Portraits of Adam*, 178.

addition, there is a symmetry with Michael demanding three times that the devil worship the *imago* of God, and Gregory providing three reasons why the devil should worship baptised followers as restored *eikones* of God.

Further symmetry can be found in the focus on purification and cleansing in both works. The demand of worship occurs in the specific context of Gregory's oration *On Baptism*, in which, not surprisingly, purification is a major theme. Likewise, scholars have shown that there is a question of how the anointing and purification combination in the primary *Adam* books relates to Christian baptismal practice, yet this cannot be answered properly until a thorough analysis of the history of the traditions of the *Adam* books has been considered. In *Life of Adam and Eve* 9, after having been banished from paradise, Adam suggests that if they spend time standing in the Tigris River to purify themselves, the Lord may then take pity on them both and allow them to re-enter paradise. After eighteen days, the devil persuades Eve to step out of the river, convincing her that her penitence and purification is unnecessary, and thus blocks her readmission.[190]

It will be apparent that we have been comparing the Latin version *Vita* rather than the Greek version, *Ap.Mos.*, due to the loss of the manuscripts for the relevant section in Greek.[191] However, the demand for Satan's worship of the *eikon* occurs in Greek in the *Writings of Bartholomew*,[192] an elusive work which attained some popularity since it was transcribed

[190] Stone notes that in *Life of Adam and Eve*, the devil is principally a deceiver, which is how Gregory presents him throughout Oration 40 (particularly in Chapters 10 and 16); see Michael E. Stone, *Adam's Contract with Satan: The Legend of the Cheirograph of Adam* (Bloomington: Indiana University Press 2002), 12–17.

[191] For reasons why the Greek tradition would have been familiar with Chapters 11–17 of the Latin and a conclusion that the fall of the devil is an integral part of all the *Adam* books, see Michael E. Stone, 'The Fall of Satan and Adam's Penance: Three Notes on the Books of Adam and Eve', *JTS*, 44, no. 1 (1993),143–95, 154–56.

[192] For an overview of scholarship on Bartholomew, see James K. Elliott, *The Apocryphal New Testament: A Collection of Apocryphal Christian Literature in an English Translation* (Oxford: Clarendon Press, 1993). Also see Jean-Daniel Kaestli and Pierre Cherix, *L'Évangile de Barthélemy d'après deux écrits apocryphes* (Turnhout: Brepols, 1993). The dating of the works is vague, which leads Elliott to suggest anywhere between second and sixth centuries. Also see Émil Turdeanu, *Apocryphes slaves et roumains de l'Ancien Testament*, vol. 5, SVTP (Leiden: Brill, 1981). For a dating somewhere in the third century, see Felix Scheidweiler, 'The Gospel of Bartholomew' in Edgar Hennecke, Wilhelm Schneemelcher, and R. McL. Wilson (eds.), *New Testament Apocrypha: Volume One* (London: Lutterworth, 1963), 484–508.

in Latin and Coptic, with Greek being the original language.[193] Stone argues that the missing chapters of this scene in *Ap.Mos.* would have been known by the author of the *Writings of Bartholomew*. Thus, it is possible that Gregory received the tradition via the *Writings of Bartholomew*.[194] However, since the dating of this literature is sketchy, I suggest this tentatively. Gregory's apparent use of this tradition builds on my argument that his doctrine of theosis was informed strongly by Judeo-Christian ideas, rather than solely Stoic or Platonic thought.

In light of the *Vita* tradition, we return once more to the question, 'How is it that Gregory, who despises idolatry, would advocate that a human *eikon* should receive worship?' Responding to this, it is possible that Gregory was aware of the tradition in which the *eikon* was offered worship by angels, and more specifically, the devil's refusal to worship the *eikon* made by God. As we have already explored, on certain occasions, Gregory presents the human *eikon* as though she is comparable with a pagan *eikon*, yet with a striking difference: God breathes spirit into her and creates her according to the true *Eikon*, Christ. Yet again, in this scene, where he demands worship from the devil, Gregory approaches the human *eikon* as though she is literally a visible *eikon* of God. This means that Christ receives the glory when his *eikon* is worshipped in his place.

Gregory's use of language in his demand of worship challenges further the common supposition that he identifies the *eikon* with the spiritual intellect, rather than the *eikon* as a unity of body and soul. According to this, Gregory's sense of self could be understood only in terms of a disembodied intellect when he states, 'I am an *eikon* of God'. However, when we consider the occasions upon which Gregory also identifies the *eikon* as the whole human person, we may assume that Gregory means his unified body and soul.[195]

Gregory departs notably from the *Vita* tradition, which itself concludes with the death of Adam. Gregory offers hope of restoration in that the

---

[193] James K. Elliott provides an evaluation of the recent German translations of the New Testament Apocrypha; see 'The "New" Hennecke', *JSNT*, 35, no. 3 (2013), 285–300. For a linguistic discussion on 'Proskynesis' and 'Adorare', where Berte M. Marti argues that the two words are the literary equivalent of one another, read 'Proskynesis and Adorare', *Language*, 12 (1936), 272–82.

[194] For a comparison of the *Gospel of Bartholomew* that points towards the missing chapters in *Ap.Mos.*, see Stone, *History of Lit. of Adam and Eve*, 21, n.60.

[195] Also see Or. 34.12 (SC 318, 218). For different senses of self in ancient writers, see Richard Sorabji, *Self: Ancient and Modern Insights about Individuality, Life, and Death* (Chicago: University of Chicago Press, 2006), 32–53.

eikon is worthy of worship from the devil once more because of the healing actuated by Christ, effected through the Holy Spirit at baptism. Gregory expects that the *eikon* should receive worship from the devil as a sign of her identity, which is 'becoming a god'; a god who is fit to receive worship on behalf of her Creator. His suggestion of the devil's worship of the *eikon* strengthens my argument that Gregory anticipates an onto-logical transformation through the process of theosis and denotes that the human person functions in a divine manner. It also emphasises both how theosis is constantly under threat, and that the *eikon* herself remains vulnerable.

The divinity conferred through baptism does not mean that the Chris-tian is invincible, which is where the paradoxical existence of human life becomes apparent once more. On the one hand, the baptised believer is restored to her created divine potential and worthy of worship by the devil, but on the other hand, she is still extremely vulnerable, of which the devil himself and the human person's own propensity to sin are constant reminders. For this reason, life after baptism continues to be one where the *eikon* wrestles with the world, the flesh, and the devil.

Throughout this chapter, I have built on my previous argument that the dynamic existence of the *eikon* is 'divine, yet vulnerable'. I located the argument within the prevailing concerns amongst contemporary com-mentators, which relate to the inspiration for and how to speak about Gregory's approach to theosis. Both throughout this chapter and the previous chapters, I have aimed to demonstrate that biblical and extra-biblical narratives inform and inspire Gregory's doctrine of theosis. More importantly, without a consideration of these, we would miss an import-ant thread which runs through Gregory's overall narrative of theosis. This recalls the human person as a visible *eikon* of God, who is being trans-formed through the Spirit into the likeness of Christ, the identical *Eikon*, and who is divine.

Responding to discussions regarding how to describe Gregory's inten-tion through deploying 'theosis', I argued that we should understand theosis literally, in such as way that it describes, as Elm puts it, a 'real' change occurring through the human *eikon*. I arrived at this conclusion from following four avenues of thought. Firstly, recall my argument in Chapter 3, where I demonstrated that Gregory presents God as creating the human *eikon* specifically to be vulnerable, or porous, to God. This is evident through the way in which God creates the *eikon* as a mixture of the *eikon* and dust, where the *eikon* transforms the dust to form a dynamic, unified human *eikon*. I built on this argument by considering

Charles Taylor's thesis, which demonstrates how the porous premodern worldview was radically different from the modern worldview.

Secondly, we have explored Gregory's particular doctrine of the Holy Spirit. Against the bishops, Gregory argues uniquely for the consubstantiality of the Holy Spirit with the Father and the Son; thus Gregory declares that the Holy Spirit is God. This is significant because it is the role of the Holy Spirit to deify the *eikon* through baptism. In light of this, it is impossible for the *eikon* to remain unaffected and undeified by the Holy Spirit's presence, since the Spirit transforms the human *eikon* ontologically. Thirdly, I considered baptism as the sacrament through which the Holy Spirit deifies the *eikon*. Here, I argued that Gregory understands baptism to effect a real change in the believer. Fourthly and finally, I moved on to consider the interaction between the *eikon* and the devil at baptism. I highlighted that the devil goes to great lengths to prevent baptism because he understands that baptism is integral to the theosis of the *eikon*. Here, I analysed Gregory's unusual demand for worship from the devil. Gregory's conviction that those who are baptised should receive worship confirms further his presentation of the ontological and functional divinity of the *eikon*; ontological in the sense that the presence of the Holy Spirit through baptism genuinely deifies the believer, and functional in the sense that the devil should worship the *eikon* as one should worship God.

Drawing from all the examples that I have discussed thus far, the evidence demonstrates that Gregory's concept of theosis must be understood in light of both a robust theological anthropology and pneumatology, where the human *eikon* is divine precisely because God creates her to be vulnerable (or porous) to God. The negative implications of her vulnerability are that the theosis of the human *eikon* cannot occur without a struggle, since the envious devil attempts to destroy her at every opportunity. The divinity of the *eikon* should be understood in terms of being spiritually alive, since her divinity is set apart from the divinity of pagan *eikones* precisely because she relates ontologically to God. Gregory's depiction of theosis depicts the dynamic process of God's intended ontological transformation of the human *eikon* and should be interpreted literally. This is possible only through participation in Christ's life, death, and resurrection, in which human *eikones* partake through baptism by the power of the Holy Spirit, accompanied by a life of communion with God.

Conclusion

This book has offered a new reading of Gregory Nazianzen's vision of the 'divine, yet vulnerable' human *eikon*, vis à vis the *imago Dei*. If interpreted correctly, Gregory's nuanced approach makes a significant contribution to contemporary conversations related to the *imago Dei*. Before we discuss this further, let us recall the prevailing tenets of Gregory's account. I have argued that the narrative of the human *eikon*, which we have discovered in the texts, is multifaceted, yet cohesive. Into his rich tapestry Gregory weaves ideas about the ontology, relation, function, ethics, and experience of human *eikones*. Rather than simply focusing upon the question, 'what is a human *eikon*?', Gregory depicts the human *eikon* in her day-to-day existence; this involves struggling with the 'world', the 'flesh,' and the 'devil'. Furthermore, Gregory's approach is both christological and pneumatological. He interprets human *eikones* in light of Christ, the identical *Eikon*; God who is Father, Son, and Holy Spirit; the cosmos and Creator of beings, both spiritual and 'mixed'.

A close reading of the texts has challenged the view that Gregory depicts the human *eikon* simply in light of the soul or the spiritual intellect. I have argued that Gregory's vision extends much further than this, since the *eikon* relates also to the whole human person, comprising a dynamic human *eikon*. To achieve this, we have followed two avenues of thought: a) Gregory's treatment of the unity and visibility of Christ, the identical *Eikon*, and b) the way in which Gregory plays on ideas about images and idols in relation to the human *eikon*. In relation to Christ, we observed that Gregory includes Christ's flesh in his interpretation of Christ as God's visible *Eikon*. In addition to this, Gregory's application of μίξις and κρᾶσις, with respect to the mixture of divine and human in

Christ, entails that the *Eikon* transforms the flesh/body/dust to form the unified Christ, who is 'One'. Thus, Gregory describes Christ as a unified, visible *Eikon*, which sets the stage for the entrance of a visible human *eikon*.

Furthermore, we explored the backdrop of beliefs on images and idols, arguing that it informs our understanding of the human *eikon*. Gregory's description of Christ and the human *eikon* as 'living beings' becomes significant, since this forms a key difference between human and other kinds of *eikones*. The human *eikon* is infused with the Spirit at creation, meaning that she is a 'living being', thus setting her apart from idols which are static and lifeless in comparison. Gregory develops this concept through his treatment of women who wear cosmetics. He argues that the use of cosmetics reduces the human *eikon* to an idol, which means that the *eikon* is diminishing and consequently cannot image God properly. Gregory continues to play on ideas relating to pagan images by treating the human *eikon* quite literally as a visible *eikon* of God, who should be worshipped. For example, in Chapter 1, we saw that Gregory describes Basil as though he were a visible *eikon* who warrants veneration. Following on from this, in Chapter 5, we observed that Gregory demands worship from the devil, precisely because the human person is an *eikon* of God. Through all of the above discussions, observe that the *eikon* relates not only to the soul, but also to the whole human person. This results in human *eikones* being, quite literally, visible divine *eikones* who bear the presence of God. This also means that they are dynamic, not static; thus they have the potential for spiritual growth and theosis.

Secondly, I have argued throughout the book that biblical and extra-biblical texts comprise significant sources for understanding Gregory's account of the human *eikon*. Reading the whole biblical narrative in light of Christ, the identical *Eikon*, Gregory follows the human *eikon* from her creation through to her fall and subsequent restoration and theosis. Having been banished from paradise, Gregory locates the human *eikon* within a cosmological struggle against the 'world, the flesh, and the devil', which is interpreted most coherently in light of biblical and extra-biblical themes. Although Gregory is undoubtedly influenced by philosophical sources, we must attend to his application of the biblical and extra-biblical themes if we are to appreciate the complexity of his interpretation of the human *eikon*. This is particularly crucial in understanding Gregory's consistent narrative of the spiritual warfare encountered by the human *eikon*.

The final argument, which runs through the book, relates to Gregory's description of the *eikon* as 'divine'. His declaration has often confounded commentators, primarily because of its boldness, generally resulting in two kinds of contrasting responses. Commentators either conclude that Gregory cannot really mean what he is writing; consequently, his ideas are reduced to 'empty rhetoric'. Or else they claim that Gregory does not use metaphor, and that his intention regarding theosis is 'real'. Despite a great amount of focus upon linguistic categorisation, we have been left with little clarity regarding how Gregory depicts the divinity and theosis of the *eikon*. I have argued that if we consider together a) Gregory's theological anthropology, in which God creates the human person specifically to be vulnerable (or porous) to the spiritual realm; b) Gregory's high pneumatology, and the lengths to which he goes in order to argue the consubstantial divinity of the Holy Spirit; c) Gregory's theological approach to baptism as the sacrament through which the Holy Spirit deifies the human *eikon*; and d) Gregory's interaction with the devil after baptism, in which he demands worship from his enemy, then we must take Gregory's ideas about a 'divine' *eikon* seriously. We may understand the 'divinity' of the human *eikon* as ontological, functional, ethical, relational, and experiential, since the human *eikon* participates in, and is created to function like, the identical *Eikon*, Christ. When we consider the way in which Gregory locates the human *eikon* within Christ, we must recall also Gregory's high pneumatology. The Holy Spirit, who gives life to the *eikon* at her creation, also deifies the *eikon*; thus we cannot faithfully speak of the divinity of the *eikon* without a robust account of the Spirit.

I return to the phrase 'divine, yet vulnerable' as a means of summarising Gregory's view of the human *eikon*. It is open to interpretation in order to account for Gregory's continual questions concerning human experience and to invite further investigation. The term 'vulnerable' allows both positive and negative interpretations; the human *eikon* is vulnerable (porous) to God and is 'divine', yet she is also vulnerable to the demonic powers of darkness, together with sin. 'Divine', as I have already argued, is to be understood ontologically, functionally, ethically, relationally, and experientially, since it encompasses varying aspects of existence as a human *eikon*.

This reading of Gregory's vision of the human *eikon* contributes to contemporary discussions in Western theological anthropology by serving as a critique of those interpretations that seek to place the *imago Dei* into a neat, succinct category. Gregory's approach recognises the complexity of human existence. As noted in the Introduction, contemporary commentators often view the *imago Dei* through a single lens, such as

Christology, structure, relation, or function. One of the many problems with this 'single-lens' approach is that it is reductive and exclusive. For example, one might struggle to denote as an *imago Dei* a person with a severe intellectual disability if the framework considers the *imago Dei* as the intellect alone. Most theologians would agree that this is unacceptable.[1] If one works through the remaining categories for the *imago Dei* in Western theological anthropology, corresponding critiques ensue, since no single category is wholly inclusive. Gregory's non-reductive approach to the human *eikon* avoids this trap, for he holds together a multifaceted interpretation of the *eikon,* incorporating every gender, race, age, and ability. All human persons may participate in God and function as an *eikon* of God precisely because they bear God's presence and point to their Creator. Unlike the modern concern, which debates how human persons should be distinguished over other animals with respect to the *imago Dei*, Gregory distinguishes human persons as they relate to other kinds of images and idols. Whilst space does not allow for the exploration of the implications of this, I suggest that Gregory's approach is compelling. It alters radically the debate on human uniqueness on the basis of rationality over and against other animals.

Added to this, Gregory's account is christologically and pneumatologically inclusive. Theologians such as Kathryn Tanner, John Behr, David Kelsey, and Ian McFarland have critiqued the way in which numerous interpretations of the *imago Dei* do not account for the New Testament witness, which points to Christ as the *Eikon* of the invisible God. Gregory could not be subjected to this critique, since he locates the human *eikon* consistently in the context of Christ, the 'identical *Eikon*'. Also, Gregory accounts robustly for the Spirit. As we observed in Chapter 1, he describes the creation of the 'mortal *eikon*' as becoming alive through the Spirit. In making this move, Gregory avoids an error that occurs commonly in accounts of the *imago Dei*, whereby the Holy Spirit is depicted entering the story at the point of renewal or transformation. This results in a theologically errant account, in which Christ is involved from the beginning of the life of the *eikon*, with the Spirit not appearing until further on in the story. In contrast to this, Gregory's account situates the Spirit at the beginning of the life of the human *eikon*, rendering a theologically inclusive account.

---

[1] Erinn Staley, 'Intellectual Disability and Mystical Unknowing: Contemporary Insights from Medieval Sources', *Modern Theology*, 28, no. 3 (2012), 385–401.

Finally, Gregory locates the human *eikon* in relation to the wider cosmos, in particular angels and demons. His view of human existence does not allow for the isolation of the human *eikon* from the wider cosmos; this means that the *imago Dei* is 'porous' and not 'buffered'. When discussing the *imago Dei*, commentators often consider human relationships with God and other humans only.[2] Consequently, relationships with spiritual beings are ignored and the *imago Dei* is presented as though it exists in isolation from and unaffected by spiritual beings in the wider cosmos. Drawing on the work of Charles Taylor, I have argued that this is one of the negative effects of the Enlightenment.[3] Engagement with early theologians, such as Gregory, repositions human *eikones* in light of their relationship both with God and the world which they inhabit. The manner in which Gregory situates the *eikon* within a perpetual battle with the spiritual powers of darkness reminds us that the human *eikon* does not exist in a vacuum. The *eikon* exists as porous and vulnerable to God, the cosmos, and all the spiritual beings that reside therein. Thus, Gregory's vision of life as a human *eikon* provides an unusual insight into the implications of the human experience of imaging God. It offers a heuristic interpretation of some of the challenging aspects of being an *eikon*, whilst, at the same time, creating the space for the re-enchantment of the *imago Dei*.

I close by observing that despite his extensive treatment of the human *eikon*, Gregory does not aim to provide the definitive word on this enquiry; rather, he recognises the complexity of being an *eikon* of God. As we observed in the Introduction, Gregory asks, 'Who was I at first? And who am I now? And who shall I become? I don't know clearly'.[4] We should heed his caution as we continue to wrestle with what it means for human persons to image God.

---

[2] For example, Elizabeth O'Donnell Gandolfo, *The Power and Vulnerability of Love* (Minneapolis: Fortress Press, 2015), 204.
[3] See Chapter 3.   [4] Carm. I.2.14 (PG 37, 757, 17).

Appendix

ON THE TEXTS

No complete critical edition of Gregory's texts currently exists. The extant works can be found in J.P. Migne's *Patrologia Graeca* 35–38, a reprint of the Benedictine texts edited by the Maurist monks in the late seventeenth and eighteenth centuries.[1] The texts amount to 45 orations, 244 letters, and 507 poems.[2] From Gregory's prose, Oration 35 remains disputed.[3] I have used the critically edited *Sources Chrétiennes* versions of the orations where possible and critical editions of the poems where they exist. For clarity, and as many people may have more access to *Patrologia Graeca*, I have provided *Patrologia Graeca* references for the poems, following the divisions set out by the Maurist monks in the eighteenth

---

[1] For an overview of the textual traditions of Gregory's orations, see Véronique Somers, *Histoire des collections complètes des Discours de Grégoire de Nazianze* (Louvain: Université Catholique de Louvain, Institut Orientaliste, 1997). For modern editions until 1950, see Denis M. Meehan, 'Editions of Saint Gregory of Nazianzus', *ITQ*, 3 (1951), 203–19.

[2] The tragedy entitled *Christus Patiens* appears in *Sources Chrétiennes*. The majority of contemporary scholars think that it was composed in the eleventh or twelfth century because it includes long laments by the Virgin Mary. This was a theme that did not begin to surface in Byzantine literature until the late ninth century (with the exception of the *Kontakion* by Romanos the Melodist in the sixth century). Since it is not consistent with the rest of Gregory's work, I have omitted the tragedy from this study. Furthermore, the drama does not discuss the human *eikon* (for an example of *eikon* as a non-human image, see *Christus Patiens* (SC 149, 200, line 923)). André Tulier (SC 149, 11–18) is alone in offering a defence of Gregory's authorship of *Christus Patiens*.

[3] Claudio Moreschini (SC 318, 38). Since Gregory does not speak of the human *eikon* in Oration 35, I have omitted it from this study.

century. The first book comprises theological poems which are divided into two sections: *Poemata Dogmatica* and *Poemata Moralia*; the second book comprises historical poems.[4] Whilst I have consulted the contemporary translations of Gregory's work specified in the bibliography, I have chosen to provide my own translations in order to highlight the nuances in the texts. I treat the texts as a cohesive whole for two reasons: firstly, I have not observed great developments in Gregory's argument; he is consistent in his overall emphasis and in his application of paradox as a means of drawing attention to the complexities of being a human *eikon*. Secondly, Gregory himself informs us that he edited his own work at the end of his life, which means that he would have been able to edit many discrepancies in his own thought.

GENRE AND RHETORIC

Our theologian is such a successful rhetorician that Kennedy refers to him as 'the most important figure in the synthesis of Greek rhetoric and Christianity'.[5] Whilst Gregory presents his prose in the form of sermons, the fact that he edited his work at the end of his career means that we do not have the versions which he may have preached in churches as a priest and bishop. Whoever the original audiences were, the edited forms of the orations and poems were preserved for both schools and future theologians. Gregory studied rhetoric substantially, receiving advanced training under Prohaeresius and Himerius. He was mindful of the highly charged

[4] The PG ordering of the poems in the *Poema Arcana* differs from Moreschini and Sykes (1997); for clarity, I have followed the PG numbering. For an overview of the textual history of the poems, see Abrams Rebillard, 'Speaking for Salvation', 7–11. For contested poems, see Henricus M. Werhahn, 'Dubia and Spuria bei Gregor von Nazianz' in Frank L. Cross (ed.), *Studia Patristica, 7 (Texte und Untersuchungen, 92)* (Berlin: Akademie-Verlag, 1966), 337–47. For a convincing defence of Gregory's authorship of these poems, see Christos Simelidis, *Selected Poems of Gregory of Nazianzus: I.2.17; II.1.10, 19, 32: A Critical Edition with Introduction and Commentary* (Göttingen: Vandenhoeck & Ruprecht, 2009), 40.

[5] George A. Kennedy, *A New History of Classical Rhetoric* (Princeton: Princeton University Press, 1994), 261. Further praise of Gregory's rhetoric can be found in Frances M. Young, 'The Rhetorical Schools and their Influence on Patristic Exegesis' in Henry Chadwick and Rowan Williams (eds.), *The Making of Orthodoxy: Essays in Honour of Henry Chadwick* (Cambridge: Cambridge University Press, 1989), 182–99, 186; William S.J. Harmless, *Desert Christians: An Introduction to the Literature of Early Monasticism* (Oxford: Oxford University Press, 2004), 317; Raymond Van Dam, *Kingdom of Snow: Roman Rule and Greek Culture in Cappadocia* (Philadelphia: University of Pennsylvania Press, 2002), 141–42.

dispute between rhetoric and philosophy, which was fuelled by Plato's critique of the fifth-century sophists.[6] This tension is present in Gregory's own work when, in *On His Own Life*, he explains that he places no value on displays of eloquence.[7] Whilst he utilises the literary conventions of his time, Gregory intends his ideas sincerely. Kustas affirms this in a detailed study of the effect of the 'Second Sophistic' movement on Christian writers.[8] He argues that rhetoric is the 'clothing' for Christian revelation. Orators like Gregory were concerned in conveying the Christian gospel clearly, but also to clothe it in language that is expressive of the Christian mystery. In *On His Own Verses*, Gregory offers four reasons why, later in life, he turned to verse.[9] Firstly, he explains that verse imposes a certain discipline on a writer, which he himself finds beneficial.[10] Secondly, he writes for the young since they enjoy poetry and the harshness of his instruction is sweetened by verse.[11] Thirdly, Gregory states that he wants to prove himself as good as any pagan at verse. This desire to show that Christians are able to excel in the public realm is also evident in Gregory's invectives against Julian, where he challenges the emperor by asking, 'Is poetry yours?'[12] Fourthly, Gregory finds comfort in writing poetry when he is ill.[13] Overall, his goal in writing poetry is much the same as in writing orations: to instruct his reader of what is true.[14]

---

[6] *Resp.* 607b5–6; *Gorg.* 447a-466a.

[7] Carm. 2.1.11 (PG 37, 1047, 254–58); Or. 2.104 (SC 247, 224); 27.1 (SC 250, 70–72); 34.10 (SC 318, 214–16); 40.10 (SC 358, 216–18).

[8] George Kustas, *Studies in Byzantine Rhetoric* (Thessalonike: Patriarchal Institute, 1973), 27–62.

[9] Carm. 2.1.39 (PG 37, 1329–36).

[10] Carm. 2.1.39 (PG 37, 1331–32, 34–37).

[11] Carm. 2.1.39 (PG 37, 1332, 37–42).

[12] Or. 4.108 (SC 309, 260).

[13] Carm. 2.1.39 (PG 37, 1333, 54–56).

[14] Carm. 2.1.39 (PG 37, 1333, 63).

Bibliography

GREGORY NAZIANZEN TEXTS

Bernardi, Jean. *Grégoire de Nazianze. Discours 1–3*, SC 247 (Paris: Les Éditions du Cerf, 1978).

Grégoire de Nazianze. Discours 4–5, SC 309 (Paris: Les Éditions du Cerf, 1983).

Grégoire de Nazianze. Discours 42–43, SC 384 (Paris: Les Éditions du Cerf, 1992).

Beuckmann, Ulrich. *Gregor von Nazianz: Gegen die Habsucht (Carmen 1, 2, 28) Einleitung und Kommentar*, SGKA, NF 2 (Paderborn: Ferdinand Schöningh, 1988).

Calvet-Sebasti, Marie-Ange. *Grégoire de Nazianze. Discours 6–12*, SC 406 (Paris: Les Éditions du Cerf, 1995).

Domiter, Kristijan. *Gregor von Nazianz. De humana natura (c. 1, 2, 14). Text, Übersetzung, Kommentar*, Patrologia, BSK, 6 (Frankfurt am Main: Peter Lang, 1999).

Gallay, Paul. *Grégoire de Nazianze. Discours 27-31*, SC 250 (Paris: Les Éditions du Cerf, 1978).

St. Grégoire de Nazianze. Lettres, vol. 1 (Paris: Société d'Édition, 1964).

St. Grégoire de Nazianze. Lettres. vol. 2 (Paris: Société d'Édition, 1967).

Gallay, Paul and Maurice Jourjon. *Grégoire de Nazianze. Lettres Théologiques*, SC 208 (Paris: Les Éditions du Cerf, 2013).

Jungck, Christoph. *Gregor von Nazianz: De Vita Sua. Einleitung, Text, Übersetzung, Kommentar*, WKGLS (Heidelberg: Carl WinterUniversitätsverlag, 1974).

Kertsch, Manfred. *Gregorio Nazianzeno. Sulla virtù, Carme giambico (I, 2, 10)*, (Pisa: Edizioni Ets, 1995).

Knecht, Andreas. *Gregor von Nazianz: Gegen die Putzsucht der Frauen. Verbesserter griechischer Text mit Übersetzung, motivgeschichtlichem Überblick und Kommentar*, WKGLS (Heidelberg: Carl Winter Universitätsverlag, 1972).

Kurmann, Alois. *Gregor von Nazianz: Oratio 4 gegen Julian. Ein Kommentar*, (Basel: Friedrich Reinhardt, 1988).

Meier, Beno. *Gregor von Nazianz: Über die Bischöfe (Carmen 2, 1, 12). Einleitung, Text, Übersetzung, Kommentar, SGKA. NF 2. Forschungen zu Gregor von Nazianz, Band 7* (Paderborn: Ferdinand Schöningh, 1989).

Migne, Jacques-Paul. *Patrologia cursus completus, series Graeca*, vols. 35–38 (Paris, 1857–62).

Moreschini, Claudio. *Grégoire de Nazianze. Discours 32–37*, SC 318 (Paris: Les Éditions du Cerf, 1985).

Grégoire de Nazianze. Discours 38–41, SC 358 (Paris: Les Éditions du Cerf, 1990).

Moreschini, Claudio and Donald Sykes. *Gregory of Nazianzus: Poemata Arcana*, OTM (Oxford: Clarendon Press, 1997).

Mossay, Justin. *Grégoire de Nazianze. Discours 20–23*, SC 270 (Paris: Les Éditions du Cerf, 1980).

Grégoire de Nazianze. Discours 24–26, SC 284 (Paris: Les Éditions du Cerf, 1981).

Oberhaus, Michael and Martin Sicherl. *Gregor von Nazianz: Gegen den Zorn (Carmen 1,2,25) Einleitung und Kommentar* (Paderborn: Ferdinand Schöningh, 1991).

Simelidis, Christos. *Selected Poems of Gregory of Nazianzus: I.2.17; II.1.10, 19, 32: A Critical Edition with Introduction and Commentary* (Göttingen: Vandenhoeck & Ruprecht, 2009).

Tulier, André. *Grégoire de Nazianze. La Passion du Christ*, SC 149 (Paris: Les Éditions du Cerf, 1969).

White, Caroline. *Gregory of Nazianzus: Autobiographical Poems*, CMC (Cambridge: Cambridge University Press, 1996).

OTHER ANCIENT TEXTS

Biblia Hebraica Stuttgartensia, Elliger, Karl and Wilhelm Rudolph (eds.), (Deutsche Bibelgesellschaft: Stuttgart, 1997).

Blanc, Cécile. *Origène: Commentaire sur saint Jean Livre XII*, SC 290 (Paris: Les Éditions du Cerf, 1982).

Bury, Robert Gregg. *Plato: Timaeus. Critias. Cleitophon. Menexenus. Epistles*, (Revised edition), LCL 234 (Cambridge, Massachusetts: Harvard University Press, 1952).

Camelot, Pierre Thomas and Claude Mondésert. *Clément d'Alexandrie. Les Stromates. Stromate 2*, SC 38 (Paris: Les Éditions du Cerf, 1954).

Colson, F.H. and G.H. Whitaker. *Philo.*, 10 vols. LCL (Cambridge, Massachusetts: Harvard University Press, 1929–52).

Davie, George John. *The Works Now Extant of S. Justin the Martyr. Translated with Notes and Indices* (New York: Andesite Press, 2015).

Descourtieux, Patrick. *Clément d'Alexandrie. Les Stromates. Stromate 6*, SC 446 (Paris: Les Éditions du Cerf, 1999).

Doutreleau, Louis and Henri de Lubac. *Origène. Homélies sur la Genèse*, SC 7 (Paris: Les Éditions du Cerf, 1977).

Evans, Earnest. *Tertullian. Aversus Marcionem 1 and 2* (Oxford: Clarendon, 1972).

Froidevaux, Léon M. *Irénée de Lyon. Demonstration de la prédication apostolique*, SC 62 (Paris: Les Éditions du Cerf, 1959).

Géhin, Paul. *Guillaumont, Claire, and Antoine Guillaumont. Évagre Le Pontique. Sur les Pensées*, SC 438 (Paris: Les Éditions du Cerf, 1998).

Giet, Stanislas. *Basile de Césarée. Homélies sur l'Hexaéméron*, SC 26 (Paris: Les Éditions du Cerf, 1950).

Kannengiesser, Charles. *Athanase d'Alexandrie. Sur l'incarnation du Verbe*, SC 199 (Paris: Les Éditions du Cerf, 1973).

Laplace, Jean. *Grégoire de Nysse. La création de l'homme*, SC 6 (Paris: Les Éditions du Cerf, 1944).

Lebon, J. *Athanase d'Alexandrie. Lettres à Serapion sur la divinté du Saint Espirit*, SC 15, (Paris: Les Éditions du Cerf, 1947).

Le Boulluec, Alain and Pierre Voulet. *Clément d'Alexandrie. Les Stromatas. Stromate 5*, SC 278 (Paris: Les Éditions du Cerf, 1981).

Lochman, Daniel T. and Daniel J. Nodes. *John Colet on the Ecclesiastical Hierarchy of Dionysius: A New Edition and Translation with Introduction and Notes*. SMRT (Leiden: Brill, 2013).

Macleod, Matthew D. *Lucian Amores*, vol. VIII. LCL 432 (Cambridge, MA: Harvard University Press, 1967).

Marcus, Ralph. *Josephus. Jewish Antiquities Books IX-XI*, LCL 326 (Cambridge, MA: Harvard University Press, 1937).

Mondésret, Claude and Henri Marrou. *Clément d'Alexandrie. Le pédagogue II*, SC 108 (Paris: Les Éditions du Cerf, 1965).

Murray, Augustus Taber and revised by William F. Wyatt. *Homer: The Iliad. Books 13–24*, LCL 171 (Cambridge, MA: Harvard University Press, 1999).

Nautin, Pierre. *Didymus L'Aveugle. Sur la Genèse 1*, SC 233 (Paris: Les Éditions du Cerf, 1976).

North Fowler, Harold. *Plutarch. Moralia Vol X*, LCL 321 (Cambridge, MA: Harvard University Press, 1936).

Pruche, Benoit. *Basile de Césarée. Traité du Saint-Espirit*, SC 17 (Paris: LesÉditions du Cerf, 1945).

Rolfe, John C. *Suetonius. Lives of the Caesars, Volume I: Julius. Augustus. Tiberius. Gaius. Caligula*, LCL 31 (Cambridge, MA: Harvard University Press, 1914).

Rousseau, Adelin and Louis Doutreleau. *Irénée de Lyon. Contre les Hérésies, Livre 1*, SC 263–64 (Paris: Les Éditions du Cerf, 1979).

Irénée de Lyon. Contre les Hérésies, Livre 3, SC 210–11 (Paris: Les Éditions du Cerf, 1974).

Rousseau, Adelin, Louis Doutreleau, Bertrand Hemmerdinger and Charles Mercier. *Irénée de Lyon. Contre les Hérésies, Livre 4*, SC 100 (Paris: Les Éditions du Cerf, 1965).

Rousseau, Adelin, Louis Doutreleau and Charles Mercier. *Irénée de Lyon. Contre les Hérésies, Livre 5*, SC 152–53 (Paris: Les Éditions du Cerf, 1969).

Septuaginta. Alfred Rahlfs (ed.), emended by Robert Hanhart. Rev. edn. (Stuggart: Deutsche Bibelgesellschaft, 2006).

The Greek New Testament. Barbara Aland, Kurt Aland, Johannes Karavidopoulos, Carlo M. Martini, and Bruce M. Metzger. (eds.), 4th Rev. edn. (Stuttgart: Deutsche Bibelgesellschaft, 1994).

Wilson, Nigel. *Herodoti Historiae: Libri I-IV*, OCT (Oxford: Oxford University Press, 2015).

Yunnis, Harvey. *Plato: Phaedrus*. CGLC, (Cambridge: Cambridge University Press, 2011).

TRANSLATIONS AND SECONDARY LITERATURE

Abrams Rebillard, Suzanne. 'Speaking for Salvation: Gregory of Nazianzus as Poet and Priest in His Autobiographical Poems' (Ph.D. Diss., Brown University, 2003).

Ackerman, James S. 'The Rabbinic Interpretation of Psalm 82 and the Gospel of John'. *HTR*, 59, no. 2 (1966), 186–91.

Aghiorgoussis, Maximos. 'Applications of the Theme "Eikon Theou" (Image of God) according to Saint Basil the Great'. *GOTR*, 21, no. 3 (1976), 265–88.

Alfeyev, Hilarion. 'Membership of the Body of Christ: Sacraments of Initiation'. *GOTR*, 43, no. 1–4 (1998), 565–72.

'The Deification of Man in Eastern Patristic Tradition (with special reference to Gregory Nazianzen, Symeon the New Theologian and Gregory Palamas)'. *Colloquium*, 36, no. 2 (2004), 109–22.

La chantre de la Luminère: Introduction à la spiritualité de saint Grégoire de Nazianze, (Paris: Les Éditions du Cerf, 2006).

Allen, Danielle S. *Why Plato Wrote* (Oxford: Wiley-Blackwell, 2010).

Altaner, Berthold. 'Augustinus und Gregor von Nazianz, Gregor von Nyssa' in Berthold Altaner (ed.), *Kleine patristische Schriften* (Berlin: Akademie Verlag, 1967) 277–85.

Althaus, Heinz. *Die Heilslehre des heiligen Gregor von Nazianz* (Münster: Verlag Aschendorff, 1972).

Anderson, Gary A. 'The Garments of Skin in Apocryphal Narrative and Biblical Commentary' in James L. Kugel (ed.), *Studies in Ancient Midrash* (Cambridge, MA: Harvard University Press, 2001), 101–43.

The Genesis of Perfection: Adam and Eve in Jewish and Christian Imagination (London: John Knox Press, 2001).

Anderson, Gary A., and Michael E. Stone. *A Synopsis of the Books of Adam and Eve*, 2nd rev. ed. (Atlanta, Georgia: Scholars Press, 1999).

Anderson, Gary A.; Michael E. Stone, and Johannes Tromp. *Literature on Adam and Eve: Collected Essays* (Leiden: Brill, 2000).

Annas, Julia. *Platonic Ethics, Old and New* (Ithaca: Cornell University Press, 1999).

Aristotle. *The Basic Works of Aristotle. Edited with an Introduction by Richard McKeon* (Random House: New York, 1941).

Armstrong, Arthur H. *The Cambridge History of Later Greek and Early Medieval Philosophy* (Cambridge: Cambridge University Press, 1967).

Arnold, Clint E. *Ephesians, Power and Magic: The Concept of Power in Ephesians in Light of its Historical Setting* (Cambridge: Cambridge University Press, 1989).

The Colossian Syncretism: The Interface Between Christianity and Folk Belief at Colossae (Tübingen: Mohr Siebeck, 1995).

Attridge, Harold W. *The Epistle to the Hebrews*. Hermeneia (Philadelphia: Fortress Press, 1989).

Aulén, Gustaf. *Christus Victor: An Historical Study of the Three Main Types of the Idea of Atonement*, translated by A.G. Herbert (London: SPCK, 1965).

Awad, Najeeb G. 'Between Subordination and Koinonia: Toward a New Reading of the Cappadocian Theology', *Modern Theology*, 23, no. 2 (2007), 181–204.

Ayres, Lewis. *Nicaea and Its Legacy: An Approach to Fourth-Century Trinitarian Theology* (Oxford: Oxford University Press, 2004).

Baer, Richard A. *Philo's Use of the Categories Male and Female* (Leiden: Brill, 1970).

Baghos, Mario. 'St Gregory the Theologian's Metanarrative of History', *Phronema*, 26, no. 2 (2011), 63–79.

Bahrani, Zainab. *The Graven Image: Representation in Babylonia and Assyria* (Philadelphia: University of Pennsylvania Press, 2003).

Balthasar, Hans Urs von. *Origen, Spirit and Fire: A Thematic Anthology of His Writings*, translated by Robert J. Daly (Edinburgh: T&T Clark, 2001).

Barasch, Moshe. *Icon: Studies in the History of an Idea* (New York: New York University Press, 1992).

Barbel, Joseph. *Gregor von Nazianz. Die fünf theologischen Reden* (Düsseldorf: Patmos-Verlag, 1963).

Barnes, Michel R. *The Power of God: Dunamis in Gregory of Nyssa's Trinitarian Theology* (WA, DC: Catholic University of America Press, 2001).

Barnett, Paul W. *The Second Epistle to the Corinthians* (Grand Rapids: Eerdmans, 1997).

Bartina, Sebastián. '"Cristo imagen del Dios invisible" según los papiros', *Studia Papyrologica*, 2 (1963), 13–34.

Batten, Alicia J. 'Neither Gold nor Braided Hair (1 Timothy 2.9; 1 Peter 3.3): Adornment, Gender and Honour in Antiquity', *NTS*, 55, no. 4 (2009), 484–501.

Baynes, Norman Hepburn. 'St. Anthony and the Demons', *JEA*, 40 (1954), 7–10.

Beagon, Philip M. 'The Cappadocian Fathers, Women and Ecclesiastical Politics', *VC*, 49, no. 2 (1995), 165–79.

Beale, Gregory K. *The Temple and the Church's Mission: A Biblical Theology of the Dwelling Place of God*. NSBT, (Leicester: Apollos, 2004).

Beasley-Murray, George R. *Word Biblical Commentary* (Mexico: Thomas Nelson Publishers, 2000).

Beeley, Christopher A. 'Divine Causality and the Monarchy of God the Father in Gregory of Nazianzus', *HTR*, 100, no. 2 (2007), 199–214.

Gregory of Nazianzus on the Trinity and the Knowledge of God: In Your Light We Shall See Light (Oxford: Oxford University Press, 2008).

'Gregory of Nazianzus on the Unity of Christ' in Peter William Martens (ed.), *In the Shadow of the Incarnation: Essays on Jesus Christ in the Early Church in Honor of Brian E. Daley, S.J.* (Notre Dame, IN: University of Notre Dame Press, 2008, 97–120).

'The Holy Spirit in Gregory Nazianzen: The Pneumatology of Oration 31' in Andrew Brian McGowan, Brian Edward Daley, and Timothy J. Gaden (eds.), *God in Early Christian Thought: Essays in Memory of Lloyd G. Patterson* (Leiden: Brill, 2009, 151–62).

'The Holy Spirit in the Cappadocians: Past and Present', *Modern Theology*, 26, no. 1 (2010), 90–119.

'The Early Christological Controversy: Apollinarius, Diodore, and Gregory Nazianzen'. *VC*, 65, no. 4 (2011), 376–407.

The Unity of Christ: Continuity and Conflict in Patristic Tradition (New Haven: Yale University Press, 2012).

Behr, John. *St. Irenaeus of Lyons: The Apostolic Preaching* (Crestwood, New York: St Vladimir's Seminary Press, 1997).

Asceticism and Anthropology in Irenaeus and Clement (Oxford: Oxford University Press, 2000).

The Nicene Faith, vol. 2 (Crestwood, New York: St. Vladimir's Seminary Press, 2004).

The Mystery of Christ: Life in Death (Crestwood, New York: St. Vladimir's Seminary Press, 2006).

Irenaeus of Lyons: Identifying Christianity (Oxford: Oxford University Press, 2013).

Behr-Sigel, Elisabeth. *The Ministry of Women in the Church*, translated by Fr. Stehpen Bigham (Pasadena, CA: Oakwood Publications, 1991).

Belting, Hans. *Likeness and Presence: A History of the Image Before the Era of Art*, translated by Edmund Jephcott (Chicago: University of Chicago Press, 1994).

Bergmann, Sigurd. *Creation Set Free: The Spirit as Liberator of Nature* (Grand Rapids: Eerdmans, 2005).

Berkhof, Hendrickus. *Christ and the Powers* (Scottsdale: Herald, 1962).

Berkouwer, G.C. *Man: The Image of God*. Studies in Dogmatics (Grand Rapids: Eerdmans, 1962).

Bernardi, Jean. *Saint Grégoire de Nazianze: le Théologien et son temps, 330–390. IPE* (Paris: Les Éditions du Cerf, 1995).

Besançon, Alain. *The Forbidden Image: An Intellectual History of Iconoclasm* (Chicago, IL: University of Chicago Press, 2000).

Bidlack, Bede Benjamin. *In Good Company: The Body and Divinization in Pierre Teilhard de Chardin, SJ and Daoist Xiao Yingsou* (Leiden: Brill, 2015).

Bird, Phyllis A. 'Sexual-Differentiation and Divine Image in the Genesis Creation Texts' in Kari Elisabeth Børresen (ed.), *Image of God and Gender Models in Judaeo-Christian Tradition* (Oslo: Solum Forag, 1991), 11–35.

Blackwell, Ben C. *Christosis: Pauline Soteriology in Light of Deification in Irenaeus and Cyril of Alexandria* (Tübingen: Mohr Siebeck, 2011).

Blosser, Benjamin P. *Become Like the Angels* (Washington, DC: Catholic University of America Press, 2012).

Bobrinskoy, Boris. 'The Indwelling of the Spirit in Christ: "Pneumatic Christology" in the Cappadocian Fathers', *SVTQ*, 28, no. 1 (1984), 49–65.

The Mystery of the Trinity: Trinitarian Experience and Vision in the Biblical and Patristic Tradition (Crestwood, New York: St. Vladimir's Seminary Press, 1999).

Bockmuehl, Markus. '"The Form of God" (Phil. 2: 6). Variations on a Theme of Jewish Mysticism', *JTS*, 48, no. 1 (1997), 1–23.

Boersma, Hans. *Violence, Hospitality, and the Cross: Reappropriating the Atonement Tradition* (Grand Rapids, MI: Baker Academic, 2004).

Bonner, Gerald. *The Warfare of Christ* (London; New York: Faith Press; Morehouse-Barlow, 1962).

Børresen, Kari Elisabeth. 'God's Image, Man's Image?' in Kari Elisabeth Børresen (ed.), *Image of God and Gender Models in Judaeo-Christian Tradition* (Oslo: Solum Forag, 1991), 188–207.

Børtnes, Jostein. 'Eikôn Theou: Meanings of Likeness in Gregory of Nazianzus' in Frances M. Young, Mark J. Edwards, and Paul Parvis (eds.), *Studia Patristica* 41 (Leuven: Peeters, 2006), 287–91.

'Rhetoric and Mental Images in Gregory' in Jostein Børtnes and Tomas Hägg (eds.), *Gregory of Nazianzus: Images and Reflections* (Chicago: Museum Tusculanum, 2006), 37–57.

Bourassa, François. *Excellence de la virginité: arguments patristiques* (Montréal: Facultés de théologie et de philosophies de la Compagnie de Jésus, 1953).

Bouteneff, Peter. 'St Gregory Nazianzen and Two-Nature Christology', *SVTQ*, 38, no. 3 (1994), 255–70.

Beginnings: Ancient Christian Readings of the Biblical Creation Narratives (Grand Rapids, MI: Baker Academic, 2008).

Bouyer, Louis. *The Spirituality of the New Testament and the Fathers*, translated by Mary P. Ryan (London: Burns and Oates, 1963).

Bradshaw, Paul F. *The Search for the Origins of Christian Worship: Sources and Methods for the Study of Early Liturgy* (London: SPCK, 2002).

Brakke, David. 'The Making of Monastic Demonology: Three Ascetic Teachers on Withdrawal and Resistance', *Church History*, 70, no. 1 (2001), 19–48.

'Athanasius' in Philip F. Esler (ed.), *Early Christian World* (London: Taylor & Francis, 2002), 1102–27.

Demons and the Making of the Monk: Spiritual Combat in Early Christianity (Cambridge, MA: Harvard University Press, 2009).

Talking Back: A Monastic Handbook for Combating Demons (MN: Cistercian Publications, 2009).

Brayford, Sarah A. *Genesis* (Leiden: Brill, 2007).

Brettler, Marc Z. *God is King: Understanding an Israelite Metaphor* (Sheffield: JSOT Press, 1989).

Brock, Sebastian P. 'Jewish Traditions in Syriac Sources', *JJS*, 30, no. 2 (1979), 212–32.

Ephrem, Saint. Hymns on Paradise (Crestwood, New York: St. Vladimir's Seminary Press, 1990).

Brown, David. *Divine Humanity: Kenosis Explored and Defended* (London: SCM Press, 2010).

Brown, Peter. *The Making of Late Antiquity* (Cambridge, MA: Harvard University Press, 1978).

The Body and Society: Men, Women, and Sexual Renunciation in Early Christianity (New York: Columbia University Press, 2008).

Brubaker, Leslie. *Vision and Meaning in Ninth-Century Byzantium: Image as Exegesis in the Homilies of Gregory of Nazianzus* (Cambridge: Cambridge University Press, 1999).

Bruce, Frank F. *The Epistle to the Hebrews* (Grand Rapids: Eerdmans, 1964).

Bucur, Bogdan G. 'From Jewish Apocalypticism to Orthodox Mysticism' in Augustine Casiday (ed.), *The Orthodox Christian World* (Oxford; New York: Routledge, 2012), 466–80.

Bucur, Bogdan G., and Elijah N. Mueller. 'Gregory Nazianzen's Reading of Habbakuk 3:2 and its Reception: A Lesson from Byzantine Scripture Exegesis', *Pro Ecclesia*, 20, no. 1 (2011), 86–103.

Bultmann, Rudolf. 'New Testament and Mythology' in Hans Werner Bartsch (ed.), *Kerygma and Myth: A Theological Debate* (London: SPCK, 1964), 1–44.

Burke, Kenneth. *The Rhetoric of Religion*, (Boston: Beacon Press, 1961).

Burkert, Walter. *Greek Religion*, translated by John Raffan (Cambridge, MA: Harvard University Press, 1985).

Burns, J. Patout. 'The Economy of Salvation: Two Patristic Traditions' in Everett Ferguson (ed.), *Doctrines of Human Nature, Sin, and Salvation in the Early Church* (New York: Garland, 1993), 224–46.

Burrus, Virginia. *Begotten, Not Made: Conceiving Manhood in Late Antiquity* (Redwood, CA: Stanford University Press, 2000).

Butterworth, George W. *Origen. On First Principles* (London: SPCK, 1936).

Caird, George. *Principalities and Powers* (Oxford: Clarendon Press, 1956).

Cameron, Averil. *Christianity and the Rhetoric of Empire: The Development of Christian Discourse* (Berkeley: University of California Press, 1991).

Capone, Alessandro. 'Apollonaris, Basil and Gregory of Nyssa', *ZAC*, 17, no. 2 (2013), 315–31.

Carr, Wesley. *Angels and Principalities* (Cambridge: Cambridge University Press, 1981).

Cartwright, Sophie. *The Theological Anthropology of Eustathius of Antioch* (Oxford: Oxford University Press, 2015).

Chalupa, Aleš. 'How Did Roman Emperors Become Gods? Various Concepts of Imperial Apotheosis*', *Anodos: Studies of the Ancient World*, 6, no. 7 (2007), 201–07.

Chryssavgis, John. *In The Heart Of The Desert: The Spirituality of the Desert Fathers and Mothers* (IN: World Wisdom Inc., 2008).

Church of England. *The Book of Common Prayer, 1662* (Cambridge: Cambridge University Press, 1960).

Clark, Elizabeth A. *Women in the Early Church* (Collegeville, MN: Liturgical Press, 1983).

   Reading Renunciation: Asceticism and Scripture in Early Christianity (Princeton, NJ: Princeton University Press, 1999).

Clifford, Richard J. 'The Hebrew Scriptures and the Theology of Creation', *Theological Studies*, 46, no. 3 (1985), 507–23.

   Creation Accounts in the Ancient Near East and in the Bible (WA, DC: CBAA, 1994).

Clines, David J.A. 'The Image of God in Man', *TB*, 19 (1968), 53–103.

Collins, Antoinette. 'Dualism and the (LXX) Book of Genesis', *Phronema*, 14 (1999), 45–52.

Collins, Paul M. 'Between Creation and Salvation: Theosis and Theurgy' in Vladimir Kharlamov (ed.), *Theosis: Deification in Christian Theology*, vol. 2 (Cambridge: James Clarke & Co., 2012), 192–204.

Conway-Jones, Ann. *Gregory of Nyssa's Tabernacle Imagery in its Jewish and Christian Contexts*, (Oxford: Oxford University Press, 2014).

Conzelmann, Hans. 'φῶς' in Gerhard Kittel and Gerhard Freidrich (eds.), *Φ-Ω TDNT*, vol. 9 (Grand Rapids: Eerdmans, 1974), 310–58.

Cook, Christopher C.H. *The Philokalia and the Inner Life: On Passions and Prayer* (Eugene, OR: Wipf & Stock, 2012).

Copan, Paul. 'Is Creatio Ex Nihilo a Post-Biblical Invention? An Examination of Gerhard May's Proposal', *Trinity Journal*, 17, no. 1 (1996), 77–93.

Corrigan, Kevin. *Evagrius and Gregory: Mind, Soul and Body in the 4th Century* (Surrey: Ashgate Publishing Limited, 2009).

Cortez, Marc. *Embodied Souls, Ensouled Bodies* (London: T&T Clark, 2008).

'Idols, Images and a Spirit-ed Anthropology' in Myk Habets (ed.), *A Pneumatological Account of the Imago Dei* (Minneapolis: Fortress Press, 2016), 267–82.

Costache, Doru. 'Experiencing the Divine Life: Levels of Participation in St Gregory Palamas' On the Divine and Deifying Participation', *Phronema*, 26, no. 1 (2011), 9–25.

'Seeking Out the Antecedents of the Maximian Theory of Everything: St Gregory the Theologian's Oration 38' in Doru Costache and Philip Kariatils (ed.), *The Cappadocian Legacy: A Critical Appraisal* (Redfern, NSW: St Andrew's Orthodox Press, 2013), 225–42.

Coulie, Bernard. *Les richesses dans l'oeuvre de saint Grégoire de Nazianze*, Étude littéraire et historique, PIOL 32 (Louvain: Université Catholique de Louvain, 1985).

Cousar, Charles B. *Philippians and Philemon: A Commentary. NTL* (Louisville, KY: Westminster John Knox Press, 2009).

Crouch, Carly L. 'Genesis 1:26–7 as a Statement of Humanity's Divine Parentage', *JTS*, 61, no. 1 (2010), 1–15.

'Made in the Image of God: The Creation of אדם, the Commissioning of the King and the Chaoskampf of YHWH', *JANER*, 16, no. 1 (2016), 1–21.

Crouzel, Henri. *Théologie de l'image de Dieu chez Origène* (Paris: Aubier, 1954).

Culp, Kristine. *Vulnerability and Glory* (Louisville: Westminster John Knox, 2010).

Curtis, Edward M. 'Image of God' in David N. Freeman (ed.), *ABD, H-J*, (New York: Doubleday, 1992), 389–91.

Daley, Brian. *The Hope of the Early Church: A Handbook of Patristic Eschatology* (Cambridge: Cambridge University Press, 1991).

'"Heavenly Man" and "Eternal Christ": Apollinarius and Gregory of Nyssa on the Personal Identity of the Savior', *JECS*, 10, no. 4 (2002), 469–88.

'Saint Gregory of Nazianzus as Pastor and Theologian' in Michael Welker and Cynthia A. Jarvis (eds.), *Loving God with Our Minds: The Pastor as Theologian* (Grand Rapids: Eerdmans, 2004), 106–18.

Gregory of Nazianzus (London: Taylor & Francis, 2006).

'Walking through the Word of God: Gregory of Nazianzus as a Biblical Interpreter' in J. Ross Wagner, Christopher Kavin Rowe, and A. Katherine Grieb (eds.), *The Word Leaps the Gap: Essays on Scripture and Theology in Honor of Richard B. Hays* (Grand Rapids: Eerdmans, 2008), 514–31.

Daniélou, Jean. *Primitive Christian Symbols* (Baltimore: Helicon Press, 1963).

The Angels and their Mission: According to the Fathers of the Church, translated by David Heimann (Westminster, MD: Christian Classics, Inc., 1982).

Danker, Frederick W., and Walter Bauer. *A Greek-English Lexicon of the New Testament and Other Early Christian Literature*, 3rd ed. (Chicago: University of Chicago Press, 2000).

de Lubac, Henri. *History and Spirit: The Understanding of Scripture According to Origen*, translated by Anne Englund Nash (San Francisco: Ignatius Press, 2007).

Demoen, Kristoffel. *Pagan and Biblical Exempla in Gregory Nazianzen: A Study in Rhetoric and Hermeneutics* (Turnhout: Brepols, 1996).

Dillon, Matthew, and Lynda Garland. *Ancient Greece: Social and Historical Documents from Archaic Times to the Death of Alexander* (London: Routledge, 2010).

Drever, Matthew. *Image, Identity, and the Forming of the Augustinian Soul* (Oxford: OUP, 2013).

Drew-Bear, Anette. *Painted Faces on the Renaissance Stage: The Moral Significance of Face-Painting Conventions* (Lewisburg: Bucknell University Press, 1994).

Dunkle, Brian. *Poems on Scripture: Saint Gregory of Nazianzus* (New York: St. Vladimir's Seminary Press, 2012).

Dunn, James D.G. *The Epistles to the Colossians and to Philemon*, NIGTC (Grand Rapids: Eerdmans, 1996).

The Theology of Paul the Apostle (Edinburgh: T&T Clark, 1998).

Dürr, Oliver. *Der Engel Mächte: Systematisch-theologische Untersuchung: Angelologie* (Stuttgart: Verlag W. Kohlhammer, 2009).

Edwards, Mark J. *Image, Word, and God in the Early Christian Centuries* (Surrey, England: Ashgate Publishing Ltd., 2013).

Origen Against Plato (Aldershot: Ashgate, 2002).

Egan, John P. *The Knowledge and Vision of God according to Gregory Nazianzen: A Study of the Images of Mirror and Light* (Paris: Institut catholique de Paris, 1971).

'The Deceit of the Devil according to Gregory Nazianzen' in Elizabeth A. Livingstone (ed.), *Studia Patristica* 22 (Leuven: Peeters Press, 1989), 8–13.

Ellingworth, Paul. *The Epistle to the Hebrews: A Commentary on the Greek Text* (Grand Rapids: Eerdmans, 1993).

Elliott, James K. *The Apocryphal New Testament: A Collection of Apocryphal Christian Literature in an English Translation* (Oxford: Clarendon Press, 1993).

'The "New" Hennecke', *JSNT*, 35, no. 3 (2013), 285–300.

Ellverson, Anna S. *The Dual Nature of Man: A Study in the Theological Anthropology of Gregory of Nazianzus* (Stockholm: Uppsala, 1981).

Elm, Susanna. *'Virgins of God': The Making of Asceticism in Late Antiquity* (Oxford: Clarendon Press, 1994).

'Inscriptions and Conversions: Gregory of Nazianzus on Baptism (Or. 38–40)' in Kenneth Mills and Anthony Grafton (eds.), *Conversion in Late Antiquity and the Early Middle Ages* (New York: University of Rochester Press, 2003), 1–35.

'"O Paradoxical Fusion!" Gregory of Nazianzus on Baptism and Cosmology (Orations 38–40)' in Annette Yoshiko Reed and Ra'anan S. Boustan (eds.), *Heavenly Realms and Earthly Realities in Late Antique Religions* (New York: Cambridge University Press, 2004), 296–316.

'Gregory's Women: Creating a Philosopher's Family' in Jostein Børtnes and Tomas Hägg (eds.), *Gregory of Nazianzus: Images and Reflections* (Copenhagen: Museum Tusculanum, 2006), 171–92.

'Paul as Conceived by Gregory of Nazianzus: Considerations Regarding His Antiochene Greek and Syriac *Nachleben*' in F. Bonaghi and E. Virginio (eds.), *San Paulo letto da Oriente*, SOCM 18 (Milan: Edizioni Terrae Sanctae, 2010), 109–18.

Sons of Hellenism, Fathers of the Church: Emperor Julian, Gregory of Nazianzus, and the Vision of Rome, (Berkeley: University of California Press, 2012).

'Priest and Prophet: Gregory of Nazianzus's Concept of Christian Leadership as Theosis' in Beate Dignas, Robert Parker, and Guy G. Stroumsa (eds.) *Priests and Prophets among Pagans, Jews and Christians* (Leuven: Peeters, 2013), 162–84.

Elsner, Jaś. 'Iconoclasm as Discourse: From Antiquity to Byzantium', *Art Bulletin*, XCIV, no. 3 (2012), 368–84.

Roman Eyes: Visuality & Subjectivity in Art & Text (Princeton, NJ: Princeton University Press, 2007).

Eltester, Friedrich-Wilhelm. *Eikon im Neuen Testament. BZNW* (Berlin: Topelmann, 1958).

Evdokimov, Paul. *Orthodoxy*, translated by Jeremy Hummerstone (New York: New City Press, 2011).

Faraone, Christopher A. *Talismans and Trojan Horses: Guardians and Statues in Ancient Greek Myth and Ritual* (Oxford: Oxford University Press, 1992).

Fatum, Lone. 'Image of God and Glory of Man: Women in the Pauline Congregations' in Kari Elisabeth Børresen (ed.), *Image of God and Gender Models in Judaeo-Christian Tradition* (Oslo: Solum Forag, 1991), 56–138.

Ferguson, Everett. *Demonology of the Early Christian World* (New York: Edwin Mellen Press, 1984).

Baptism in the Early Church: History, Theology, and Liturgy in the First Five Centuries (Grand Rapids: Eerdmans, 2009).

'Gregory's Baptismal Theology and the Alexandrian Tradition' in Christopher A. Beeley (ed.), *Re-Reading Gregory of Nazianzus* (WA DC: The Catholic University of America Press, 2012), 67–84.

Finn, Thomas M. *Early Christian Baptism and the Catechumenate: West and East Syria* (Collegeville, MN: Liturgical Press, 1992).

Fitzmyer, Joseph A. *Romans: A New Translation with Introduction and Commentary. AYB* (New Haven: Doubleday, 1993).

Fletcher-Louis, Crispin H.T. 'The Worship of Divine Humanity as God's Image' in Carey C. Newman, James R. Davila, and Gladys S. Lewis (eds.), *The Jewish Roots of Christological Monotheism* (Leiden: Brill, 1999), 112–28.

All the Glory of Adam: Liturgical Anthropology in the Dead Sea Scrolls (Leiden: Brill, 2002).

'2 Enoch and the New Perspective on Apocalyptic' in Andrei Orlov, Gabriele Boccaccini, and Jason Zurawski (eds.), *New Perspectives on 2 Enoch: No Longer Slavonic Only* (Leiden: Brill, 2012), 127–48.

Florovsky, Georges. 'Lamb of God', *SJT*, 4, no. 1 (1951), 13–28.

Flusser, David. *Judaism of the Second Temple Period: The Jewish Sages and Their Literature*, translated by Azzan Yadin (Grand Rapids: Eerdmans, 2009).

Forsyth, Neil. *The Old Enemy: Satan and the Combat Myth* (Princeton, NJ: Princeton University Press, 1989).

Fossum, Jarl E. *The Image of the Invisible God: Essays on the Influence of Jewish Mysticism on Early Christology* (Freiburg, Schweiz: Universitätsverlag Freiburg, 1995).

Frank, Karl S. *Angelikos bios. Begriffsanalytische und begriffsgeschichtliche Untersuchung zum "engelgleichen Leben" im frühen Mönchtum* (Münster: Aschendorff, 1964).

Froehlich, Karlfried. *Biblical Interpretation in the Early Church* (Philadelphia: Fortress Press, 1984).

Fulford, Ben. 'Gregory of Nazianzus and Biblical Interpretation' in Christopher A. Beeley (ed.), *Re-Reading Gregory of Nazianzus* (Washington, DC: The Catholic University of America Press, 2012), 31–66.

Divine Eloquence and Human Transformation: Rethinking Scripture and History through Gregory of Nazianzus and Hans Frei (Minneapolis: Augsburg Fortress, 2013).

Gallay, Paul. *La vie de Saint Grégoire de Nazianze* (Lyon: Emmanuel Vitte, 1943).

'La Bible dans l'oeuvre de Grégoire de Nazianze le Théologien' in Claude Mondésert (ed.), *Le monde grec ancien et la Bible* (Paris: Éditions Beauchesne, 1984), 313–34.

Gardner, Iain, and N.C. Lieu Samuel. *Manichaean Texts from the Roman Empire* (Cambridge: Cambridge University Press, 2004).

Garr, W. Randell. *In His Own Image and Likeness: Humanity, Divinity, and Monotheism* (Leiden: Brill, 2003).

Garrett, Susan R. *No Ordinary Angel: Celestial Spirits and Christian Claims About Jesus* (New Haven: Yale University Press, 2008).

Gavrilyuk, Paul. 'The Retrieval of Deification: How a Once-Despised Archaism Became an Ecumenical Desideratum', *Modern Theology*, 25, no. 4 (2009), 647–59.

'Creation in Early Christian Polemical Literature: Irenaeus against the Gnostics and Athanasius against the Arians', *Modern Theology*, 29, no. 2 (2013), 22–32.

Gelpi, Donald L. *The Firstborn of Many: Synoptic Narrative Christology*, vol. 1 (Marquette: Marquette University Press, 2001).

Gilbert, Peter. 'Person and Nature in the Theological Poems of St. Gregory of Nazianzus' (Ph.D. Diss., Catholic University of America, 1994).
On God and Man: The Theological Poetry of St. Gregory of Nazianzus (Crestwood, New York: St. Vladimir's Seminary Press, 2001).
Giulea, Dragoş A. 'The Cappadocian Paschal Christology: Gregory Nazianzen and Gregory of Nyssa on the Paschal Divine Image of Christ', *JAC*, 12 (2009), 475–501.
Pre-Nicene Christology in Paschal Contexts: The Case of the Divine Noetic Anthropos (Leiden: Brill, 2014).
Gleason, Maud W. *Making Men: Sophists and Self-Presentation in Ancient Rome* (Princeton, NJ: Princeton University Press, 1995).
Goehring, James E. *Ascetics, Society, and the Desert: Studies in Early Egyptian Monasticism* (Harrisburg, PA: Trinity Press International, 1999).
Gokey, Francis X. *The Terminology for the Devil and Evil Spirits in the Apostolic Fathers* (Washington: AMS Press, 1961).
Golitzin, Alexander. 'Adam, Eve and Seth: Pneumatological Reflections on an Unusual Image in Gregory of Nazianzus's Fifth Theological Oration', *ATR*, 83, no. 3 (2001), 537–46.
'Recovering the "Glory of Adam": "Divine Light" Traditions in the Dead Sea Scrolls and the Christian Ascetical Literature of Fourth-Century Syro-Mesopotamia' in James R. Davila (ed.), *The Dead Sea Scrolls as Background to Postbiblical Judaism and Early Christianity: Papers from an International Conference at St. Andrews in 2001* (Leiden: Brill, 2003), 275–308.
Gorman, Michael J. *Inhabiting the Cruciform God: Kenosis, Justification, and Theosis in Paul's Narrative Soteriology* (Grand Rapids: Eerdmans, 2009).
Gregg, Robert C. *Consolation Philosophy: Greek and Christian Paideia in Basil and the Two Gregories* (Philadelphia: Philadelphia Patristic Foundation, 1975).
'Gregory Nazianzen's Opponents in Oration 31' in Robert C. Gregg (ed.), *Arianism: Historical and Theological Reassessments* (Eugene, Oregon: Wipf & Stock, 2007), 321–26.
Grenz, Stanley J. *The Social God and the Relational Self: A Trinitarian Theology of the Imago Dei* (Louisville, KY: Westminster John Knox Press, 2001).
Grillmeier, Alois. *Christ in Christian Tradition: From the Apostolic Age to Chalcedon (451)* vol. 1, translated by John S. Bowden. 2nd revised ed. (London: Mowbray, 1965).
Gross, Jules. *The Divinization of the Christian according to the Greek Fathers*, translated by Paul Onica (Anaheim, CA: A&C Press, 2002).
Guiley, Rosemary. *The Encyclopedia of Demons and Demonology* (New York: Facts On File, Infobase Publishing, 2009).
Hahn, Scott W., and David Scott. *Temple and Contemplation: God's Presence in the Cosmos, Church, and Human Heart* (Steubenville, OH: St Paul Center for Biblical Theology, 2008).
Hanson, Richard P.C. *The Search for the Christian Doctrine of God: The Arian Controversy 318–381* (Edinburgh: T&T Clark, 1988).
Harakas, Stanley S. 'Presuppositions for Ethical Method in St. Gregory the Theologian's Five Theological Orations', *GOTR*, 55, no. 1–4 (2010), 89–126.

Harmless, William S.J. *Desert Christians: An Introduction to the Literature of Early Monasticism* (Oxford: Oxford University Press, 2004).

Harnack, Adolf. *History of Dogma. Translated by James Millar*, vol. 3 (London: Williams & Norgate, 1897).

Harris, Harriet A. 'Should We Say that Personhood is Relational?', *SJT*, 51, no. 2 (1998), 214–34.

Harris, Murray J. *The Second Epistle to the Corinthians: A Commentary on the Greek Text* (Grand Rapids: Eerdmans, 2005).

Harrison, Nonna Verna. 'Perichoresis in the Greek Fathers', *SVTQ*, 35, no. 1 (1991): 53–65.

'Feminine Man in Late Antique Ascetic Piety', *Union Seminary Quarterly Review*, 48, no. 3–4 (1994), 49–71.

'The Maleness of Christ', *SVTQ*, 42, no. 2 (1998), 111–51.

'Women, Human Identity, and the Image of God: Antiochene Interpretations', *JECS*, 9, no. 2 (2001), 205–49.

'Women and the Image of God according to St. John Chrysostom' in Paul M. Blowers (ed.), *Dominico Eloquio: Essays on Patristic Exegesis in Honor of Robert Louis Wilken* (Grand Rapids: Eerdmans, 2002), 259–79.

'Gregory Nazianzen's Festal Spirituality: Anamnesis and Mimesis', *Philosophy & Theology*, 18, no. 1 (2006), 27–51.

Gregory Nazianzen: Festal Orations, PPS. Crestwood (New York: St. Vladimir's Seminary Press, 2008).

Harrison, Verna E.F. 'Male and Female in Cappadocian Theology', *JTS*, 41, no. 2 (1990), 441–71.

'Poverty, Social Involvement, and Life in Christ according to Saint Gregory the Theologian', *GOTR*, 39, no. 1–2 (1994), 151–64.

'Illumined from All Sides by the Trinity' in Christopher A. Beeley (ed.), *Re-Reading Gregory of Nazianzus: Essays on History, Theology, and Culture* (WA, DC: Catholic University of America Press, 2012), 13–30.

Haykin, Michael A. *The Spirit of God: The Exegesis of 1 and 2 Corinthians in the Pneumatomachian Controversy of the Fourth Century* (Leiden: Brill, 1993).

Hays, Richard B. *Echoes of Scripture in the Letters of Paul* (New Haven: Yale University Press, 1989).

Herring, Stephen L. 'A "Transubstantiated" Humanity: The Relationship between the Divine Image and the Presence of God in Gen. I 26f', *Vetus Testamentum*, 58 (2008), 1–15.

Divine Substitution: Humanity as the Manifestation of Deity in the Hebrew Bible and the Ancient Near East (Göttingen, Germany: Vandenhoeck & Ruprecht, 2013).

Hiebert, Robert J.V. 'Septuagint: Origins and Significance' in Craig A. Evans, Joel N. Lohr, and David L. Petersen (eds.), *The Book of Genesis: Composition, Reception, and Interpretation* SVT (Leiden: Brill, 2012), 405–26.

Hildebrand, Stephen M. *Saint Basil the Great: On the Holy Spirit*. PPS (Crestwood, New York: St. Vladimir's Seminary Press, 2011).

Hoag, Gary G. 'Decorum and Deeds in 1 Timothy 2:9–10 in light of *Ephesiaca* by Xenophon of Ephesus', *Ex Auditu*, 27 (2011), 134–60.

Hoehner, Harold W. *Ephesians: An Exegetical Commentary* (Grand Rapids, MI: Baker Academic, 2002).

Hofer, Andrew O.P. *Christ in the Life and Teaching of Gregory of Nazianzus* (Oxford: Oxford University Press, 2013).

Holman, Susan. *The Hungry Are Dying: Beggars and Bishops in Roman Cappadocia* (Oxford: Oxford University Press, 2001).

'Out of the Fitting Room: Rethinking Patristic Social Texts on "The Common Good"', in Johan Leemans, Brian J. Matz and Johan Verstraeten (eds.), *Reading Patristic Texts on Social Ethics: Issues and Challenges for Twenty-First Century Christian Social Thought* (Washington, DC: Catholic University of America Press, 2011), 103–23.

Houdret, Jean-Philippe. 'Palamas et le Cappadociens', *Istina*, 19 (1974), 260–71.

Hughes, Philip Edgcumbe. *The True Image: The Origin and Destiny of Man in Christ* (Grand Rapids; Leicester: Eerdmans; Inter-Varsity Press, 1989).

Hultgård, Anders. 'God and Image of Woman in Early Jewish Religion' in Kari Elisabeth Børresen (ed.), *Image of God and Gender Models in Judaeo-Christian Tradition* (Oslo: Solum Forag, 1991), 35–55.

Hunt, Hannah. *Clothed in the Body: Asceticism, the Body and the Spiritual in the Late Antique Era* (Surrey: Ashgate Publishing Limited, 2012).

'"Clothed in the Body": The Garment of Flesh and the Garment of Glory in Syrian Religious Anthropology' in Markus Vincent (ed.), *Studia Patristica 64* (Leuven: Peeters Press, 2013), 167–76.

Hunter, David G. 'The Paradise of Patriarchy: Ambrosiaster on Woman as (Not) God's Image', *JTS*, 43, no. 2 (1992), 447–69.

Hurtado, Larry W. *Lord Jesus Christ: Devotion to Jesus in Earliest Christianity* (Grand Rapids: Eerdmans, 2005).

Jenson, Robert W. *The Triune Identity: God according to the Gospel* (Philadelphia: Fortress Press, 1982).

Jervell, Jacob. *Imago Dei: Gen 1,26f. im Spätjudentum, in der Gnosis und in den paulinischen Briefen* (Göttingen: Vandenhoeck and Ruprecht, 1960).

Johnson, Elizabeth A. 'Redeeming the Name of Christ' in Catherine LaCugna (ed.), *Freeing Theology: The Essentials of Theology in Feminist Perspective* (San Francisco: Harper-San Francisco, 1993), 115–37.

Johnson, Luke Timothy. *Hebrews: A Commentary* (Louisville, KY: Westminster John Knox Press, 2006).

Johnson, Maxwell E. *The Rites of Christian Initiation: Their Evolution and Interpretation* (MI: Liturgical Press, 2007).

Johnson, Michael D. 'Life of Adam and Eve' in James H. Charlesworth (ed.), *The Old Testament Pseudepigrapha* (Garden City, New York: Doubleday, 1985), 249–95.

Jónsson, Gunnlaugur A. *The Image of God: Genesis 1:26–28 in a Century of Old Testament Research*, CBOTS (Stockholm: Almqvist & Wiksell, 1988).

Kaestli, Jean-Daniel, and Pierre Cherix. *L'Évangile de Barthélemy d'après deux écrits apocryphes* (Turnhout: Brepols, 1993).

Kalleres, Dayna. 'Demons and Divine Illumination: A Consideration of Eight Prayers by Gregory of Nazianzus', *VC*, 61, no. 2 (2007), 157–88.

Kannengiesser, Charles. *Handbook of Patristic Exegesis: The Bible in Ancient Christianity*, vol. 1 (Leiden: Brill, 2003).

Kariatlis, Philip. '"What then? Is the Spirit God? Certainly!" St Gregory's Teaching on the Holy Spirit as the Basis of the World's Salvation', *Phronema*, 26, no. 2 (2011), 81–102.

Kelly, Henry Ansgar. *The Devil at Baptism: Ritual, Theology, and Drama* (Ithaca: Cornell University Press, 1985).

Satan: A Biography (Cambridge: Cambridge University Press, 2006).

Kelly, John N.D. *Early Christian Doctrines* (New York: Continuum, 1977).

Kelsey, David. *Eccentric Existence: A Theological Anthropology* (Louisville: Westminster John Knox, 2009).

Kennedy, George A. *A New History of Classical Rhetoric* (Princeton: Princeton University Press, 1994).

Aristotle: On Rhetoric (Oxford: Oxford University Press, 2006).

Keydell, Rudolf. 'Die Unechtheit der Gregor von Nazianz zugeschriebenen Exhortatio ad Virgines', *BZ*, 43, no. 2 (1950), 334–37.

Kharlamov, Vladimir. 'Rhetorical Application of Theosis in Greek Patristic Thought' in Michael J. Christensen and Jeffrey A. Wittung (eds.), *Partakers of the Divine Nature: The History and Development of Deification in the Christian Traditions* (Grand Rapids, Mi: Baker Academic, 2007), 115–31.

'Basil of Caesarea and the Cappadocians on the Distinction between Essence and Energies in God and its Relevance to the Deification Theme' in Vladimir Kharlamov (ed.), *Theosis: Deification in Christian Theology*, vol. 2 (Cambridge: James Clarke & Co., 2012), 100–45.

Kim, Heerak Christian. *The Jerusalem Tradition in the Late Second Temple Period: Diachronic and Synchronic Developments Surrounding Psalms of Solomon 11* (Maryland: University Press of America, 2007).

Kimbriel, Samuel. *Friendship as Sacred Knowing* (Oxford: Oxford University Press, 2014).

Kitzinger, Ernst. 'The Cult of Images in the Age before Iconoclasm', *DOP*, 8 (1954), 83–150.

Koonce, Kirsten. 'Agalma and Eikon', *American Journal of Philology*, 109, no. 1 (1988), 108–10.

Kovacs, Judith L. '"Now Shall the Ruler of This World Be Driven Out": Jesus' Death as Cosmic Battle in John 12:20–36', *JBL*, 114, no. 2 (1995), 227–47.

Kraemer, Ross Shepherd. *When Aseneth Met Joseph: A Late Antique Tale of the Biblical Patriarch and His Egyptian Wife, Reconsidered* (Oxford: Oxford University Press, 1998).

Krueger, Derek. *Liturgical Subjects: Christian Ritual, Biblical Narrative, and the Formation of the Self in Byzantium* (Philadelphia, PA: University of Pennsylvania Press, 2014).

Kugel, James L. *Traditions of the Bible: A Guide to the Bible As It Was at the Start of the Common Era* (New York: Harvard University Press, 2009).

Kuhn, Harold Barnes. 'The Angelology of the Non-Canonical Jewish Apocalypses', *JBL*, 67, no. 3 (1948), 217–32.

Kustas, George. *Studies in Byzantine Rhetoric* (Thessalonike: Patriarchal Institute, 1973).

Lambden, Stephen N. 'From Figleaves to Fingernails: Some Notes on the Garments of Adam and Eve in the Hebrew Bible and Select Early Postbiblical Jewish Writings' in Paul Morris and Deborah Sawyer (eds.), *A Walk in the Garden: Biblical, Iconographical and Literary Images of Eden* (Sheffield: JSOT Press, 1992), 74–90.

Lampe, Geoffrey W.H. *Patristic Greek Lexicon* (Oxford: Clarendon Press, 1961).

The Seal of the Spirit: A Study in the Doctrine of Baptism and Confirmation in the New Testament and the Fathers, 2nd ed. (London: SPCK, 1967).

Lampert, Evgeny. *The Divine Realm: Towards a Theology of the Sacraments* (London: Faber and Faber, 1944).

Lane Fox, Robin. *Pagans and Christians* (Harmondsworth: Viking, 1986).

Lane, William L. *Hebrews 1–8*. WBC (Dallas, Texas: Word Books, 1991).

Langton, Edward. *Essentials of Demonology: A Study of Jewish and Christian Doctrine, its Origin and Development* (London: Epworth, 1949).

Lee, Michelle M. *Body, Dress, and Identity in Ancient Greece* (Cambridge: Cambridge University Press, 2015).

Leonhardt-Balzer, Jutta. 'The Ruler of the World, Antichrists and Pseudo-Prophets: Johannine Variations on an Apocalyptic Motif' in Catrin H. Williams and Christopher Rowland (eds.), *John's Gospel and Imitations of Apocalyptic* (London: T&T Clark, 2013), 180–99.

Letham, Robert. *The Holy Trinity: in Scripture, History, Theology, and Worship* (Phillipsburg, NJ: P&R Publishing, 2004).

Levison, John R. *Portraits of Adam in Early Judaism: from Sirach to 2 Baruch.* JSPSS (Sheffield: JSOT, 1988).

Leys, Roger. *L'image de Dieu chez Saint Grégoire de Nysse: Esquisse d'une doctrine* (Paris: Desclée de Brouwer, 1951).

Liddell, Henry George, Robert Scott, and Henry Stuart Jones. *A Greek-English Lexicon*, 9th with supplement ed. (Oxford: Clarendon Press, 1940, reprinted 1973).

Limberis, Vasiliki M. *Architects of Piety: The Cappadocian Fathers and the Cult of the Martyrs* (Oxford: Oxford University Press, 2011).

Litwa, David. *Becoming Divine: An Introduction to Deification in Western Culture* (Eugene, Oregon: Wipf & Stock, 2013).

Long, Anthony A., and David N. Sedley. *The Hellenistic Philosophers: Volume 1, Translations of the Principal Sources with Philosophical Commentary. Cambridge* (New York: Cambridge University Press, 1987).

Longenecker, Richard N. *Biblical Exegesis in the Apostolic Period* (Grand Rapids: Eerdmans, 1999).

Lossky, Vladimir. *In the Image and Likeness of God* (Crestwood, New York: St. Vladimir's Seminary Press, 1974).

The Vision of God, 2nd ed. (Crestwood, New York: St. Vladimir's Seminary Press, 1983).

Lot-Borodine, Myrrha. *La Déification de l'homme, selon la doctrine des Pères grecs* (Paris: Les Éditions du Cerf, 1970).

Louth, Andrew. *Denys the Areopagite* (London: Continuum, 2001).

'The Fathers on Genesis' in Craig A. Evans, Joel N. Lohr, and David L. Petersen (eds.), *The Book of Genesis: Composition, Reception, and Interpretation* (Leiden: Brill, 2012), 561–78.

Ludlow, Morwenna. 'Demons, Evil and Liminality in Cappadocian Theology', *JECS*, 20, no. 2 (2012), 179–211.

Ludlow, Morwenna, and Scot Ray Douglass (eds.) *Reading the Church Fathers.* (New York: T&T Clark, 2011).

Macaskill, Grant. 'Adam Octipartite/Septipartite' in Richard Bauckham, James R. Davila, and Alexander Panayotov (eds.), *Old Testament Pseudepigrapha: More Noncanonical Scriptures* (Grand Rapids: Eerdmans, 2013), 3–21.

MacCormack, Sabine. *Art and Ceremony in Late Antiquity* (Berkeley: University of California Press, 1981).

MacLeod, David J. 'The Finality of Christ: An Exposition of Hebrews 1:1–4', *Bibliotheca Sacra*, 162, no. 646 (2005), 210–30.

Mantzaridis, Georgios I. *The Deification of Man* (Crestwood, New York: St. Vladimir's Seminary Press, 1984).

Maritz, Petrus J. 'Logos Articulation in Gregory of Nazianzus' in Hendrick F. Stander (ed.), *Acta Patristica et Byzantina* (Pretoria: University of Pretoria, Department of Ancient Languages, 1995), 99–108.

Marti, Berte M. 'Proskynesis and Adorare', *Language*, 12 (1936), 272–82.

Martin, Bruce L. *Christ and the Law in Paul* (Eugene, OR: Wipf & Stock, 2001).

Martin, Dale B. *The Corinthian Body* (New Haven: Yale University Press, 1999).

Inventing Superstition (Cambridge, MA: Harvard University Press, 2004).

'When Did Angels Become Demons?', *JBL*, 129, no. 4 (2010), 657–77.

Martos, Joseph. *Doors to the Sacred: A Historical Introduction to Sacraments in the Christian Church* (London: SCM Press, 1981).

Maslov, Boris. 'The Limits of Platonism: Gregory of Nazianzus and the Invention of Theosis', *GRBS*, 52 (2012), 440–68.

'οἰκείωσις πρὸς θεόν: Gregory of Nazianzus and the Heteronomous Subject of Eastern Christian Penance', *ZAC*, 16 (2012), 311–43.

Matz, Brian J. 'Philippians 2:7 as Pastoral Example in Gregory Nazianzen's Oration 12', *GOTR*, 49, no. 3–4 (2004), 270–90.

'Deciphering a Recipe for Biblical Preaching in *Oration 14*' in Christopher A. Beeley (ed.), *Re-Reading Gregory of Nazianzus* (Washington, DC: The Catholic University of America Press, 2012), 49–66.

Gregory of Nazianzus (Grand Rapids, MI: Baker Academic, 2016).

May, Gerhard. *Creatio Ex Nihilo* (New York: T&T Clark, 2004).

McDonnell, Killan, and George T. Montague. *Christian Initiation and Baptism in the Holy Spirit: Evidence from the First Eight Centuries* (MI: Liturgical Press, 1991).

McFadyen, Alistair I. *The Call to Personhood: A Christian Theory of the Individual in Social Relationships* (Cambridge: Cambridge University Press, 1990).

McFarland, Ian A. *The Divine Image: Envisioning the Invisible God* (Philadelphia: Fortress Press, 2005).

McGrath, Alister E. *Scientific Theology: Nature*, vol. 1 (Edinburgh: T&T Clark, 2002).

McGuckin, John A. '"Perceiving Light from Light in Light" (Oration 31.3): The Trinitarian Theology of Saint Gregory the Theologian', *GOTR*, 39, no. 1–2 (1994), 7–32.

St. Gregory of Nazianzus: An Intellectual Biography (Crestwood, New York: St. Vladimir's Seminary Press, 2001).

'The Strategic Adaptation of Deification in the Cappadocians' in Michael J. Christensen and Jeffery A. Wittung (eds.), *Partakers of the Divine Nature: The History and Development of Deification in the Christian Traditions* (Madison: Fairleigh Dickinson University Press, 2007), 95–114.

McLeod, Frederick G. *The Image of God in the Antiochene Tradition* (Washington, DC: Catholic University of America Press, 1999).

McLynn, Neil. 'The Other Olympias: Gregory Nazianzen and the Family of Vitalianus' in Neil McLynn (ed.), *Christian Politics and Religious Culture in Late Antiquity* (Surrey: Ashgate Publishing Ltd, 2009), 227–46.

Meehan, Denis M. 'Editions of Saint Gregory of Nazianzus', *ITQ*, 3 (1951), 203–19.

Three Poems (Washington, DC: Catholic University of America Press, 1987).

Meeks, Wayne. *The Origins of Christian Morality: The First Two Centuries* (New Haven: Yale University Press, 1993).

Merki, Hubert. ὁμοίωσις θεῷ. *Von der platonischen Angleichung an Gott zur Gottähnlichkeit bei Gregor von Nyssa* (Freiburg: Paulusverlag, 1952).

Meyendorff, John. *Byzantine Theology: Historical Trends and Doctrinal Themes* (USA: Fordham University Press, 1983).

Michaelis, Wilhelm. 'κοσμοκράτωρ' in Geoffrey William Bromiley (ed.), *Θ-Κ TDNT*, vol 3 (Grand Rapids: Eerdmans, 1966), 913–14.

Michopoulos, Tasos Sarris. 'Mimisometha Nomon Theou: Gregory the Theologian's Ontology of Compassion', *GOTR*, 39, no. 1–2 (1994), 109–21.

Middleton, Richard J. '"The Liberating Image?" Interpreting the Imago Dei in Context', *CSR*, 24, no. 1 (1994), 8–25.

The Liberating Image: The Imago Dei in Genesis 1 (Grand Rapids, MI: Baker Publishing Group, 2005).

Milbank, John. 'The Double Glory, or Paradox versus Dialectics: On Not Quite Agreeing with Slavoj Žižek' in Creston Davis (ed.), *The Monstrosity of Christ* (Massachusetts: MIT, 2009), 110–233.

Miles, Margaret. 'Image' in Mark C. Taylor (ed.), *Critical Terms for Religious Studies* (Chicago: University of Chicago Press, 2008), 160–72.

Miller, Patricia Cox. *The Corporeal Imagination: Signifying the Holy in Late Ancient Christianity* (PA: University of Pennsylvania Press Incorporated, 2012).

Milovanović-Barham, Čelica. 'Sailing to Sophistopolis: Gregory of Nazianzus and Greek Declamation', *JECS*, 13, no. 2 (2005), 187–232.

Misch, Georg. *A History of Autobiography in Antiquity* (London: Routledge, 1950).

Molac, Philippe. *Douleur et transfiguration. Une lecture du cheminement spirituel de saint Grégoire de Nazianze* (Paris: Les Éditions du Cerf, 2006).

'"A-t-il commis une faute en étant pour toi miséricordieux? Pour moi, c'est très admirable!" la Christologie dans le deuxième poème dogmatique de Grégoire de Nazianze', *BLE*, 109, no. 4 (2008), 307–38.

Moreschini, Claudio. *Filosofia e letteratura in Gregorio di Nazianzo* (Milan: Vita e Pensiero, 1997).

'Nuove considerazione sull'origenismo di Gregorio Nazianzo' in Mario Giradi and Marcello Marin (eds.), *Origene e l'alessandrinismo cappadoce (III-IV secolo)* (Bari: Edipuglia, 2002), 207–18.

Moreschini, Claudio; Ivano Costa, Carmelo Crimi, and Giovanni Laudizi. *Gregorio Nazianzeno: Poesie*, vol. 1 (Roma: Città Nuova Editrice, 1994).

Mosser, Carl. 'The Earliest Patristic Interpretations of Psalm 82, Jewish Antecedents, and the Origin of Christian Deification', *JTS*, 56, no. 1 (2005), 30–74.

Mosshammer, Alden A. 'Non-Being and Evil in Gregory of Nyssa', *VC*, 44 (1990), 136–67.

Muehlberger, Ellen. *Angels in the Religious Imagination of Late Antiquity* (IN: Indiana University, 2008).

Mueller, Elijah N. 'Temple and Angel: An Outline of Apocalyptic Themes in John of Damascene' in Robert J. Daly (ed.), *Apocalyptic Thought in Early Christianity* (Grand Rapids, MI: Baker Publishing Group, 2009), 240–49.

Mumford, James. *Ethics at the Beginning of Life: A Phenomenological Critique* (Oxford: Oxford University Press, 2013).

Muraoka, Takamitsu. *A Greek-English Lexicon of the Septuagint* (Leuven: Peeters, 2009).

Myers, Ben. 'Atonement and the Image of God' in *Los Angeles Theology Conference* (Los Angeles, 15–16 January 2015).

Nasrallah, Laura. 'The Earthen Human, the Breathing Statue: The Sculptor God, Greco-Roman Statuary, and Clement of Alexandria' in Konrad Schmid and Christopher Riedweg (eds.), *Beyond Eden: The Biblical Story of Paradise [Genesis 2–3] and its Reception History* (Tübingen: Mohr Siebeck, 2008), 110–40.

Nellas, Panayiotis. *Deification in Christ: Orthodox Perspectives on the Nature of the Human Person* (Crestwood, New York: St. Vladimir's Seminary Press, 1987).

Noble, Thomas A. 'Gregory Nazianzen's Use of Scripture in Defence of the Deity of the Spirit', *TB*, 39 (1988), 101–23.

'The Deity of the Holy Spirit according to Gregory of Nazianzus' (Ph.D. Diss., Edinburgh, 1989).

Nock, Arthur D. 'A Diis Electa' in Zeph Stewart (ed.), *Essays on Religion and the Ancient World* (Oxford: Clarendon Press, 1972), 232–76.

'Notes on Ruler-Cult I–IV' in Zeph Stewart (ed.), *Essays on Religion and the Ancient World* (Oxford: Clarendon Press, 1972), 134–59.

Norét, Jacques. 'Grégoire de Nazianze, l'auteur le plus cité, après la Bible, dans la littérature ecclésiastique byzantine' in Justin Mossay (ed.), *Symposium Nazianzenum 2* (Schöningh: Paderborn, 1983), 259–66.

Norris, Frederick W. 'Gregory Nazianzen's Doctrine of Jesus Christ', (Ph.D. Diss., Yale, 1970).

Faith Gives Fullness to Reasoning: The Five Theological Orations of Gregory Nazianzen (Leiden: Brill, 1990).

'Deification: Consensual and Cogent', *SJT*, 49, no. 4 (1996), 411–28.

'Gregory Contemplating the Beautiful: Knowing Human Misery and Divine Mystery through and Being Persuaded by Images' in Jostein Børtnes and Tomas Hägg (eds.), *Gregory of Nazianzus: Images and Reflections* (Copenhagen: Museum Tusculanum, 2006), 19–36.

O'Brien, Peter T. *Colossians, Philemon* WBC. (Waco, TX: Word Books, 1982).

O'Donnell Gandolfo, Elizabeth. *The Power and Vulnerability of Love* (Minneapolis: Fortress Press, 2015).

Opperwall, Daniel G. 'The Holy Spirit in the Life and Writings of Gregory of Nazianzus' (Ph.D. Diss., Open Access Dissertations and Theses: McMaster, 2012).

Orlov, Andrei A. *From Apocalypticism to Merkabah Mysticism: Studies in the Slavonic Pseudepigrapha* (Leiden: Brill, 2007).

Otis, Brooks. 'The Throne and the Mountain: An Essay on St. Gregory Nazianzus', *CJ*, 56, no. 4 (1961), 146–65.

Patlagean, Evelyne. 'Remarques sur la production et la diffusion des apocryphes dans le monde byzantin', *Apocrypha*, 2 (1991), 155–64.

Patmore, Hector M. *Adam, Satan, and the King of Tyre: The Interpretation of Ezekiel 28:11–19 in Late Antiquity* (Leiden: Brill, 2012).

Peers, Glenn. *Subtle Bodies: Representing Angels in Byzantium* (CA: University of California Press, 2001).

Pelikan, Jaroslav. *Christianity and Classical Culture: The Metamorphosis of Natural Theology in the Christian Encounter with Hellenism.* (New Haven; London: Yale University Press, 1993).

Peters, Francis E. *Greek Philosophical Terms: A Historical Lexicon* (New York: New York University Press, 1967).

Peterson, Erik. 'Theologie des Kleides', *BM*, 16 (1934), 347–56.

Pettorelli, Jean-Pierre, Jean-Daniel Kaestli, Albert Frey, and Bernard Outtier. *Vita latina Adae et Evae*, CCSA. vol. 19 (Turnhout: Brepols, 2013).

Pinault, Henri. *Le Platonisme de Saint Grégoire de Nazianze: Essai sur le relations du Christianisme et de l'Hellénisme dans son oeuvre théologique* (La Roche-sur-Yon: G. Romain, 1925).

Plagnieux, Jean. *Saint Grégoire de Nazianze théologien* (Paris: Éditions Franciscaines, 1951).

Plato. *Complete Works* (Indianapolis: Hackett, 1977).

Platt, Verity J. *Facing the Gods: Epiphany and Representation in Greco-Roman Art, Literature and Religion* (Cambridge: Cambridge University Press, 2011).

Popov, Ivan P. 'The Idea of Deification in the Early Eastern Church', translated by Boris Jakim, in Vladimir Kharlamov (ed.), *Theosis: Deification in Christian Theology*, vol. 2 (Cambridge: James Clarke & Co., 2012), 42–82.

Portmann, Franz Xaver. *Die göttliche Paidagogia bei Gregor von Nazianz: eine dogmengeschichtliche Studie* (St. Ottilien: EOS Verlag der Erzabtei St. Ottilien, 1954).

Price, Richard, and Michael Gaddis. *The Acts of the Council of Chalcedon* (Liverpool: Liverpool University Press, 2005).

Prüum, Karl. 'Reflexiones theologicae et historicae ad usum Paulinum termini "eikon"', *Verbum Domini*, XL (1962), 232–57.

Ramelli, Ilaria L.E. 'Evagrius and Gregory: Nazianzen or Nyssen? Cappadocian (and Origenian) Influence on Evagrius', *GRBS*, 53 (2013), 117–37.

The Christian Doctrine of Apokatastasis: A Critical Assessment from the New Testament to Eriugena (Leiden: Brill, 2013).

Reed, Annette Yoshiko. 'The Trickery of the Fallen Angels and the Demonic Mimesis of the Divine: Aetiology, Demonology, and Polemics in the Writings of Justin Martyr', *JECS*, 12, no. 2 (2004), 141–71.

Reno, Russell R. *Genesis* (London: SCM Press, 2010).

Richard, Anne. *Cosmologie et théologie chez Grégoire de Nazianze* (Paris: Institut d'Études Augustiniennes, 2003).

Richards, Jay Wesley. 'Can a Male Savior Save Women?: Gregory of Nazianzus on the Logos' Assumption of Human Nature', *CSR*, 28, no. 1 (1998), 42–57.

Ricoeur, Paul. 'The Model of the Text: Meaningful Action Considered as a Text', *NLH*, 5, no. 1 (1973), 91–117.

Riley, Greg J. 'Devil' in Karen Van Der Toorn, Bob Beckling, and Peter W. Van Der Horst (eds.), *Dictionary of Deities and Demons in the Bible* (Leiden: Brill, 1999), 244–49.

Rist, John. *Plotinus: The Road to Reality* (Cambridge: Cambridge University Press, 1967).

Stoic Philosophy (Cambridge: Cambridge University Press, 1969).

Ritter, Adolf-Martin. *Das Konzil von Konstantinopel und sein Symbol* (Göttingen: Vandenhoeck & Ruprecht, 1965).

Robinson, Dominic. *Understanding the 'Imago Dei': The Thought of Barth, von Balthasar and Moltmann* (Surrey: Ashgate Publishing Limited, 2011).

Rösel, Martin. *Übersetzung als Vollendung der Auslegung*, BZAW (Berlin: de Gruyter, 1994).

Rousse, Jacques. 'Les anges et leur ministère selon Saint Grégoire de Nazianze', *MSR*, 22 (1965), 133–52.

Rousseau, Philip. *Basil of Caesarea* (Los Angeles, CA: University of California Press, 1994).

Rowe, William. 'Adolf Von Harnack and the Concept of Hellenization' in Wendy Helleman (ed.), *Hellenization Revisited: Shaping a Christian Response within the Greco-Roman World* (Lanham, MD: University Press of America, 1994), 69–97.

Ruether, Rosemary Radford. *Gregory of Nazianzus, Rhetor and Philosopher* (Oxford: Clarendon Press, 1969).

'Misogynism and Virginal Feminism in the Fathers of Church' in Rosemary Radford Ruether (ed.), *Religion and Sexism* (New York: Simon and Schuster, 1974), 150–83.

'Can a Male Savior Save Women?' in Rosemary Radford Ruether (ed.), *To Change the World: Christology and Cultural Criticism* (New York: Crossroad, 1981), 45–56.

'The Liberation of Christology' in Ann Loades (ed.), *Feminist Theology: A Reader* (Louisville: Westminster John Knox, 1990), 138–48.

Runia, David T. *Philo in Early Christian Literature: A Survey* (Minneapolis: Fortress Press, 1993).

Philo of Alexandria, on the Creation of the Cosmos according to Moses: Introduction, Translation and Commentary (Leiden: Brill, 2001).

Russell, Daniel C. 'Virtue as "Likeness to God" in Plato and Seneca', *JHP*, 42, no. 3 (2004), 241–60.

Russell, Jeffrey B. *Satan: The Early Christian Tradition* (New York: Cornell University Press, 1987).

Russell, Norman. *The Doctrine of Deification in the Greek Patristic Tradition* (Oxford: Oxford University Press, 2004).

Rybarczyk, Edmund J. *Beyond Salvation: Eastern Orthodoxy and Classical Pentecostalism on Becoming Like Christ* (Carlisle: Paternoster Press, 2004).

Saïd, Suzanne. 'Deux noms de l'image en grec ancien: idole et icône', *CRAI*, 131, no. 2 (1987), 309–30.

Sand, Alexander. 'νοῦς' in Horst Balz and Gerhard Schneider (eds.), *Exegetical Dictionary of the New Testament: Vol 2* (Grand Rapids: Eerdmans, 1991), 478–79.

Sanders, James. 'Why the Pseudepigrapha?' in James H. Charlesworth and Craig A. Evans (eds.), *The Pseudepigrapha and Early Biblical Interpretation* (Sheffield: JSOT Press, 1993), 13–19.

Sasse, Hermann. 'κόσμος' in Gerhard Kittel (ed.), *Θ-Κ TDNT*, vol. 3 (Grand Rapids: Eerdmans, 1971), 867–98.

Scheidweiler, Felix. 'The Gospel of Bartholomew' in Edgar Hennecke, Wilhelm Schneemelcher, and R. McL. Wilson (eds.), *New Testament Apocrypha: Volume One* (London: Lutterworth, 1963), 484–508.

Schlier, Heinrich. *Principalities and Powers in the New Testament* (West Germany: Herder and Herder, 1961).

Schüle, Andreas. 'Made in the "Image of God": The Concepts of Divine Images in Gen 1–3', *ZAW*, 117, no. 1 (2005), 1–20.

Schultz, Daniel R. 'The Origin of Sin in Irenaeus and Jewish Pseudepigraphical Literature', *VC*, 32, no. 3 (1978), 161–90.

Schweizer, Eduard. 'σάρξ' in Gerhard Kittel and Gerhard Freidrich (eds.), *Σ TDNT*, vol. 7 (98–151. Grand Rapids: Eerdmans, 1971).

Scibona, Concetta Giuffré. 'How Monotheistic is Mani's Dualism?', *Numen*, 48, no. 4 (2001), 444–67.

Scroggs, Robin. *The Last Adam: A Study in Pauline Anthropology* (Philadelphia: Fortress Press, 1966).

Sedley, David. 'The Ideal of Godlikeness', in Gail Fine (ed.), *Plato Volume 2: Ethics, Politics, Religion and the Soul* (Oxford: Oxford University Press, 1999), 309–28.

Sekulovski, Goran. 'L'homme à l'image du Christ? Les fondements christologiques de l'anthropologie de Grégoire de Nazianze', *BLE*, CXV, no. 2 (2014), 231–42.

Shaw, Teresa M. *The Burden of the Flesh: Fasting and Sexuality in Early Christianity* (Minneapolis: Fortress Press, 1998).

Shoemaker, Stephen J. 'Early Christian Apocryphal Literature' in Susan A. Harvey and David G. Hunter (eds.), *The Oxford Handbook of Early Christian Studies* (Oxford: Oxford University Press, 2008), 521–48.

Sinkewicz, Robert E. *Evagrius of Pontus: The Greek Ascetic Corpus* (New York: Oxford University Press, 2003).

Smith, John Clark. *Origen. Homilies on Jeremiah; Homily on 1 Kings 28* TFC (WA, DC: Catholic University of America Press, 1998).

Smith, Warren. *Passion and Paradise: Human and Divine Emotion in the Thought of Gregory of Nyssa* (New York: The Crossroad Publishing Company, 2004).

Somers, Véronique. *Histoire des collections complètes des Discours de Grégoire de Nazianze* (Louvain: Université Catholique de Louvain, Institut Orientaliste, 1997).

Sorabji, Richard. *Emotion and Peace of Mind* (Oxford: Oxford University Press, 2000).

Self: Ancient and Modern Insights about Individuality, Life, and Death (Chicago: University of Chicago Press, 2006).

Sperling, S. David. 'Belial' in Karel Van Der Toorn, Bob Beckling, and Pieter W. Van Der Horst (eds.), *Dictionary of Deities and Demons in the Bible* (Leiden: Brill, 1999), 169–71.

Špidlík, Tomáš. *Grégoire de Nazianze* (Roma: Pont. Institutum Studiorum Orientalium, 1971).

Spinks, Bryan D. *Early and Medieval Rituals and Theologies of Baptism: From the New Testament to the Council of Trent* (Aldershot: Ashgate, 2006).

Staley, Erinn. 'Intellectual Disability and Mystical Unknowing: Contemporary Insights from Medieval Sources', *Modern Theology*, 28, no. 3 (2012), 385–401.

Steenberg, David. 'The Case against the Synonymity of Morphe and Eikon', *JSNT* 34 (1988), 77–86.

'The Worship of Adam and Christ as the Image of God', *JSNT*, 39 (1990), 95–109.

Steenberg, Matthew C. 'Children in Paradise: Adam and Eve as "Infants" in Irenaeus of Lyons', *JECS*, 12, no. 1 (2004), 1–22.

Of God and Man: Theology as Anthropology from Irenaeus to Athanasius (New York: T&T Clark, 2009).

Steiger, Peter D. 'The Image of God in the Commentary *On Genesis* of Didymus the Blind' in Frances M. Young, Mark J. Edwards, and Paul Parvis, (eds.), *Studia Patristica* 42 (Leuven: Peeters Publishers, 2006), 243–48.

Steiner, Deborah. *Images in Mind: Statues in Archaic and Classical Greek Literature and Thought* (Princeton, NJ: Princeton University Press, 2001).

Stemmer, Peter. 'Perichorese. Zur Geschichte eines Begriffs', *Archiv für Begriffsgeschichte*, 27 (1983), 9–55.

Sterk, Andrea. *Renouncing the World Yet Leading the Church: The Monk-Bishop in Late Antiquity* (Cambridge, MA: Harvard University Press, 2004).

Stewart, Peter. 'The Image of the Roman Emperor' in Rupert Shepherd and Robert Maniura (eds.), *Presence: The Inherence of the Prototype within Images and Other Objects* (Hants.: Ashgate, 2006), 245–58.

Stone, Michael E. *A History of the Literature of Adam and Eve* (Atlanta: Scholars Press, 1992).

'The Fall of Satan and Adam's Penance: Three Notes on the Books of Adam and Eve', *JTS*, 44, no. 1 (1993), 143–95.

Adam's Contract with Satan: The Legend of the Cheirograph of Adam (Bloomington: Indiana University Press, 2002).

Storin, Bradley K. 'In a Silent Way: Asceticism and Literature in the Rehabilitation of Gregory of Nazianzus', *JECS*, 19, no. 2 (2011), 225–57.

Stout, Ann M. 'Jewellery as a Symbol of Status in the Roman Empire' in Judith L. Sebesta and Larissa Bonfante (eds.), *The World of Roman Costume* (Madison: University of Wisconsin, 1994), 77–100.

Stuckenbruck, Loren T. 'The Origins of Evil in Jewish Apocalyptic Tradition: The Interpretation of Genesis 6:1–4 in the Second and Third Centuries BC' in Christoph Auffarth and Loren T. Stuckenbruck (eds.), *The Fall of the Angels* (Leiden: Brill, 2004), 87–118.

Studer, Basil. *Trinity and Incarnation: The Faith of the Early Church* (Edinburgh: T&T Clark, 1993).

Sykes, Donald A. 'The Poema Arcana of Saint Gregory Nazianzen', *JTS*, 21, no. 1 (1970), 32–42.

Szymusiak, Jan M. *Éléments de théologie de l'homme selon saint Grégoire de Nazianze* (Rome: Pontificia Universitas Gregoriana, 1963).

'Pour une chronologie des discours de S. Grégoire de Nazianze', *VC*, 20 (1966), 183–89.

'Grégoire le théologien, disciple d'Athanase' in Charles Kannengiesser (ed.), *Politique et théologie chez Athanase d'Alexandrie. Actes du Colloque de Chantilly* (Paris: Beauchesne, 1974), 359–63.

Tanner, Kathryn. *Christ the Key* (Cambridge: Cambridge University Press, 2010).

Tavard, George H. *Woman in Christian Tradition* (London: University of Notre Dame Press, 1973).

Taylor, Charles. *Sources of the Self: The Making of the Modern Identity* (New York: Cambridge University Press, 1989).

A Secular Age (Cambridge, MA: Harvard University Press, 2007).

Telepneff, Gregory. 'Theopascite Language in the Soteriology of Saint Gregory the Theologian', *GOTR*, 32, no. 4 (1987), 403–16.

Thomas, Gabrielle. 'Gregory Nazianzen on the Devil and the Image of God: "Worship me!"' in Marcus Vincent and Allan Brent (eds.), *Studia Patristica* 74 (Leuven: Peeters Press, 2016), 181–90.

Tobin, Thomas H. *The Creation of Man: Philo and the History of Interpretation.* Catholic Biblical Quarterly Monograph Series (Washington, DC: Catholic Biblical Association of America, 1983).

Todd, Robert B. *Alexander of Aphrodisias on Stoic Physics: A Study of the De Mexitione with Preliminary Essays, Text, Translation and Commentary* (Leiden: Brill, 1976).

Tollefsen, Torstein Theodor. 'Theosis according to Gregory' in Jostein Børtnes and Tomas Hägg (eds.), *Gregory of Nazianzus: Images and Reflections* (Copenhagen: Museum Tusculanum, 2006), 257–70.

Torrance, Alexis. 'Precedents for Palamas' Essence-Energies Theology in the Cappadocian Fathers', *VC*, 63, no. 1 (2009), 47–70.

Torrance, Thomas F. *Trinitarian Faith: The Evangelical Theology of the Ancient Catholic Faith* (Edinburgh: T&T Clark, 1998).

Tov, Emanuel. 'The Septuagint' in Martin J. Mulder and Harry Sysling (eds.), *Mikra: Text, Translation, Reading and Interpretation of the Hebrew Bible in Ancient Judaism and Early Christianity* (Assen, Philadelphia: Fortress Press, 1988), 161–88.

Towner, Wayne Sibley. *Genesis* (Louisville: Westminster John Knox Press, 2001).

Trigg, Joseph W. *Origen* (London: Routledge, 1998).

'Knowing God in the Theological Orations of Gregory of Nazianzus' in Lloyd G. Patterson, Andrew Brian McGowan, Brian Daley, and Timothy J. Gaden (eds.), *God in Early Christian Thought: Essays in Memory of Lloyd G. Patterson*, SVC (Leiden: Brill, 2009), 83–104.

Trisoglio, Francesco. 'Filone Alessandrino e l'esegesi cristiana: contributo alla conoscenza dell'influsso esercitato da Filone sul IV secolo, specificatamente in Gregorio de Nazianzo', *ANRW II*, 21, no. 1 (1984), 588–730.

'Il demonio in Gregorio di Nazianzo' in Eugenio Corsini (ed.), *L'autunno del diavolo. "Diabolos, Dialogos, Daimon" convegno di Torino 17/21 ottobre 1988, volume primo* (Milano: Bompiani, 1990), 249–65.

San Gregorio di Nazianzo: Un contemporaneo vissuto sedici secoli fa. (Torino: Effatà Editrice, 2008).

Tsirpanlis, Constantine N. 'The Doctrine of Katharsis: Contemplation and Kenosis in St Gregory of Nazianzus', *PBR*, 3 (1984), 5–17.

Van Dam, Raymond. *Kingdom of Snow: Roman Rule and Greek Culture in Cappadocia* (Philadelphia: University of Pennsylvania Press, 2002).

Van Kooten, George H. 'Image, Form and Transformation. A Semantic Taxonomy of Paul's "Morphic" Language' in Rieuwerd Buitenwerf, Harm W. Hollander, and Johannes Tromp (eds.), *Jesus, Paul, and Early Christianity: Studies in Honour of Henk Jan De Jonge* (Leiden: Brill, 2008), 213–42.

Paul's Anthropology in Context: The Image of God, Assimilation to God and Tripartite Man in Ancient Judaism, Ancient Philosophy and Early Christianity (Tübingen: Mohr Siebeck, 2008).

Van Wolde, Ellen J. 'The Text as an Eloquent Guide: Rhetorical, Linguistic and Literary Features in Genesis 1' in Craig A. Evans, Joel N. Lohr, and David L. Petersen (eds.), *The Book of Genesis: Composition, Reception, and Interpretation* (Leiden: Brill, 2012), 134–52.

VanderKam, James C. '1 Enoch, Enochic Motifs, and Enoch in Early Christian Literature' in James C. VanderKam and William Adler (eds.), *The Jewish Apocalyptic Heritage in Early Christianity* (Assen; Minneapolis: Van Gorcum; Fortress, 1996), 33–101.

Vasiliu, Anca. *Eikôn* (Paris: PUF, 2010).

Vinson, Martha Pollard. *St. Gregory of Nazianzus: Select Orations* (WA, DC: Catholic University of America Press, 2003).

Vivian, Tim, Apostolos N. Athanassakis, and Rowan A. Greer. *Athanasius. The Life of Antony* (Kalamazoo, MI: Cistercian Publications, 2003).

Vogt, Kari. '"Becoming Male": A Gnostic and Early Christian Metaphor' in Kari Elisabeth Børresen (ed.), *Image of God and Gender Models in Judaeo-Christian Tradition* (Oslo: Solum Forag, 1991), 172–87.

von Rad, Gerhard. *Genesis*, translated by John H. Marks. OTL. rev. ed. (Philadelphia: Westminster, 1972).

Ware, Kallistos. 'The Meaning of "Pathos" in Abba Isaias and Theodoret of Cyrus' in Elizabeth A. Livingstone (ed.), *Studia Patristica* 20 (Leuven: Peeters Press, 1989), 315–22.

'The Trinity: Heart of Our Life' in James S. Cutsinger (ed.), *Reclaiming the Great Tradition* (Downers Grove, IL: Intervarsity Press, 1997), 125–46.

Weber, Max. *Sociology of Religion* (Boston: Beacon Press, 1963).

Wenham, Gordan J. *Genesis 1–15*. WBC (Waco: Word, 1987).

Wesche, Kenneth Paul. 'The Union of God and Man in Jesus Christ in the Thought of Gregory of Nazianzus', *SVTQ*, 28, no. 2 (1984), 83–98.

'"Mind" and "Self" in the Christology of Saint Gregory the Theologian: Saint Gregory's Contribution to Christology and Christian Anthropology', *GOTR*, 39, no. 1–2 (1994), 33–61.

'The Doctrine of Deification: A Call to Worship', *Theology Today*, 65, no. 2 (2008), 169–79.

Westermann, Claus. *Genesis 1–11: A Continental Commentary*, translated by John Scullion (Minneapolis: Fortress Press, 1994).

Wevers, John W. *Text History of the Greek Genesis* (Göttingen: Vandenhoeck & Ruprecht, 1974).

Wickham, Lionel, and Frederick Williams. *St. Gregory of Nazianzus: On God and Christ: The Five Theological Orations and Two Letters of Cledonius.* PPS (Crestwood, New York: St. Vladimir's Seminary Press, 2002).

Widengren, Geo. *Mani and Manichaeism* (London: Weidenfield and Nicolson, 1961).

Wiebe, Phillip. *God and Other Spirits: Intimations of Transcendence in Christian Experience* (Oxford: Oxford University Press, 2004).

Wilckens, Ulrich. 'χαρακτήρ' in Gerhard Kittel and Gerhard Freidrich (eds.), *Φ-Ω TDNT*, vol. 9 (Grand Rapids: Eerdmans, 1974), 418–23.

Williams, Anna N. 'Light from Byzantium: The Significance of Palamas' Doctrine of Theosis', *Pro Ecclesia*, 3, no. 4 (1994), 483–96.

The Ground of Union: Deification in Aquinas and Palamas (Oxford: Oxford University Press, 1999).

The Divine Sense: The Intellect in Patristic Theology (Cambridge: Cambridge University Press, 2007).

Williams, Rowan. *The Wound of Knowledge: Christian Spirituality from the New Testament to St. John of the Cross*, 2nd ed. (London: Darton, Longman and Todd, 1991).

Wimbush, Vincent L. and Richard Valantasis. *Asceticism* (Oxford: Oxford University Press, 2002).

Windley-Daoust, Susan. *The Redeemed Image of God: Embodied Relations to the Unknown Divine* (Maryland: University Press of America, 2002).

Wink, Walter. *Unmasking the Powers: The Invisible Forces That Determine Human Existence* (Philadelphia.: Fortress Press, 1986).

Winkler, Gabriele. 'The Original Meaning of the Prebaptismal Anointing and its Implications' in Maxwell E. Johnson (eds.), *Living Water, Sealing Spirit* (Collegeville, MN: The Liturgical Press, 1995), 58–81.

Winslow, Donald F. 'Orthodox Baptism – A Problem for Gregory of Nazianzus' in Elizabeth A. Livinsgstone (ed.), *Studia Patristica* 14 (Berlin: Akademie-Verlag, 1976), 371–74.

The Dynamics of Salvation: A Study in Gregory of Nazianzus (Cambridge, MA: Philadelphia Patristic Foundation, 1979).

Wolfson, Harry A. *The Philosophy of the Church Fathers; Faith, Trinity and Incarnation*, vol. 1 (Cambridge, MA: Harvard University Press, 1956).

Wright, Nicholas T. 'ἁρπαγμός and the meaning of Philippians 2:5–11', *JTS*, 37, no. 2 (1986), 321–52.

Wyß, Bernhard. 'Gregor von Naziang: ein griechisch-christlicher Denker des vierten Jahrhunderts', *Museum Helveticum*, 6 (1949), 177–210.

'Gregor von Naziang', *RAC*, 12 (1983), 793–863.

Yarnold, Edward. *The Awe-Inspiring Rites of Initiation: The Origins of the R.C.I.A.*, 2nd ed. (Edinburgh: T&T Clark, 1994).

Young, Frances M. *From Nicaea to Chalcedon: A Guide to the Literature and Its Background* (London: SCM Press, 1983).

'The Rhetorical Schools and their Influence on Patristic Exegesis' in Henry Chadwick and Rowan Williams (eds.), *The Making of Orthodoxy: Essays in Honour of Henry Chadwick* (Cambridge: Cambridge University Press, 1989), 182–99.

The Making of the Creeds (London: SCM Press, 1991).

Biblical Exegesis and the Formation of Christian Culture (Cambridge: Cambridge University Press, 1997).

'God's Image: The 'Elephant in the Room' in the Fourth Century?' in Allen Brent and Markus Vinzent (eds.), *Studia Patristica* 50 (Leuven: Peeters Publishers, 2011), 57–72.

God's Presence: A Contemporary Recapitulation of Early Christianity (Cambridge: Cambridge University Press, 2013).

Ysebaert, Joseph. *Greek Baptismal Terminology: Its Origins and Early Development* (Nijmegen: Dekker and Van de Vegt, 1962).

Zizioulas, John. *Being as Communion: Studies in Personhood and the Church* (Crestwood, New York: St. Vladimir's Seminary Press, 1985).

General Index

Scripture Index

Old Testament

CPSIA information can be obtained
at www.ICGtesting.com
Printed in the USA
BVHW082052070223
658071BV00004B/30